3/92

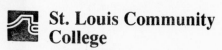

JAMES MILTON TURNER
and the Promise of America

Missouri Biography Series
William E. Foley, Editor

JAMES MILTON TURNER
and the Promise of America

The Public Life of a
Post–Civil War Black Leader

Gary R. Kremer

Univerity of Missouri Press
Columbia and London

Copyright © 1991 by
The Curators of the University of Missouri
University of Missouri Press, Columbia, Missouri 65201
Printed and bound in the United States of America
5 4 3 2 1   95 94 93 92 91

Library of Congress Cataloging-in-Publication Data

Kremer, Gary R.
    James Milton Turner and the promise of America : the public life
of a post-Civil War Black leader / Gary R. Kremer.
        p.   cm. — (Missouri biography series)
    Includes bibliographical references and index.
    ISBN 0-8262-0780-4 (alk. paper)
    1. Turner, John Milton. 2. Diplomats—United States—Biography.
3. Afro-American politicians—Missouri—Biography. 4. Politicians—
United States—Biography. 5. Afro-Americans—History—1877–1964.
6. United States—Foreign relations—Liberia. 7. Liberia—Foreign
relations—United States. 8. Missouri—Politics and government—
1865–1950. I. Title. II. Series.
E664.T88K74   1991
973.8′092—dc20
[B]   90–29876
                                                                   CIP

∞™ This paper meets the requirements of the
American National Standard for Permanence of Paper
for Printed Library Materials, Z39.48, 1984.

Designer: Kristie Lee
Typesetter: Connell-Zeko Type & Graphics
Printer: Thomson-Shore, Inc.
Binder: Thomson-Shore, Inc.
Typeface: Sabon

TO MY PARENTS
Bernard S. and Gertrude A. Kremer
Who Taught Me about the Promise of America

CONTENTS

ACKNOWLEDGMENTS

This book, like all others, is a product of the generous help and assistance of many people. My mentor, Lorenzo J. Greene, introduced me to the historical figure James Milton Turner. I wish he were still here to see the final result. William E. Parrish, whose books on post–Civil War Missouri provided me with a starting point for studying Turner's life, gave me countless hours of his time; in the process, he became more to me than a helpful scholar—he became a good friend. Lawrence O. Christensen, another good friend whose interest in Turner rivals my own, has also been extremely generous in his assistance. In particular, he discovered the letters that are the foundation of Chapter II. Indeed, that chapter is as much his as mine.

Many other scholars have been helpful in reading portions of the manuscript, in sharing their research with me, or in simply offering stimulating conversation and encouragement. I appreciate the support of Elizabeth Caldwell Beatty, Robert L. Beisner, Roger H. Brown, Donald H. Ewalt, Jr., William E. Foley, John Hope Franklin, Thomas E. Gage, Willard B. Gatewood, James W. Goodrich, Antonio F. Holland, Alan M. Kraut, Allen Lichtman, John Marszalek, August Meier, Joe M. Richardson, Nell Irvin Painter, Joel Williamson, and Kathleen Wojciehowski.

Numerous librarians and archivists have tolerated my persistent questions and, more often than not, been able to help me find answers. I especially want to thank the staffs of the following repositories: the Library of Congress, the National Archives, The State Historical Society of Missouri, the Western Historical Manuscript Collection at the University of Missouri–St. Louis, the Arkansas Historical Commission, the Missouri Historical Society, the Missouri State Archives, the Kingdom of Callaway Historical Society, the Oklahoma Historical Society, and the Moorland-Spingarn Research Center. Librarians at the following institutions have helped me considerably: Lincoln University of Missouri, the University of Oklahoma, the American University, the University of Missouri. Melvina Conley of the St. Louis Circuit Court Archives has been especially helpful.

Earlier versions of Chapters III and IX appeared in article form in the *Missouri Historical Review* as follows: "Background to Apostasy:

James Milton Turner and the Republican Party," *Missouri Historical Review* 71 (October 1976): 59–75, and "World of Make Believe: James Milton Turner and Black Masonry," *Missouri Historical Review* 74 (October 1979): 50–71. Both articles are copyrighted by and reprinted with the permission of The State Historical Society of Missouri. Chapter VII appeared in altered form as "For Justice and a Fee: James Milton Turner and the Cherokee Freedmen," *The Chronicles of Oklahoma* 57 (Winter 1980–1981): 377–91. That article, likewise, is copyrighted and reprinted with the permission of the Oklahoma Historical Society. I wish to express my gratitude to both Societies for allowing me to use previously published material.

Patrick H. Huber, my research associate, provided invaluable assistance. Janet M. Kremer and Sharon N. Kremer typed and retyped the entire manuscript with great patience and good humor.

Lisa Dugan Kremer read and critiqued the manuscript, thereby helping me to produce a better book than I would have produced without her. I appreciate, also, the equanimity with which our children, Randy, Sharon, and Becky, tolerated the presence of an additional person in the house; James Milton Turner, it seems, has become part of the family.

Finally, I wish to thank Missouri's Secretary of State, Roy D. Blunt, for allowing me time away from my duties at the Missouri State Archives so that I could finish this book. Likewise, my co-workers at the State Archives have been wonderfully supportive.

Deficiencies that remain in this study stand as a testimony to my own intransigence more than to the quality of help that I have received.

JAMES MILTON TURNER
and the Promise of America

I pray you . . . receive my little book in all charity, studying my words with me, forgiving mistake and foible for sake of the faith and passion that is in me, and seeking the grain of truth hidden there.

W. E. B. DuBois, "The Forethought,"
Souls of Black Folk, 1903

PROLOGUE
A Niche in the Temple of Time

The Negro has been with us from the very beginning of the history of our State, and, indeed, of the nation itself. Surely, he must somewhere, at some time and somehow, have carved his humble niche in the temple of time.

—James Milton Turner
"Dred Scott Eulogized,"
April 18, 1882

This account of the public life of James Milton Turner has been in progress for so long that it has developed a history of its own. I discovered the historical figure James Milton Turner slightly more than two decades ago, in an undergraduate black history course taught by Lorenzo J. Greene at Lincoln University. I was a sociology major studying under the redoubtable Oliver Cromwell Cox, on my way, I thought, to a career as a social worker.

I was troubled, however, by the two dominant problems of my generation: the Vietnam War and the civil rights movement. In fact, I had enrolled in a black history course because I wanted to understand the momentous events of the midsixties—the sit-ins, boycotts, riots— and the recalcitrant racism that caused them, from the perspective of time. What happened to me, however, was that over the course of the semester, I came to view the discipline of history differently than ever before.

I had never been eager to study history; it had always been presented to me as a finite body of information (names, dates, places) to be memorized and then regurgitated back on a test. Soon, however, history was to become for me, in that overused word that dominated academic discussions in the 1960s, "relevant." So much so that I changed my major from sociology to history and decided that I

1

wanted to spend my professional career teaching and inspiring students of history. The discipline of history gave me, instead of the tedious chore of memorizing a body of information, a way of making sense of the world in which I lived. It became, in William Appleman Williams's well-known phrase, "a way of learning," rather than simply something to be learned. With that discovery came an excitement that always accompanies newly gained insight. In a time (the 1960s) and a place (the United States) when so much seemed chaotic and without reason, the world had become intelligible at last.[1]

I discovered history at precisely the same time that I discovered James Milton Turner. Indeed, there was a connection, for while the discipline of history provided me with a method for understanding why things occurred, Turner's life seemed to touch on and mirror many of the things I wanted to understand.

In trying to understand race relations in the 1960s, during the Second Reconstruction, for example, I found Turner's speeches, delivered one hundred years earlier, to be timeless. His demands for black political equality and educational opportunity for all races during the First Reconstruction seemed to be messages for Americans across the ages.

The more I discovered about Turner's life, the more intrigued I became. How, I wanted to know, did a black man living in the state of Missouri, with such deep southern roots and strong traditions of racial segregation and discrimination, become so effective in establishing schools for blacks after the Civil War? What drove him to battle the guardians of the status quo? How did he manage to wield such political power in the Republican party of Missouri at a time when blacks were just beginning to be allowed to vote and did not have the protection of federal troops as they did in the former Confederate states? Indeed, Missouri never experienced a period of "Black Reconstruction" as did states with black majorities (South Carolina, Mississippi, Louisiana) or near majorities (Alabama, Florida, Georgia). What was the source of Turner's power in a state whose black population was less than 7 percent of the total?

When I discovered that Turner had been appointed a foreign diplomat by Pres. Ulysses S. Grant in 1871 I became even more intrigued. How could a man born a slave become the representative of the United States in a foreign land? And then, when I began reading

1. William Appleman Williams, ed., *History as a Way of Learning*.

Turner's dispatches to Secretary of State Hamilton Fish, I found more reflections of the late twentieth century in the nineteenth.

The American arrogance of power displayed in the Vietnam War of the 1960s had its nascence in the latter half of the nineteenth century. One of its early manifestations appeared in Liberia during Turner's ministership to that West African country (1871–1878). In 1875 a civil war broke out between the native Grebo tribe and the descendants of blacks who had established the Liberian colony two generations earlier. That war, in which the United States took a great interest, threatened the destruction of the lives and life-style of African-Americans in Africa. At James Milton Turner's urging, the United States government entered the conflict and actually sent a military force to Liberia to suppress the rebellious Africans. Paradoxically, Turner's action demonstrated an almost unrestrained faith in America's ability to provide a model of how people should live, even as his own people were being denied basic civil rights back home.

Turner's optimism, however, did not long survive his return to the United States. Much changed in this country between 1871 and 1878, especially in the federal commitment to protect black civil rights in the former slave states. Optimism turned to disillusionment for Turner and other black leaders as they saw a reinvigorated racism in the former slave states, unrestrained by federal power.

My discovery of Turner's disillusionment with the Republican party, and then with America itself, coincided with the emergence of the Black Nationalism movement in this country during the late 1960s and early 1970s. Again I was struck by the prescience of Turner's words and deeds. When he struggled with the question of whether or not blacks should leave the United States and wrote that American-born blacks were more American than African, urging them to remain in the South and fight for their rights there, he articulated a position that was at the core of a debate over the same issue one hundred years later. And then, just as the controversy emerged over the American Indian Movement and tribal rights in the 1970s, I discovered Turner's role as an advocate for the Cherokee freedmen during the 1880s.

I had known little about slavery in the Indian Territory prior to the Civil War; consequently, I found myself fascinated with the decades' long debate over tribal rights—who had them, and what they meant—that went on throughout the 1880s and 1890s. Turner, in Barbara Tuchman's phrase, served as my "prism of history": by inquiring into his long, eventful life, I saw the light of my inquiry refracted in many different and revealing directions.[2]

In the late 1970s, I began to consider the possibility of writing a book-length study of Turner's life. To my surprise, and dismay, most of the people with whom I discussed the idea assured me that there were not enough sources available to produce a book. Always the critics told me that I would never be able to write a conventional, book-length study of consequence without finding a cache of private Turner papers. Always I responded, usually to myself, "How, under any circumstances, could anyone write a conventional biography of one who seemed so unconventional?" I continued digging into Turner's life and career, hoping to find that mother lode of private papers, but pursuing other research topics in the meantime. Turner always seemed to be on my mind, and periodically I turned up new sources.

Meanwhile, other scholars were adding to the literature on post–Civil War black leadership, and their books and essays helped me to ask new questions about Turner's life. As I read through the ever-growing volume of literature on late nineteenth-century black life, I was struck by similarities in the lives of many of the leaders—similarities that seemed to shed light on the course of post–Civil War black life in America. I found particularly instructive the "tentative model" of postwar leadership offered by August Meier in his afterword to a collection of essays entitled *Southern Black Leaders of the Reconstruction Era*. Meier wrote of these leaders:

> They were men of relatively fortunate origins, compared to the mass of their Negro constituents. They were likely, but not necessarily, to have come to prominence through work in the Freedmen's Bureau, the Union leagues, the church, or the school. As a class they were relatively well-educated, ambitious men. They were likely to be successful artisans, farmers, and professionals, and in a few cases at least achieved considerable wealth. However they achieved power, they all operated from a black base. Yet all found it necessary . . . to find allies among whites.[3]

2. Barbara Tuchman, *Practicing History,* 80–91.

3. The literature on post–Civil War black leadership has grown quite extensive. For an introduction to this literature, see the following: Howard N. Rabinowitz, ed., *Southern Black Leaders of the Reconstruction Era;* Leon F. Litwack and August Meier, *Black Leaders of the Nineteenth Century;* August Meier, "Afterword: New Perspectives on the Nature of Black Political Leadership during Reconstruction," in Rabinowitz, *Southern Black Leaders of the Reconstruction Era,* 401.

A disproportionate number of the black leaders who emerged out of the immediate postwar period had been, like Turner, free blacks before the war. As such, they felt themselves superior to the former slaves. Indeed, as Leon Litwack has written, "Some blacks who had been free before the war resented being called 'freedmen' and tried in every way to dissociate themselves from the former slaves." These black leaders, "freemen," were also much better educated than their "freedmen" counterparts, many of them schooled in the religiously oriented institutions of numerous Christian denominations such as Oberlin College, in Ohio, which Turner attended.[4]

The black leaders of the postwar period placed great faith in education as a panacea for black progress, particularly vocational education, an idea that received its clearest articulation in the writings first of Frederick Douglass and later Booker T. Washington. Postwar leaders also tended to be elitist, often criticizing the black masses for having failed to imbibe the white middle-class values of the late nineteenth century.[5]

Ironically, this elitism often alienated the black leaders of the Reconstruction era from the black masses in the 1880s and beyond. This alienation, combined with a resurgence of racism in America generally and in the "Redeemed" South particularly, left black "leaders" with few followers. A surprising number of these once-powerful leaders dropped almost totally from sight, many of them, like Turner, wielding little or no power in the last decade or two of their lives. For example, Peter Humphries Clark, who rose to prominence as a black leader in Ohio in the era of Reconstruction, moved to St. Louis to become a schoolteacher in 1888. As his biographer David A. Gerber has written, "So completely did [Clark] disappear from the public eye that on the few occasions when word of his work in the St. Louis schools or of his presence at some family celebration reached the black press in Ohio, people were surprised to learn that he was still alive."[6]

4. Leon W. Litwack, *Been in the Storm So Long: The Aftermath of Slavery,* 513. For "The Education of the Elite," see Willard B. Gatewood, *Aristocrats of Color,* 250–71.

5. Philip S. Foner, ed., *The Life and Writings of Frederick Douglass;* Booker T. Washington, *Up from Slavery;* the elitism of the black leaders of the Reconstruction era is a major theme of Litwack and Meier, eds., *Black Leaders of the Nineteenth Century.*

6. David Gerber, "Peter Humphries Clark," in Litwack and Meier, eds., *Black Leaders of the Nineteenth Century,* 190.

In reading the secondary works on black leaders of the nineteenth century, I was encouraged to discover that most of these essays and books were produced without benefit of large collections of private papers. One book in particular, John Hope Franklin's masterful biography of George Washington Williams, convinced me, beyond doubt, that a large collection of private papers was not necessary to document a public life.[7]

This study of Turner's life has been a long time in the making, but it seems even more important to me now than it did two decades ago that it should be written. Turner was, unquestionably, the dominant black political figure in Missouri during the generation after the Civil War. And yet, slightly more than a century later, he is little remembered by historians and unknown to everyday Missourians, even those whose political party he once served so faithfully. The fact that so much material about Turner's public career is extant argues for, not against, the telling of his life story. Indeed, much about Turner's private life and thought remains undiscovered. Since he was a public figure, however, his life has been easier to document than the vast majority of nineteenth-century Missouri blacks.

Additionally, Turner's significance as a historical figure transcends his own experiences. His life personalizes what historian Rayford Logan called the betrayal of the negro. Turner possessed, in the 1860s and 1870s, a deep and abiding faith in America. The Civil War, he believed, had purged the land of its sins and allowed the country to realize what had always been its promise: the creation of a social and political environment in which merit, not race or any other accident of birth, mattered.[8]

But in the late 1870s, the promise soured. It is easy for us to see in retrospect what Turner could not see up close: he was supporting ideas and attitudes that the American public was not willing to embrace. Turner, like so many other black leaders of the era, wanted a federal solution to problems in which the federal government was no longer interested. The Compromise of 1877, embodying, as it did, the abandonment of black interests in the South, signaled an end to the use of federal power to protect black civil and political rights.

---

7. John Hope Franklin, *George Washington Williams: A Biography.*
8. The classic work on the Republican party's abandonment of blacks after the 1877 Compromise is Rayford W. Logan, *The Betrayal of the Negro: From Rutherford B. Hayes to Woodrow Wilson.*

In Turner's home state of Missouri, the fiery orator lost his power base when the Radical Republicans were turned from power in the early 1870s. By middecade, when he looked to centralized authority to reinforce his vision of a free and equal America, Missourians were institutionalizing localism in the form of the conservative 1875 Constitution. Locally, Missourians' racial attitudes had changed little in the previous decade; the difference between 1865 and 1875 was that by the latter date, Missourians were unrestrained in their racist practices by either federal or state authority.

It was a bitter reality for the hopeful Turner to accept. He spent several years vacillating between acceptance and rejection, belief and disbelief, hope and despair. In the end, despair won. Indeed, the despair and the frustration are understandable only when measured against the hope and optimism of earlier years.

At root, Turner was not a radical or revolutionary who wanted to turn America upside down. The words written by historian R. J. M. Blackett about postwar black leaders generally apply to Turner—his "was a leadership of change, not fundamental radical reorganization, but reformation, advocating the fulfillment of America's revolutionary republican principles."[9]

Like so many other black leaders who had been acculturated to white middle-class values, Turner believed in his country and the principles for which it claimed to stand. He believed in the rule of law, not of men. He believed in a literal interpretation of the Declaration of Independence: "All men are created equal and endowed by their Creator with certain inalienable rights, and that among those rights are the right to life, liberty, and the pursuit of happiness." In short, he believed in the promise of America, the promise that he tried to help his country fulfill. His odyssey, for that reason alone, is worth recording: it encapsulates and mirrors an era of the American experience. Indeed, the words Turner uttered on the occasion of his eulogy of Dred Scott in 1882 seem a fitting justification for an account of his life: "[He] carved his humble niche in the temple of time."

9. R. J. M. Blackett, *Beating against the Barriers, Biographical Essays in Nineteenth-Century Afro-American History,* 401.

CHAPTER I
Time and Place

[I] do hereby Emancipate and forever set free from my Service and that of the Services of any of my Home claiming under or after me my maid servant Hannah, and all and every of the heirs of her body born after this date. Also, her son James Milton Turner, now a boy in his fourth year who is also of a brown or copper Colour.

—Theodosia Young
December 5, 1843

In 1911, four years before James Milton Turner's death, the *St. Louis Post-Dispatch* ran an interview of nearly four thousand words with the distinguished black Missourian. Turner spent a considerable part of that interview talking about his ancestry and early childhood in pre–Civil War Missouri. It is the closest thing we have to a Turner autobiography.

Born in St. Louis County on a plantation twelve miles west of the city, Turner claimed to be descended from African royalty. Eager to be identified as more than an ex-slave descended from slaves, Turner professed that his father's ancestry could be traced to a Moorish prince and his mother's to the "Vey tribe in Africa, which is said to have invented a system of writing and elaborated a grammar."[1]

Turner's father, John, according to the interview, was a Virginia native and a nephew of the famous Nat Turner, whose 1831 insurrection spread terror throughout the South. Indeed, John Turner came to Missouri because of the insurrection, spirited away by his young master, Benjamin Tillman, who feared for his slave's life. Financial problems beset Tillman in St. Louis, so he sold John Turner to Frederick

1. *St. Louis Post-Dispatch,* July 9, 1911. This interview appears in its entirety as Appendix A.

Colburn, who allowed John to work as "Black John the Horse Doctor" in the St. Louis area and to keep part of his earnings. Tillman had taught John the science of "veterinary surgery." Eventually John Turner bought his freedom from Colburn. He married Hannah, the slave of the Reverend Aaron Young, who with his wife, Theodosia, had moved from Kentucky to Missouri in 1819. Hannah had been a wedding present to Theodosia. John Turner was eager to purchase his wife, but the asking price of three thousand dollars was too high. Consequently, he conspired with an abolitionist doctor to gain Hannah's freedom. As it happened, Hannah Turner had broken a bone in one of her wrists. The attending physician agreed to report to her master that the hand would have to be amputated. Once the report was made, the Reverend Mr. Young lowered the asking price for Hannah to four hundred dollars, well within John Turner's range. James Milton, then in his fourth year, was thrown into the bargain for an extra fifty dollars.

While this version of James Milton Turner's emancipation is appealingly dramatic, it is almost certainly inaccurate. Extant court records make no mention of a fee being involved in the emancipation of Hannah Turner or her son—in fact, no reason is given for the emancipation. Likewise, Theodosia was the one who freed mother and child, not the Reverend Mr. Young. A St. Louis Circuit Court "deed of emancipation" filed on March 12, 1844, identifies Hannah Turner as thirty-seven years old in that year. The court approved the emancipation, "it appearing to the satisfaction of the Court that said Hannah Turner is a person of sound mind and body and is fully capable of supporting herself."[2]

No mention of John Turner is made in the deed of emancipation. Neither he nor Hannah Turner appears in the 1850 federal census. The 1860 census lists John Turner as sixty-four years old and Virginia born. Hannah Turner appears as aged sixty and Kentucky born. John's occupation is listed as "Horse Farrier" and Hannah's as "Washer Woman." Two females, perhaps daughters of James Milton's brother, appear on the census: Josephine, age seventeen, and Anna, age five. According to the census, John Turner owned five hundred dollars of real estate and fifty dollars of personal property. On April 23, 1861, John Turner acquired a free license, which allowed him to

2. Records of the St. Louis Circuit Court, 1843–1844, 416, Civil Courts Building, St. Louis, Missouri.

remain in the county as a free person of color, for a five-hundred-dollar bond. Unlike most free blacks of the period, he was able to sign his own name, although neither he nor Hannah was literate. A description of him appears on the license as follows: "5'4″, 61 [years old], dark scar on nose, small scar between eyes, Horse Doctor." John Turner died of typhoid on December 14, 1864. Hannah Turner remained in St. Louis and lived into the 1870s.[3]

The 1911 interview with James Milton Turner is an intriguing reminiscence. It is also highly exaggerated, so much so that it invites skepticism on every point. There is no evidence that Turner ever traced his ancestral lineage to its African roots, or that he was related to the famous Nat Turner. By the time he granted the interview, his disillusionment and frustration with American life were so great that he felt compelled to embellish both his accomplishments and the background against which they occurred. Tired of being denied the respect to which he felt entitled, Turner fabricated a past that he thought would impress readers and gain for himself much-sought-after recognition.

The Missouri into which Turner was born in 1839 had grown dramatically over the previous decade, in large part because of a concentration of Americans from Kentucky, Tennessee, and Virginia. Those southerners, attracted by virgin soil and a pro-slavery constitution that brought the state into the Union as part of the Missouri Compromise, came to their new homeland to develop commercial plantation crops. By 1850, the first year that the Bureau of the Census tabulated nativity data, persons born in free states who had moved to Missouri numbered 76,592, compared to 187,518 persons born in slave states. The newly arrived southern migrants carried with them a commitment to southern culture and southern ways, including a belief in the institution of slavery. Even those upland South migrants who did not bring slaves with them and never owned blacks tended to believe in slavery as a social and economic institution. Quite naturally, as the population of southerners increased so did the population of slaves. During the decade preceding James Milton Turner's birth,

3. "Population Schedules of the 8th Census of the United States" (1860), St. Louis, Missouri, Ward 04, 0201; P. Dexter Tiffany Papers, Bonds for Free Negroes, Missouri Historical Society, St. Louis, Missouri; *Missouri Republican,* December 18, 1864. Hannah Turner's name appears in *Gould's St. Louis Directory* through 1872. Her residence is listed as 213 Almond Street.

the black population of Missouri increased by 130 percent. The anxiety generated by this increase, combined with the fear emanating from the growing agitation of abolitionists during middecade, prompted Missouri lawmakers to pass restrictive legislation against blacks.[4]

Several laws passed in the 1830s curtailed the rights of free blacks, such as James Milton Turner's father, and defined their inferiority to whites. In 1835, the Missouri legislature declared it illegal for any free black to possess a firearm "or weapon of any kind," without first obtaining a license from a justice of the peace in the county where he resided. That same legislature also required county courts to bind out as apprentices or servants all free Negroes and mulattoes between the ages of seven and twenty-one years. No colored apprentice could be placed in the company of a free white worker, except by the consent of the parent or guardian of the white apprentice. To place a black man alongside a white man in the learning of the same trade was considered a dangerous first step toward emancipation.

The year 1835 also saw the Missouri legislature try to restrict the movement of free blacks into and within the state. Lawmakers declared that in order to reside in a Missouri county a free Negro had to obtain a license from the county court. The license was, in effect, a permit to remain in the county so long as one behaved. A black applicant for a permit had either to post a bond ranging from one hundred to one thousand dollars or have some white person act as security for him. Further evidence of hostility toward free blacks manifested itself in 1837, when the Missouri General Assembly passed, without a single dissenting vote in the House, a law prohibiting the spread of abolitionist doctrines or literature. Violators convicted for a third time under this statute were subject to a life sentence in prison.[5]

But if Missouri, as a whole, was a place where southern sentiments dominated and state laws restricted black life, St. Louis was another story. St. Louis was an exciting place to be in 1850. In the pre-railroad days, when river transportation reigned supreme, St. Louis's location on the Mississippi River, at the mouth of the Mis-

4. The family tradition of Turner's owner records that he was born on May 16, 1840. In 1871, however, upon receipt of a commission to Liberia as Minister Resident and Consul-General, he told Secretary of State Hamilton Fish that he was born on August 22, 1839. Gary R. Kremer, "A Biography of James Milton Turner," 25; Perry McCandless, *A History of Missouri, 1820–1860,* 37; Russell Gerlach, *Settlement Patterns in Missouri,* 20.

5. Lorenzo J. Greene et al., *Missouri's Black Heritage,* 48–49.

souri, gave it distinct trade and business advantages. Immigrants and migrants came to the city in droves. One of America's fastest growing cities between 1840 and 1850, St. Louis saw its population increase by 373 percent, to 77,860 people. Among the newcomers to St. Louis were many people who were opposed to slavery. In particular the number of German immigrants, notorious for their opposition to slavery, grew daily. The *Niles Register* estimated in December 1837 that as many as 7,000 Germans lived in St. Louis. The German population of the city had grown to 22,534 in 1850, nearly 30 percent of the city's total.[6]

Not only was the number of opponents to slavery growing in St. Louis, but people who had slaves there tended to use them differently than slave owners elsewhere in the state. In this prosperous, growing city, slaves were likely to be used in a wide variety of nonagricultural tasks as valets, butlers, handymen, carpenters, maids, nurses, and cooks. Working in such capacities greatly facilitated the possibility of self-purchase for slaves. John Turner's work as a "farrier" and "horse doctor" was a case in point. By 1850, when James Milton Turner was approximately ten years old, there were 2,618 free blacks in Missouri, more than half of them in the St. Louis area.[7]

In fact, there arose in St. Louis what Cyprian Clamorgan, a contemporary black writer, called a "Colored Aristocracy." That group of free blacks, according to Clamorgan, "command[ed] several millions of dollars." Although they could not vote, they exercised power and attained status through their wealth. They were "by means of wealth, education, or natural ability . . . the elite of the colored race." Even though Turner's family never entered this antebellum aristocracy, presumably they, like most other free blacks in St. Louis, took this elite group, with its high degree of respectability and self-reliance, as a model.[8]

Certainly John and Hannah Turner made sure that their son received a good education. Exactly when James Milton Turner began school is unknown, but by 1847, when he was only eight, Missouri had adopted a law specifically prohibiting the education of blacks.

6. James Neal Primm, *The Lion of the Valley: St. Louis, Missouri*, 172–73.
7. Greene et al., *Missouri's Black Heritage*, 56.
8. Lawrence O. Christensen, ed., "Cyprian Clamorgan: The Colored Aristocracy of St. Louis," 10–11. Christensen points out that Clamorgan's figures are open to question, since the Manuscript Census of 1860 for St. Louis indicates that free blacks held only $221,498 worth of real and personal property.

Anyone operating a school or teaching reading and writing to any Negro or mulatto could be punished by a fine of not less than $500 and up to six months in jail. Turner gained much of his early education in a clandestine school run by the Reverend John Berry Meachum.[9]

Born a slave in Virginia on May 3, 1789, Meachum eventually purchased his own freedom and that of his father. He migrated to St. Louis in 1815 and worked as a carpenter and a cooper. He became the protégé of Rev. John Mason Peck, who came to St. Louis in 1817 as one of the first missionaries sent to Missouri by the Baptist Board of Foreign Missions for the United States. A native of Litchfield, Connecticut, Peck organized a Sunday School for blacks in St. Louis in 1818. That Sunday School became the nucleus of the First African Baptist Church, which Meachum pastored from 1827 until his death in 1854.[10]

Meachum accepted and promoted the notion of vocational education for blacks. Like most nineteenth-century Americans, he saw such training as a key to progress for the lower classes, white as well as black. One historian has called Meachum "the most outspoken Missourian in favor of education for blacks" during the antebellum period. That same scholar has also described Meachum as "the Booker T. Washington of antebellum Missouri." In August 1846, at a time when Turner was enrolled in the primary grades under Meachum's tutelage, Meachum wrote an "Address to the Colored Citizens of the United States." That address included the following advice typical of the era, and especially typical of white-influenced black preachers and teachers:

> In order that we might do more for our young children I would recommend MANUAL LABOR SCHOOLS to be established in the different states, so as the children could have free access to them. And I would recommend in these schools pious teachers, either white or colored, who would take all pains with the children to

9. The best account of the development of black education in Missouri remains Robert I. Brigham, "The Education of the Negro in Missouri." *History of the Central Baptist Church of St. Louis* (pamphlet, no date), cited in Noah Webster Moore, "James Milton Turner, Diplomat, Educator, and Defender of Rights, 1840–1915," 195; Donnie D. Bellamy, "The Education of Blacks in Missouri Prior to 1861."

10. Noah Webster Moore, "John Berry Meachum: St. Louis Pioneer, Black Abolitionist, Educator and Preacher."

bring them up in piety and in industrious habits. We must endeavor
to have our children look up a little, for there are too many to lie in
idleness and dishonor.

According to Meachum, education was supposed to prepare young
people for participation in economic life, as well as instill in them
universal principles of right conduct. Industrial education, in this
view, offered the best hope for the unity and eventual uplift of blacks.

By 1846, the Reverend Mr. Meachum's African Baptist Church
had a membership of five hundred free blacks and slaves, including
John and Hannah Turner and their family, with Sunday School attendance in excess of one hundred and fifty. Meachum was intensely
opposed to slavery and encouraged free blacks to buy the freedom of
their not-so-fortunate brethren in bondage, a practice in which he
engaged. Until freedom came, he counseled, blacks should try to take
care of themselves and to prepare for emancipation.[11]

Preparation through education was not always so easy, however.
The Missouri law against black education was enforced sporadically.
Purportedly, Turner was present in Meachum's school in the base-
ment of the African Baptist Church when law-enforcement officials
burst in and arrested one of the white teachers, charging him with
breaking the law by teaching blacks "reading, writing, and figuring."
Sometime later Meachum's school closed and he built a steamboat-
school that operated from the middle of the Mississippi River, a location that was not subject to state law. Thereafter, students traveled to
and from the boat by means of a skiff. Meachum continued the operation of this school until his death in 1854.[12]

Turner stopped going to Meachum's school some time before the
latter's death. Exactly when or why that happened is unclear. None-
theless, he continued to pursue knowledge informally while working
as an office boy at six dollars a month for different St. Louis businessmen. In 1911 he recalled that he had satisfied his passion for
learning by studying the books of those men secretly, all the while
keeping "a watchful ear cocked for the footsteps of those who might
detect him and denounce him to the authorities."[13]

11. The information in this and the preceding two paragraphs is from Bellamy, "The Education of Blacks in Missouri Prior to 1861," 149–50.
12. Ibid.; *St. Louis Post-Dispatch,* July 9, 1911.
13. *St. Louis Post-Dispatch,* July 9, 1911.

Sometime around 1854 or 1855 Turner again returned to formal education, this time at Oberlin College in Ohio. There is no record of Turner ever paying a bill at Oberlin. Consequently, it seems likely that he obtained room and board from a professor, as was customary at the time. George B. Vashon, son of the first African-American to graduate from Oberlin and a longtime friend of Turner, reported that Turner was cared for at the Ohio school by Dr. James Harris Fairchild, an abolitionist professor who later became president of Oberlin in 1866. Fairchild was one of a few whites with whom black students boarded. Of Turner's Oberlin career, Vashon reported only that the young scholar made progress "some what beyond the average."[14]

No other record of Turner's experiences at Oberlin exists. Still, it is hard to imagine that that hotbed of abolitionism and moral righteousness did not affect him. He must have heard endless arguments in favor of abolition and endorsements of equal rights and education for blacks. Something of the flavor of that atmosphere can be gleaned from the life of the antislavery emissary Stephen Blanchard, who came to Missouri from Oberlin as an American Missionary Association representative in September 1859. Historian Joe M. Richardson has described Blanchard as "the most active missionary in Missouri." Using the medium of the church pulpits opened to him and the *St. Joseph Free Democrat,* which published his articles, Blanchard launched an intense antislavery campaign based upon a conviction of biblical opposition to slavery. Blanchard's behavior was typical of AMA representatives who considered themselves to be "Christian abolitionists" responsible for "divesting freedmen of the shackles of ignorance, superstition and sin."

That same atmosphere also fostered in Turner a religiously based opposition to the institution of slavery. AMA workers saw the Civil War as God's punishment for southern adherence to slavery. God's wrath would be appeased, they reasoned, "only when blacks were recognized as equal to whites." This view of the Civil War as a God-

14. For Oberlin's role as an educator of antebellum blacks, see Juanita D. Fletcher, "Against the Consensus: Oberlin College and the Education of American Negroes"; Walter G. Robinson, Jr., "Blacks in Higher Education in the United States before 1865." For Fairchild's Oberlin career, see William and Aimee Lee Cheek, *John Mercer Langston and the Fight for Black Freedom, 1829–1865.* Vashon's statement is contained in *Colored Democrat,* October 16, 1920.

sent punishment and of the slave owners as sinners explains Turner's extreme opposition to rebel reenfranchisement in postwar Missouri. Indeed, it seems reasonable to conclude that the AMA and Oberlin had a great effect upon Turner. Unquestionably, he continued to be in contact with people from Oberlin for many years after the war and sent his stepdaughter to school there in the 1870s.[15]

Turner's stay at Oberlin ended in either 1856 or 1857, although why he left is unclear. Vashon reported in 1920 that Turner returned home to his family because his father had died, but this turns out not to be the case. Whatever the cause of J. Milton Turner's return to Missouri, he found himself in the peculiar position of being an educated black man in a slave state. An 1859 *St. Louis Directory* lists him as a "Porter." In the 1860 census he is described as a twenty-one-year-old "Porter," living apart from his parents and possessing $30 worth of personal property. Vashon reported that Turner served as a "bootblack and general factotum" for the federal forces under Nathaniel Lyon and Francis P. Blair when they attacked a group of southern sympathizers encamped just west of St. Louis at Camp Jackson in 1861. According to Vashon, Turner came into the city with Captain Blair and a short time later joined the Union effort. He reportedly entered the Civil War as a body servant to Col. Madison Miller, a St. Louis railroad entrepreneur. Present at the battle of Wilson's Creek, he said he witnessed the death of Gen. Nathaniel Lyon. He also claimed to have participated in the battles of Pea Ridge, Belmont, Island No. 10, Paducah, Fort Henry, and Corinth. At the battle of Shiloh, he received a hip wound that, according to Vashon, caused him to limp the rest of his life.[16]

It was apparently at the battle of Shiloh also that Colonel Miller was seriously wounded and captured by the Confederates. Turner, thinking that the colonel had been killed, returned to Missouri with four thousand dollars that Miller had given him for safe-keeping. He gave the money to Mrs. Miller, who was the sister of Thomas B. Fletcher, a man who later became Missouri's Radical governor. Un-

15. Material in this and the preceding paragraph is drawn from Joe M. Richardson, "The American Missionary Association and Black Education in Civil War Missouri."

16. *St. Louis Directory* (1859), 477; "Population Schedules of the 8th Census of the United States" (1860), St. Louis, Missouri, Ward 04, 0194; *Colored Democrat,* October 16, 1920; *St. Louis Post-Dispatch,* July 9, 1911.

doubtedly, this Miller-Fletcher family connection facilitated Turner's entry into postwar Radical Missouri politics.[17]

Some weeks after Turner's return to St. Louis, Miller showed up in the city on parole from a Confederate prison. According to Turner, Miller was overwhelmed at finding his money waiting for him and rewarded his former body-servant with $500. Turner's direct involvement with the war ended at that point. He remained in St. Louis, where he claimed to devote much of his time to helping slaves escape to the North. Often at night, he said in the *Post-Dispatch* interview, he tied a skiff containing a fugitive slave to the stern of a steamboat so that it might be towed to the Illinois shore of the Mississippi River and freedom.[18]

Missouri's slaves gained their legal freedom three months before Lee surrendered to Grant at Appomattox. On January 11, 1865, a constitutional convention dominated by Radical Unionists who sought to chart Missouri's postwar future passed an ordinance ending the "peculiar institution" in the state. Later in the day, Gov. Thomas B. Fletcher issued a formal emancipation proclamation. Blacks celebrated the event throughout the state. On Saturday, January 14, St. Louisans turned out by the thousands for a day of festivities that included a number of parades and a sixty-gun salute. A contemporary observer described the rejoicing as follows: "Blacks assembled in their churches singing songs of deliverance and Thanksgiving. As the leaders prayed, the congregation in unison cried, 'Bless de Lawd, Amen, Glory Hal'lual, We're free.'"[19]

In Missouri, much of the hope for black political and civil rights lay in the hands of a state government controlled by Radical Republicans. Missouri's Radicals traced their origins to an 1862 split in the state's Unionist party. Theirs was the faction that supported emancipation at that early date, as opposed to others in the party who wanted gradual emancipation, and still others who opposed emancipation altogether. Missouri's wartime provisional government imposed a strict proscription against southern sympathizers that limited the ballot to Unionists.

17. *St. Louis Post-Dispatch,* July 9, 1911.

18. G. W. Randolph, Confederate Secretary of War to Col. James Kent, May 28, 1862, *War of the Rebellion,* series 2, 3:885; *St. Louis Post-Dispatch,* July 9, 1911.

19. William E. Parrish, *A History of Missouri, 1860–1875,* 116–17; Galusha Anderson, *The Story of a Border City during the Civil War,* 34.

While the Radical-dominated January convention quickly passed an emancipation ordinance, a resolution to the problem of what to do with blacks once they were freed was not so easily reached. There were three major concerns: Should blacks be allowed to testify against whites in court cases? Should blacks be allowed to vote and to hold office? Should the state provide educational opportunities for blacks at public expense?

After considerable debate, the convention resolved the first question by deciding "that no person can, on account of color, be disqualified as a witness." Radicals moved more cautiously on the suffrage issue. The vast majority of Missourians remained hesitant about the black franchise. Even the Radicals' leader, Charles Drake, was skeptical about including a black suffrage plank in the constitution, fearing that it would cause the entire document to be rejected by Missouri voters. Consequently, the privileges of voting and officeholding were limited to qualified white males. Finally, the convention cleared the way for state-established schools for blacks by including a provision stating that the General Assembly "may" establish schools "for the children of African descent." Funds for all public schools were to be appropriated "in proportion to the number of children without regard to color."[20]

Only the proposals for black suffrage and officeholding had been soundly rejected by the constitutional convention. It was to those issues that Missouri blacks addressed themselves in the fall of 1865. They were not alone in that endeavor. Throughout the former slaveholding states in 1865, blacks gathered in conventions and mass meetings organized to try to make their newfound freedom practicable. Speeches were made at these gatherings, testimonials given, and memorials presented, all in an effort to persuade state and federal lawmakers to grant blacks civil and political rights. It was, for most American blacks, their "political debut." The meetings recognized the relative powerlessness and vulnerability of the freedmen and called upon state conventions and legislatures to help them.[21]

In Missouri, this "convention movement," as it came to be called, manifested itself in the formation of an Equal Rights League. The

20. Material from this and the preceding two paragraphs is drawn from William E. Parrish, *Missouri under Racial Rule, 1865–1870,* 2–3, 117–18; see also, Margaret Dwight, "Black Suffrage in Missouri, 1865–1877."
21. Litwack, *Been in the Storm So Long,* 507.

league was a black organization that cooperated with various white philanthropic agencies attempting to advance the rate of assimilation and adjustment of the freedmen to their new condition. A parent organization, the National Equal Rights League, had been formed in October 1864, with black leader John Mercer Langston as its president. Langston, like Turner, a former Oberlin student, was a fierce advocate of black emancipation and equal rights. Turner and Langston had, in fact, met at Oberlin. The organizational meeting of the Missouri Equal Rights League was held in St. Louis on October 3, 1865. A large number of black men and women attended, including most of the best-known black leaders in the state. According to a newspaper account, the mass meeting was "called for the purpose of advancing the rights of the race and promoting the interests of the colored people in the State."[22]

The meeting began with an election of officers. The Reverend G. P. Wells was elected chairman, and Blanche K. Bruce, later elected the first black United States senator from Mississippi, was chosen secretary. The Reverend Wells spoke to the crowd assembled, endorsing the league and calling for a defense of the rights of black people. He was followed in his remarks by State Representative Enos Clarke, a white man, who not only endorsed the right for blacks to vote but also counseled those assembled to lobby actively for black suffrage. Clark, an Ohio native who had strong abolitionist credentials, also suggested the appointment of an executive committee to distribute information among the people. In addition, he recommended the establishment of a newsletter to publicize the group's claims.[23]

At some point during the evening, James Milton Turner, then approximately twenty-six years old, gave the crowd what the *Missouri Democrat* described as "a most fervid and pertinent speech in advocacy of the rights of his race." This is the first documented instance of Turner taking a leadership role among Missouri blacks.

---

22. *Tri-Weekly Missouri Democrat,* October 4, 1865. For more on Langston, see Cheek and Cheek, *John Mercer Langston and the Fight for Black Freedom.*

23. Bruce spent 1864 and 1865 in Hannibal, Missouri, teaching school. Although he left Missouri in 1866, he did not move to Mississippi until 1869. William C. Harris, "Blanche K. Bruce of Mississippi: Conservative Assimilationist," in Rabinowitz, ed., *Southern Black Leaders of the Reconstruction Era,* 5–6. The account of the meeting in this and the following two paragraphs is taken from the *Tri-Weekly Missouri Democrat,* October 4, 1865.

Although his speech was only one of many at the gathering, he seems, even at this early stage in his career, to have clearly articulated many of the aspirations of the blacks in his audience. Turner's speech was followed by the assembly's unanimous adoption of a series of resolutions designed to seek support for its cause through traditionally American, patriotic arguments.

In those propositions, the black Missourians called attention to their plight as freedmen, without the rights and privileges of the elective franchise, and charged that such a condition was little better than the oppression they had suffered under slave masters. They emphasized that the denial of the franchise that they experienced was due not to a lack of patriotism on their part or a lack of commitment to their country during the war. Rather, they said, they had been "proscribed alone and singly on account of [their] color." They decided unanimously to "demand those rights and privileges which rightfully and logically belong to us as freedmen, and as those who have never deserted the flag of our common country in the hour of its darkest peril." Likewise, they suggested that their future safety and prosperity would be best insured by the establishment of the principle of equality before the law for all people, regardless of color. They endorsed the idea of disallowing the rebellious states to return to the Union until they had pledged support for the principle of "the universal right to the ballot box." Finally, they chose a seven-man executive committee to carry out the spirit of their resolutions. The members of this committee included the following: Henry McGee, Col. Francis Robinson, Moses Dickson, J. Bowman, Samuel Helms, Dr. George Downing, and George Wedley. This committee was specifically charged with the responsibility of planning a series of mass meetings, procuring black speakers, and preparing an address to the black people of Missouri.

Less than two weeks later, one of the mandates of the mass meeting was met when an approximately twenty-seven-hundred-word *Address to the Friends of Equal Rights* appeared in local newspapers and was printed separately for distribution throughout the state. Although Turner had not been a member of the original executive committee, his name now appeared on the document as the secretary for the organization. He had assumed that position shortly after the organizational meeting. Perhaps his "fervid and pertinent" speech at the October 3 meeting prompted the other committee members to solicit his support. Whether he was enlisted or pressed his services upon the other members of the league, Turner continued to serve as secretary of the executive committee throughout its existence.[24]

The *Address,* which drew heavily from one of the American people's most hallowed documents, the Declaration of Independence, began with a reference to the Civil War as a holy battle between an advanced civilization and a relic of barbarism. It acknowledged a debt of gratitude to God for his deliverance and asked him to secure for black people the liberties and privileges "which are enjoyed by every other American citizen." Those rights and privileges, the *Address* asserted, could only be found in the exercise of the right of suffrage. Without the vote, black people were being forced to submit to taxation without representation and were having to obey laws that they had no voice in framing. Several times the *Address* equated the plight of black freedmen with that of the American colonists who rebelled against the arbitrary and dictatorial rule of England. The principle that ought to be employed, it argued, should always be "the consent of the governed."

Black demands for political equality, the *Address* continued, were not excessive: "We ask not for social equality with the white man, as is often claimed by the shallow demagogue; for a higher law than human must forever govern social relations. We ask only that privilege which is now given to the very poorest and meanest of white men who come to the ballot-box." The petitioners reminded their readers that they were citizens of the state and the nation and that their toil had enriched both. They recalled that thousands of black soldiers had "bared their breasts to the remorseless storm of treason, and by hundreds went down to death in the conflict while the franchised rebel . . . [the] bitterest enemy of our right to suffrage, remained . . . at home, safe, and fattened on the fruits of our sacrifice[,] toil and blood." The State of Missouri and the nation could, the *Address* argued, benefit from black votes against "disorganizing elements" just as they had benefited from black muskets during the Civil War.

The freedmen expressed doubt about the wisdom and the benevolence of their former masters, and added that it was those masters, along with the "Northern Copperheads," who had fought for the previous four years to enslave their bodies and souls. Hence, they mis-

24. Information on the *Address* in this and the following five paragraphs is taken from the *Tri-Weekly Missouri Democrat,* October 16, 1865.

trusted the paternalistic politicians who "are so anxious to do for us our voting, to perform all our legislation and to accept all our political responsibilities. . . . If we are to be nursed and strengthened into manhood solely at the hands of others, we ask in the name of God that it be done by our friends, and not by our enemies."

The phrase "nursed and strengthened into manhood" was a tacit acknowledgment of how poorly a slave society had prepared freedmen for competition in a white world. The petitioners hastened to assure their readers that black people did not want to become burdens upon society. Consequently, they pleaded, why not assist blacks to develop the skills that were expected of white citizens of the United States. If black people were weak because of their prior servitude, why not give them the help they needed to be strong? If they were ignorant, give them "the lessons of experience . . . which is ever deemed essential to white man's advancement." If they were poor, allow them to accumulate their own capital, start their own businesses, and, by their vote, support laws favorable to their own commerce.

The committee warned that the question of what do with black people in the immediate postwar period would become the greatest issue before the Republic. The *Address* closed with a request of the friends of black rights to help the executive committee by contributing money to its campaign. In the meantime, the committee concluded, "Let our trust be confided in Him whose just Providence has wrested the lash from our taskmaster and through our great and good Lincoln given to our oppressed people, a universal emancipation."

Some fifteen months later, Turner, as secretary for the committee, presented a report of the league's first year of activity. The occasion was another mass meeting, this time held on the anniversary of the emancipation of Missouri's slaves. Turner indicated that the *Address to the Colored People of Missouri* had been distributed and favorably received, and that the committee had corresponded with a number of the "more distinguished" black speakers in the state, "with a view to secure their services in a canvass of this State." The committee hired the president of the National Equal Rights League, John M. Langston of Ohio, who began a tour on November 27, 1865, by delivering a speech at the meeting place of the Turnverein Society, Turner's Hall, in St. Louis. He followed that speech with engagements at Hannibal, Macon City, Chillicothe, St. Joseph, Kansas City, Sedalia, and Jefferson City. Everywhere he went the message was the same: he pleaded for black suffrage and for black access to education. He closed his campaign on January 9, 1866, in Jefferson City, where the Hall of the House of Representatives was opened to him and he spoke before the members of the legislature and others.[25]

In addition to Langston's efforts, the report continued, James Milton Turner had also carried a similar message throughout the state, especially the southeastern portion. This area, sometimes called the "Bootheel" or the "Cotton Delta," had a large concentration of slaves before the war. Turner was particularly active in the areas surrounding the towns of Cape Girardeau, Commerce, and Jackson. Persistent rebel sympathies there were evident by the opposition he encountered. On one occasion he was forced "to escape for his life at midnight, barefooted in the snow, leaving his shoes behind him."[26]

The committee also circulated a petition throughout the state, imploring the legislature to provide suitable schools for black children and endorsing an amendment to the constitution that would remove the word *white* and, in so doing, proclaim the legal equality of all the state's citizens. That petition gained the signatures of four thousand black persons, at which point it was turned over to Rep. Enos Clarke, for presentation to the legislature. Hence, the report offered "hope for more liberality in the present Legislature now in session" and encouraged friends of the black cause to continue confronting legislators with petitions and appeals "for equal justice towards all who are loyal to the state and government without respect to the *color* of the *loyalists'* skin."

The report also recounted the difficulties under which the committee had labored. One pressing problem was the burden of expenses. Those present at the meeting were informed that the league had incurred debts totaling $2,221.82. Donations, subscriptions, and proceeds from entertainments had brought in $900.25, leaving a balance to be paid of $1,321.57. Lastly, the committee expressed its gratitude to the many friends who had supported the league and asked for continued support in the effort "to awaken an enlightened public sentiment" so that free schools and the right to vote would soon be open to black people in the state.

25. *Missouri Democrat,* January 15, 1867; Cheek and Cheek, *John Mercer Langston and the Fight for Black Freedom,* 294, 445–46.
26. Information in this and the following three paragraphs is taken from the *Missouri Democrat,* January 15, 1867.

The committee emphasized that "we mean to make our freedom *practical*," adding that it saw education as the chief means by which that could be done. Convinced that the responsibilities of citizenship could be best fulfilled by an educated citizenry, it sought to establish schools for blacks wherever possible. It was toward that effort that James Milton Turner turned his energy in the latter part of the decade.

CHAPTER II
Education to Uplift the Race

I take pleasure in being able to announce that the colored people generally are frugal and temperate, very anxious to be taught (for which they are apparently ready to make considerable sacrifice), as also in the acquisition of tracts of land for farming purposes. This desire I have at all times encouraged.

—James Milton Turner
to Col. F. A. Seely
February 20, 1870

The American Missionary Association, the Christian philanthropic organization, was a major force in establishing schools for black Missourians during the Civil War. The AMA began its first school for blacks in St. Louis in 1862 but later extended its efforts throughout the state. After the war, with its resources limited, and feeling a greater need for its services in the more southern states, the AMA appealed to a federal agency, the Bureau of Refugees, Freedmen, and Abandoned Lands (the Freedmen's Bureau), to take over and continue its educational efforts in Missouri. Ultimately, the Freedmen's Bureau did so and solicited the assistance of James Milton Turner. Between 1868 and 1870, Turner spent most of his time either teaching in or establishing schools for blacks throughout the state.[1]

It is safe to assume that given his responsibilities with the Equal

1. Richardson, "American Missionary Association," 433–48. For the role of the AMA in black education generally during this period, see Joe M. Richardson, *Christian Reconstruction: The American Missionary Association and Southern Blacks, 1861–1890*. This chapter draws heavily on Lawrence O. Christensen's essay, "Schools for Blacks: J. Milton Turner in Reconstruction Missouri," 121–35.

Rights League and his Oberlin background, Turner aspired to be involved with the AMA and its efforts on behalf of blacks, especially in the St. Louis area. In early 1867, Turner had married a woman who had a daughter by a previous marriage, and although his wife was from Ohio, the couple and the child were living in St. Louis. He must have known Jacob R. Shipherd, the AMA western-district secretary, because on October 17, 1867, Shipherd wrote to Enoch K. Miller, an AMA agent in Arkansas, telling him that Turner, "a very intelligent col'd man desires a good place where he and his wife could find support." Soon after the Shipherd-Miller letter, Shipherd wrote to F. A. Seely, chief disbursing officer for the Freedmen's Bureau in Missouri, asking him "to immediately supervise the schools and other interests of the AMA in Missouri." Shortly thereafter, the AMA and the Freedmen's Bureau cooperated in attempting to improve educational opportunities for blacks in the state.[2]

Turner, meanwhile, had found employment in a black public school in Kansas City. The March 17, 1868, minutes of the city's school board show that a decision was made to hire Turner "to teach the colored school in Kansas City, Missouri at $60 per month. Time to commence April 16, 1868." A cash book for the remainder of 1868 reveals that Turner was paid sixty-five dollars for his services on May 5, 1868, and an additional sixty-five dollars on June 27 of that same year. Turner spent the next year teaching at a black school in Boonville, a Missouri River town in Cooper County that harbored a large population of southerners and their descendants. Turner's advocacy of educational opportunities for blacks as secretary of the Missouri Equal Rights League, combined with his role as a teacher, helped him to develop a reputation as a leading spokesman for black education in the state.[3]

2. Testimony of Estelle B. Montgomery and Lillie M. Mason, *Charles W. Turner et al. v. Miltonia Turner Hill et al.,* Circuit Court of St. Louis, June Term, 1916, Records of the Circuit Court, Division 2, Civil Courts Building, St. Louis, Missouri. Hereafter referred to as "Case No. 2884B." J. R. Shipherd to E. K. Miller, October 17, 1867, Enoch K. Miller Papers, Arkansas Historical Commission, Little Rock, Arkansas; J. R. Shipherd to F. A. Seely, December 2, 1867, Record Group 105, Bureau of Refugees, Freedmen, and Abandoned Lands, Missouri Chief Disbursing Officer, Letters Received, Registered, vol. 2, 1867–1869, E-W, National Archives, Washington, D.C. Hereafter referred to as "Freedmen's Bureau Letters."

3. Minutes of the School Board of Kansas City for March 17, 1868; cash book for the School Board of Kansas City, 1868, 17, 21, Missouri Valley Room Collec-

On May 17, 1869, Richard B. Foster, the white founder and first principal of the all-black Lincoln Institute, delivered an "Address upon Colored Schools" before the State Teachers' Association meeting in St. Louis. Foster suggested the importance of Turner's role in establishing black schools by commenting that "he, instead of myself, ought to have delivered this address to you." Foster's speech detailed the woeful condition of black education in Missouri. He estimated that out of a pool of fifty thousand black school-age children, only about five thousand of them were attending school. He concluded that black schools were not adequate for the needs of black children: "We may as well accept the fact that the colored schools of this State are mostly in poor condition; too few in number, little thought of, little cared for."[4]

Soon after Foster's speech, Freedmen's Bureau Commissioner Oliver Otis Howard directed F. A. Seely to draft for his signature a letter to Missouri officials urging the state to take steps to advance the cause of black education. Seely, in turn, solicited the assistance of James Milton Turner to investigate the condition of black education in Missouri. Over the course of the next several months, Turner traveled across the state and reported what he found to Seely. As historian Lawrence O. Christensen has written, Turner's reports "allow us to see conditions in Reconstruction Missouri from a unique perspective, through the eyes of a very perceptive black observer."[5]

Appropriately, Turner began his investigation with a visit to Lincoln Institute, a school viewed by many as a key to black progress in postwar Missouri. Foster had spoken in May of the need for a black normal school to train black teachers and had suggested Lincoln as a possibility. Lincoln Institute was the product of the vision and sacrifice of black Missouri soldiers who enlisted in the Union cause during the Civil War. Those soldiers who made up the Sixty-second and Sixty-fifth United States Colored Infantries, which were stationed in Texas at the war's end, raised over five thousand dollars in money and pledges early in 1866 to establish a school for blacks in Missouri. They entrusted their money to Foster, an officer in the Sixty-second,

tion, Kansas City Public Library, Kansas City, Missouri; J. W. McClurg to U. S. Grant, April 26, 1869, Applications and Recommendations for the Grant Administration, Record Group 59, National Archives, Washington, D.C. Hereafter referred to as "Applications and Recommendations for the Grant Administration."

4. Antonio F. Holland and Gary R. Kremer, eds., "Some Aspects of Black Education in Reconstruction Missouri: An Address by Richard B. Foster," 190.

5. Christensen, "Schools for Blacks," 123.

and sent him to their home state to establish the school. Upon his
arrival, he made an abortive effort to establish a school in St. Louis,
but failing to get the kind of support he hoped for, he moved west to
Jefferson City. Foster chose the Missouri capital because the eman-
cipationist Radical Republicans were firmly in control of state government there, and he hoped for a more sympathetic response than he
had received in St. Louis. What he found was community hostility,
particularly evident over the housing issue: "I applied to the colored
Methodist Church for their house," he wrote in 1871, "but the minister refused, alledging as a reason that the teacher would be white. . . .
I applied to the white Methodist Church," he continued, "but the minister refused, alleging as a reason that the scholars would be black."[6]

In spite of this hostility, Lincoln Institute opened its doors to black
students in the fall of 1866. The Radical General Assembly had passed
a series of comprehensive laws earlier in 1866 that included a measure
requiring each township or city board of education to establish and
maintain schools for blacks in jurisdictions where black school-age
children numbered twenty or more. School terms for blacks were to be
equal in length to those for whites, unless attendance dropped below
twelve, in which case the black school could be closed for a period of
up to six months. Where there were fewer than twenty black children
in a district, school boards were allowed to provide for black educational needs as they saw fit. By the time Turner visited the school in
1869, the institute was still without a permanent facility but was hoping to obtain a legislative appropriation that would allow it to become
Missouri's publicly supported black normal school.[7]

While in Jefferson City, Turner contacted Radical Republican
Thomas A. Parker, the state superintendent of schools, who encouraged him in his work for the Freedmen's Bureau and, as Turner wrote
Seely, "promised to issue me a commission delegating to me all necessary power in the matter." Parker expressed an immediate need for
Turner's services in Randolph County, and Turner responded that he
was "eager for the work." Realizing that he could not operate schools
by himself he informed Seely that he would "write to Oberlin this day
& ask for teachers." Armed with the state superintendent's blessing,

---

6. Richard B. Foster, *Historical Sketch of Lincoln Institute,* 6, 10.
7. Parrish, *A History of Missouri,* 161–65. In 1868 the legislature lowered
the number of students needed to begin a school to fifteen and the average attendance requirement to ten.

Turner's job grew from just investigating and reporting the condition of black education in Missouri to actively enforcing compliance of the 1866 state law.[8]

Turner's relationships with the Freedmen's Bureau and the state superintendent of schools represented important developments for the black educator. They reaffirmed his vision of a nation and state that were righting past wrongs. Unlike the antebellum days, government and laws were no longer the enemies of blacks, no longer obstacles to blacks in pursuit of "life, liberty, and happiness." Quite the contrary, Turner believed that the government was using its power as an instrument of social change, and that as a government agent, he could play a viable part.

Turner threw himself into his work as only a man with a mission can. He traveled in circles that blacks had rarely before frequented, reporting in September 1869 that he had spoken with the governor about a suspicious murder in Fayette. Writing from Jefferson City on September 7, 1869, he told Seely he was leaving "by night train" for Boonville, where "there [are] 3 or 4 places within a few miles of Boonville upon which I can operate successfully." He had to hurry, however, because he was expected in Sedalia by week's end, adding that he wanted "to visit Huntsville, Marshall & Saline, etc. but have not the money please hasten check."[9]

The next seven months were heady days for Turner. The former slave, who had spent the bulk of his life living in a state that restricted the mobility of even free blacks, now enjoyed the opportunity to move about the state at will. He also must have experienced immense satisfaction when writing an implicitly threatening letter on the "Office of State Superintendent Public Schools" letterhead and being able to invoke the name of Parker, a prominent state official: "Prof. Parker requested me to ask you if the proper officers have taken any steps toward opening-colored-school this ensuing term at Fredrich town & Mine Lamotte." Missouri law gave the state superintendent the authority to assume school-board powers when local boards failed to comply with provisions for black schools. His letters sometimes carried an air of hauteur, as when he wrote Seely from Huntsville that he

---

8. Turner to F. A. Seely, July 17, 1869 and August 3, 1869, Freedmen's Bureau Letters. To avoid overusing [sic], I have reproduced all quotations from Turner precisely as they were recorded.
9. Turner to Seely, September 7, 1869, ibid.

had "succeeded in organizing or frightening the Rebel B[oard] of
Ed[ucation] at this place to reopen the Colored School." Both whites
and blacks had warned him about going to Roanoke, in the heart of
Little Dixie's Howard County. Unafraid, he told Seely that he was on
his way there, adding, "I shall know all its dangers in about 2 hours."[10]

On October 15, Turner reported to Seely that he had visited more
than half a dozen communities in west-central Missouri over the previous week. At Tipton, in Moniteau County, he found school officials
who were willing to open a school for blacks but undermined its
effectiveness by hiring "an incompetent and very ignorant Negro man
as teacher." Following Turner's complaints, the board of education replaced the black instructor with "a very good teacher and a white
man." In Sedalia, Turner encountered "a very poorly organized school"
run by "Mr. Carter, a competent teacher" whom the Freedmen's Bureau agent found "useing a cowhide quite liberally." Turner requested
Carter to banish the cowhide. At Otterville, east of Sedalia, Turner
also "found matters sadly neglected." Board of Education members
contended that there were not enough blacks in the district to require
a school. Turner quickly made his own count, concluded that the
board was wrong, and threatened the chairman that he was going to
report the matter to Superintendent Parker unless the board established a public school for blacks. To his surprise, Turner did find one
board member who supported his position, someone whom he described as "a Massachusetts man and a liveing practical Yankee much
more radical than I am."[11]

One of his most difficult cases occurred in Fulton, Missouri, the
seat of government for the rabidly secessionist Kingdom of Callaway
County, so called because so many of its citizens continued to support
the Confederacy even after the State of Missouri took a formal pro-
Union stance in the early days of the Civil War. Turner's major nemesis
in Fulton was the county superintendent of schools, Thomas A. Russell,
whose "*meaness*," Turner asserted, "extend[ed] to the entire county."

Turner confronted Superintendent Russell about the county's
practice of hiring less-than-competent teachers for black schools,
whereupon the latter told him he refused to examine any "colored
person as teacher." Russell told Turner that he would hire anyone

10. Turner to Daniel Peterson, August 27, 1869, ibid.; Turner to Seely, September 17, 1869, ibid. Parrish, *A History of Missouri,* 165.
11. Turner to Seely, October 15, 1869, ibid.

who applied for the job and that, in his judgment, "any such colored person need not so far as He is concerned know the English Alphabet." Turner pledged to take "this *extraordinary* case" to Superintendent Parker for resolution and told Seely he thought "the old idiot [Russell] should be in the Fulton lunatic Asylum instead of the Fulton Schools." Turner also found a lack of cooperation among other county officials whose help he sought, especially the "ungentlemanly clerk of County Court" who refused to provide him enumeration records without being paid. All in all, Turner pronounced Fulton *"the meanest place and people I ever have seen."*[12]

On another occasion Turner encountered a board official in Otterville, A. M. Gibbs, who offered an elaborate explanation for why the school district still provided no facilities for blacks. Not to be taken in by polite falsehoods, Turner informed Seely, "I saw quite easily that this statement was merely that of a man caught in an overt act." After concluding that there were approximately forty school-age children in the district and that the board had enough money to finance a black school for four to six months, Turner confronted the school official, who finally agreed to set up a school, if Turner provided a teacher. Finding teachers for the schools he hoped to open was a never-ending problem for Turner. Earlier he had written Seely, "In travelling I find many localities in which Schools would be opened but for want of teachers." He continually looked to the AMA, especially Charles H. Howard, to help him find teachers willing to come to Missouri and teach black students. Charles H. Howard was the brother of Freedmen's Bureau Commissioner Oliver O. Howard and replaced Jacob R. Shipherd as AMA western-district secretary in late 1868. In addition, he was also Inspector of Schools for the Freedmen's Bureau. This combination of positions undoubtedly made him an important contact.[13]

On October 25, Turner informed Seely that he had written to Howard, asking that Howard send him three more teachers, including one to replace his wife, who was seriously ill with a "congestive chill which the physician thinks will terminate in a Typhoid fever." Mrs. Turner conducted the school for blacks in Boonville. Turner indicated that he was on his way to Westport, in the extreme western part of the state.[14]

En route to Westport by train, Turner's pocketbook containing

12. Turner to Seely, October 23, 1869, ibid.
13. Turner to Seely, October 16, 20, 21, 1869, ibid.
14. Turner to Seely, October 25, 1869, ibid.

sixty-five dollars was lost or stolen. He wired Seely for a fifty-dollar advance against his salary of one hundred dollars per month and checked into a fine Kansas City hotel, the Broadway, which apparently did not make a practice of providing rooms to blacks. Turner commented to Seely, with some surprise and no little satisfaction, that he "did not think it possible" for him to get a room there. He further informed Seely that he would be attending a "Convention of Colored men now sitting in Topeka," after which he would go, as requested by Superintendent Parker, to Liberty in Clay County and Independence in Jackson County, "places," Turner wrote, "that have threatened to lynch me."[15]

Also while on his way to Westport, Turner wrote a letter to Dr. E. P. Childs of Vineland, in Jefferson County, to remind Dr. Childs of his visit there earlier "in the interest of [the] Colored School." Something of Turner's dogged determination can be seen in his request that Childs "do me the kindness to reply . . . without delay & inform me has there been any action taken in the matter by the Bd. of Ed.?" Childs responded with a note written on the bottom of Turner's letter, indicating "that a colored school is now being kept here successfully I believe, in their *completed* school house." The letter was signed "Respectfully, E. P. Childs." Whatever respect he received—be it lodging in an exclusively white hotel or a courteous gesture—Turner believed it was due in large part to his position as a representative of state government, and he did not hesitate to use the state superintendent of schools to bring pressure to bear on local officials.[16]

Turner returned home to Boonville on November 4 to check on his ailing wife and was pleased to find her "in improved health." The next day, while still in Boonville, he wrote Seely that it was imperative that there be established in Missouri a normal school "for colored students that we may be prepared to furnish teachers for our schools from our own midst. Every day experience that I have in my present work," he continued, "convinces me more each day that this is a necessity." By way of illustration, Turner noted that two weeks had gone by since he had written to Charles H. Howard, asking "for several teachers," and "as yet they have not come." He had, he said, immediate need for four teachers from Howard. Increasingly aware that the establishment of a normal school for blacks was a political

15. Turner to Seely, October 27, 1869, ibid.
16. Turner to Seely, November 1, 1869, ibid.

problem requiring a political solution, Turner said that he would soon be in St. Louis "for the purpose of encouraging preliminaries" for the establishment of an "*Educational Convention* of colored men of the State of Missouri."[17]

On November 6, Turner was in Lone Elm Prairie where he was confronted with yet another problem. There the number of black children in the township numbered fifty. Officials at Lone Elm were willing to provide a school with available money, but the black population was spread over such a wide geographic area that it was difficult to find, as Turner wrote, "a site sufficiently central to be accessible to the greatest number of colored children in the Township." On November 8, he wrote to Seely that he was proposing to leave for Jefferson City so that he could meet with Superintendent Parker because he had "10 or 12 cases for his official interference."[18]

The following day, Turner hired a buggy and drove from Boonville to Arrow Rock, in Saline County, where he undertook the investigation of an alleged fraud that resulted in an insufficient amount of money coming to the school district to build a new building for black students. The matter struck Turner as suspicious, and he decided to deal with it on several fronts. Mr. Wilhelm, the board spokesman, told Turner that because the board had not gotten the money due it a new building could not be built. He offered, instead, "to use money belonging to white children & open a school in [a] colored church building now in course of erection and run the same four months." Turner was uncertain that he could trust the board spokesman. "I think," he wrote Seely, "old man Wilhelm talks most too kind to be relied upon."

To ensure that Wilhelm delivered on his promise, Turner decided to ask Superintendent Parker "to send him a 20 day notice" that a school for blacks had to be in operation or the board would be in violation of state law. Additionally, Turner "called a meeting of colored people & made them promise to complete the House in 15 days." At the meeting also, Turner "told the colored people to tease old man Wilhelm untill he gives them a school that he may be rid of them." Finally, Turner vowed to travel the twenty miles to the county seat of Marshall and "look up the money that is lost . . . and if necessary shall sue for its recovery." He told Seely that he believed that a

17. Turner to Seely, November 5, 1869, ibid.
18. Turner to Seely, November 6, 8, 1869, ibid.

school would be in operation in Arrow Rock "in about twenty-five or thirty days." Turner traveled to Marshall, then caught the ten o'clock train for Jefferson City, where he met with Superintendent Parker. He assured Seely soon thereafter that Parker was "preparing to move on Fulton, Fayette, Roanoke and Rocheport and all such places."[19]

In December, Turner went to Washington, D.C., to attend the Colored National Labor Union Convention as the Missouri representative. The gathering, presided over by Isaac Myers, sought to find ways to organize recently freed black workers. As historian Eric Foner noted, however, the meeting was "composed mostly of politicians, religious leaders, and professionals, rather than sons of toil." The resolutions endorsed by the convention offer insight into Turner's political and social philosophy at the time. They represented ideals he would endorse time and time again as a political campaigner in the following year.[20]

According to the resolutions of the convention, God had created labor as the natural heritage of all men. The most efficient and productive way to utilize labor was capitalism. Harmony should always exist between capitalists and laborers. In fact, each individual should strive to become a capitalist. Several steps could be taken to achieve that goal: avoid intemperance; pursue education; encourage industrious habits among blacks; and teach trades and professions to black children. The convention also proclaimed the basic soundness of the American economic system, asserting that the republican form of government could and "should be administered for the benefit of all." The phrase "the benefit of all" reflected the hope that blacks would not be hindered by racist laws and other strictures in their quest to become capitalists.[21]

Turner served the convention as a member of the committee on education and as one of its vice-presidents. The committee on education, in its report to the convention, recounted at length the gallant effort blacks had made to acquire an education—laws against their efforts at learning notwithstanding—and concluded that "education is the necessary condition of the most efficient labor." Turner also

19. Turner to Seely, November 9, 12, 1869, ibid.

20. Eric Foner, *Reconstruction, 1863–1877*, 480. For the proceedings of the convention, see Philip S. Foner and Ronald L. Lewis, eds., *The Black Worker: A Documentary History from Colonial Times to the Present.*

21. *The New Era*, January 13, 1870; *The Elevator*, December 24, 1869.

offered a resolution that foreshadowed his relations with former rebels back on the campaign trail in Missouri. The conventioneers had heard Sen. J. W. D. Bland speak in favor of doing away with a test oath for officeholders in the state of Virginia. Turner adhered to his long-held conviction that rebels were evil men in need of chastisement when he appealed to the blacks assembled to "distinctly disavow all responsibility for the sentiments expressed here . . . by Senator J. W. D. Bland apologizing for the negro-hating, unreconstructed rebels of Virginia."[22]

Turner launched his political-activist campaign as the defender of black rights in the state of Missouri almost immediately upon his return from Washington. It was an assertive, even defiant, campaign by a man who saw himself not groveling at the feet of political power brokers, but rather as a flexible, independent, and potentially powerful supporter of whatever would enhance the achievement of his vision of a nonracist, reconstructed America. His attitude and demeanor in a speech delivered at a Jefferson City convention in January 1870 set the tone. He called the gathering of Missouri's blacks to pressure legislators into providing state aid for Lincoln Institute. Superintendent Thomas A. Parker had written of the desperate need for black teachers in his annual report to the legislature of 1869 and emphasized that that need could be met by providing state support for Lincoln Institute. Nothing had come of the suggestion, however. Turner pursued the issue by making it clear to the Radicals that they should support his proposed legislation if they were serious about meeting the needs of black people. He warned them that blacks would be watching their actions, and if the Radical party did not respond to black requests, the party could not count on black support. The next month the Missouri General Assembly enacted a law granting five thousand dollars annually in state aid to the Lincoln Institute under the condition that the institute trustees first agree to convert the school into a facility for the training of black public school teachers. In addition, Lincoln had to raise the equivalent of fifteen thousand dollars in the form of cash, buildings, grounds, or a combination of all three.[23]

22. Foner and Lewis, eds., *The Black Worker*, 60; *The New Era*, January 13, 1870.

23. *Missouri Democrat*, January 24, 1870; "Special Report on Schools for Colored Children," *Fourth Report of the Superintendent of Public Schools of the State of Missouri, 1869*, 34–37; Parrish, *Missouri under Radical Rule*, 131–32.

Meanwhile, Turner continued his work on behalf of black education for the Freedmen's Bureau. In early February of 1870 he made a trip to southeast Missouri, the Bootheel, an area of large slave holdings before the war and strong prosouthern sentiment during and after it. In New Madrid, Missouri, Turner found little support among whites for a black school. Indeed, he wrote Seely on February 5, there were "but 2 school officers in this entire county of whom I can learn a thing," and one of them, the county superintendent, he described as "a rabid Dem[ocrat]."

What Turner did find, however, was a black community that impressed him in its accomplishments, most of which he attributed to a black schoolteacher named Robert Stokes, who accompanied him on his investigation. After looking at Stokes's schoolhouse and grounds and observing his behavior, Turner pronounced Stokes to be "*by far* the most enterprising & generally useful colored man I have met in all Missouri." According to Turner, Stokes had organized a "benevolence & mutual benefit" society and asked him to address their meeting. Turner found the members of the group to be "fine looking and . . . *highly intelligent*."

Turner described farming operations of blacks that resulted in them "shipping thousands of bushels of grain from this point to New Orleans & other large crops of castor beans & cotton to the St. Louis market." He was particularly impressed with "the Hopkings brothers" who owned "the neighborhood mill together with 250 acres of good farm land *well* improved." He pronounced it "a thrifty community of colored men" and wrote that it was plain to see that "they owe this direction of their energies to the indefatigable perserverance of Robt. W. Stokes."

New Madrid County blacks had erected a "little board [school]-house by themselves." Turner said it was "the very *best* school building in the county" and commented that "unfinished and humble as [it] is . . . it gives the most strikeing evidence of the love of the teacher for his pupils." He was especially impressed with how Stokes had "spared no pains to make his school attractive to the children":

> He has with his own hands grubbed the yard clean of more than 80 stumps of trees, whitewashed the house, dug & built the water closet, cut the railings and made the fence, which is also neatly white washed. In summer he has a beautiful garden the relics of which is easily seen. He has filled this garden with about 30 differ-

ent kinds of flowers many of which are rare exotics some having been brought from Africa for this School.

Turner noted that after spending time in southeast Missouri, he had become aware that "it would be impossible for Stokes's school to exist were it not for the determination of the number of colored people in its immediate neighborhood." He urged Seely to help Stokes's school remove a six-hundred-forty-five-dollar debt: "To give permanence to this school or to plant it firmly as the germ of a new life for this *anti-progressive* region does seem to me an indispensable necessity of the public safety." One manifestation of this "anti-progressivism," Turner noted, was that some local landowners visited the St. Louis House of Refuge and took "colored boys . . . and virtually enslav[ed] them on their farms—without compensation."[24]

Turner soon headed north to St. Louis, stopping along the way at Commerce and Perryville. Then, abruptly, his services were terminated on February 28, 1870, presumably because the Freedmen's Bureau was scaling back its educational efforts throughout the former slave states. There was some talk about him being rehired the next month, and Turner wrote Seely indicating his eagerness to return to work for the bureau in spite of the fact that in March he had taken a job at Lincoln Institute where, he wrote, "My salary is more here by $20 per month & personal comforts are superior by 95 per cent but as I remarked I think the good I can accomplish in the Bureau of a much more general nature & therefore more beneficial."[25]

What Turner accomplished in the seven months of his employment with the Bureau was impressive. In his final report to Seely he noted that he had traveled "between eight and ten thousand miles" and had been "instrumental in calling into use between seven and nine thousand dollars belonging to colored children as their *pro rata* share of the common school fund." He had also "caused directly and indirectly the erection of seven or eight schoolhouses and opened thirty-two schools in various parts of the State."

His problems with respect to the establishment of black schools

24. Information in this and the preceding four paragraphs is drawn from Turner to Seely, February 7, 1870, ibid.

25. Turner to Seely, February 28, March 12, 14, 17, 1870., ibid. Turner and black preacher Moses Dickson worked as fundraisers for Lincoln Institute through the spring and summer of 1870. *Missouri State Times*, September 9, 1870.

had been great. He noted that "one of the greatest obstacles, is the fact that in such sections where the largest number of colored people are found there is a preponderance of disloyal and former slave holding peoples, who in most cases are opposed to the establishment of these [black] schools." But it was not just white racism that had hindered Turner's efforts. He observed in his final report to Seely that he had encountered much opposition among blacks to his effort to place white teachers in black schools. Such opposition existed throughout the former slave states, not just in Missouri. As Eric Foner has written, "There is abundant evidence that blacks preferred black teachers for their children as well as black churches and ministers."[26]

Additionally, Turner's letters to Seely in 1869–1870 reveal a paternalism that he no doubt felt toward the ex-slaves. He distrusted blacks to take care of themselves. Steeped in the middle-class values of white Christian America, he sought to transfer those values to Missouri freedmen by means of Oberlin-educated white teachers. There is some evidence that suggests some blacks resented what they perceived to be Turner's high-handed snobbery. In 1870 the *Boonville Eagle* commented on Turner's lack of popularity in the black community of that small town during 1869 when he conducted a school for blacks there. The *Eagle* reported that Turner had become "exceedingly obnoxious to the colored people," and noted that "in this community, where he is well-known, the colored people have no use for him."[27]

The problems he encountered with blacks and whites notwithstanding, Turner took heart in his successes and noted with pride that "the colored people generally are frugal and temperate, very anxious to be taught (for which they are apparently ready to make considerable sacrifice) as also for the acquisition of tracts of land for farming

26. Turner to Seely, February 28, 1870, Letters Received, Freedmen's Bureau Records, Educational Division, A-F, January–December, 1870, M803, roll 10, frames 0428–34. Seely, who submitted his report on Turner's activities before the latter had had a chance to submit a final report, estimated that Turner had been instrumental in "the establishment of from twenty to twenty-five schools and bringing into use from five to six thousand dollars of public funds" (Seely, Missouri School Report, January 1, 1870). Seely noted that Turner was paid five hundred dollars for his services, along with $374.49 for traveling expenses. Foner, "Black Reconstruction Leaders at the Grassroots," in Litwack and Meier, *Black Leaders of the Nineteenth Century*, 225.

27. *Boonville Eagle,* quoted in the *Fulton Telegraph,* August 12, 1870.

purposes." He observed that he had "at all times encouraged . . . cooperative effort[s] by groups of several families." Where those ventures had been successful, "he noticed a superior manliness and independence of thought and action, comparing favorably with the servility which the past condition of many necessarily engendered."[28]

It was clear to Turner that much remained to be done insofar as black education was concerned. In early August, six months after he had so highly praised Robert Stokes and other New Madrid blacks for their educational efforts, arsonists set fire to Stokes's school, totally destroying it. A note left behind "warned off" Stokes "under pain of being 'treated' in 'the same way'!" Stokes and the blacks of his community were disheartened, of course, "but they desire to rebuild their house and improve upon their former effort." Ironically, the schoolhouse had apparently been burned because it was being used as a meeting place for blacks gathering to discuss the issue of amnesty for former supporters of the Confederacy.[29]

The issue of forgiving and reenfranchising the rebels was destined to become the major campaign issue of the 1870 political season, and it was that issue to which James Milton Turner turned his considerable efforts. His travels about the state on behalf of black education had given him a firsthand view of the work that needed to be done to secure the victory of freedom. Former rebels who ruled unrestrained by the power and force of law in some areas threatened the fulfillment of freedom. He believed the key to the future for blacks lay in outside power, exercised by the Radical Republicans whom he assumed shared his vision of the promise of America. He had every reason to make that assumption. A Radical-run Missouri had made him an agent of the government, thereby enhancing his prestige, and ensuring his ability to travel freely about the state. He mingled with highly elected officials, including the governor, and stayed overnight in a hotel that had previously been unavailable to him. Moreover, the Radicals supported his successful efforts to force former rebels to comply with the mandate to establish black schools. To make sure that the Radicals stayed in power, Turner threw himself into the 1870 political campaign with the same intensity and commitment that had marked his work for the Freedmen's Bureau.

28. Turner to Seely, February 7, 1870, Freedmen's Bureau Letters.
29. Robert Stokes to Seely, August 25, 1870, ibid.

CHAPTER III
The Politics of Mutual Benefit

Some men claim that the ratification of the 15th amendment ended the mission of the Republican party. I contend the mission of the party will not be complete until the word white is stricken from the constitution of every State in this Union and all men placed on perfect equality before the law of the country.

—J. Milton Turner
April 12, 1870

During the period of Radical Reconstruction in Missouri, which extended from the end of the Civil War until 1870, the Radical Republicans needed black support and made extensive efforts to gain it. The motives of the Republicans who aligned themselves with blacks were utilitarian and shortsighted. Their support of black causes reflected more the precariousness of Missouri politics than genuine concern for black people.

The Radicals' strategy was to identify and then latch onto a black leader who could coalesce a potentially powerful black vote. They found such a man in James Milton Turner: his beliefs matched the Radicals' opportunism, and he interpreted the Radicals' overtures as evidence of their commitment to equal rights for all blacks. He viewed the Radical wing of the Republican party not only as an effective vehicle for his own advancement, but, indistinguishably, as a means by which all black people could realize the promise of America. Thus convinced, he actively campaigned for the Radical causes and candidates. His almost fanatical commitment to the Radical party had mixed results, however. On the one hand, the Radicals rewarded his unfailing support by facilitating his appointment by the president as minister to Liberia. On the other hand, a good deal of controversy

swelled up around him, and many blacks feared his hard-line opposition to the reenfranchisement of rebels would jeopardize future concessions to blacks. Some even began to question whether he was not
more concerned with his own personal advancement than he was
with the status of freedmen.

Turner's political activism had begun, of course, with his work on
behalf of the Missouri Equal Rights League during the period 1865–
1867. He and other league members lobbied the general assembly for
the black franchise during the 1867 legislative session. As a result of
their effort, the Radical legislature passed a constitutional amendment that proposed to eliminate the word *white* as a qualification for
suffrage. The amendment was submitted to Missouri voters for ratification in 1868. As historian Margaret Dwight wrote, "Blacks attempted to convince whites to vote for the suffrage amendment by
campaigning, making speeches, and writing letters to the editors."
Indeed, James Milton Turner was one of the most active of the amendment's supporters and spent a considerable amount of his own money
traveling across the state making speeches and answering questions.[1]

Radical candidate Joseph W. McClurg was elected governor by an
approximately twenty-thousand-vote margin in the 1868 election.
Still, opposition to black suffrage was intense, and the proposed
black voting rights amendment was defeated 75,053 to 55,236. Consequently, Missouri's black citizens did not gain the right to vote until
the ratification of the Fifteenth Amendment two years later. The rejection of the 1868 amendment illustrated the growing lack of unity
within the Republican party. The most important issue of disagreement was the insistence of Charles D. Drake, a Radical leader and
also a United States senator, that the party continue its stand against
reenfranchising former rebels. Many would-be supporters of the
black franchise refused to support black suffrage until disenfranchised rebels were allowed to vote. A more liberal and tolerant faction
of Republicans led by Missouri senator Carl Schurz, owner of a St.
Louis German-language newspaper, formed around this issue.

The ratification of the Fifteenth Amendment by the requisite
number of states gave blacks the right to vote in early February 1870.
Confident of the support of this new bloc of voters, the Liberal wing
of the Republican party felt less afraid of reenfranchising rebels, so

1. Parrish, *Missouri under Radical Rule,* 136; Dwight, "Black Suffrage in
Missouri, 1865–1877," 88–89.

they pushed through the legislature a proposal to submit three amendments to Missouri voters the following fall: the first would modify the test oath to a simple declaration of support for state and national constitutions, thereby making it possible for former rebels who intended to support the existing state and national governments to have all citizenship rights restored to them; the second would eliminate the test oath completely for jurors; and the third would repeal the test oath as a requirement for officeholding and remove all racial barriers to political office. Before the eventual ratification of the Fifteenth Amendment, however, the Radicals had been wooing James Milton Turner for nearly a year in an effort to move newly enfranchised blacks solidly into the Radical camp. Turner had gained a good deal of publicity working with the Missouri Equal Rights League and as an advocate of the 1868 amendment, even before he began working with the Freedmen's Bureau, the American Missionary Association, and the State Department of Education. By early 1869 he was confident that his leadership ability among Missouri's blacks gave him certain powers of leverage within the official Republican party structure. In April and May of that year, a number of Missouri Radicals, convinced of Turner's powers of persuasion, sent letters of recommendation, endorsing his attempt to gain the position of Minister Resident and Consul General to Liberia. These letters of recommendation attest to the value the incumbent Radicals placed on the black vote, and their desire to reward someone whom they believed could deliver it.[2]

Charles D. Drake sent the first letter. He described Turner as "a colored gentleman who, in my opinion, is well-qualified for the place." Moreover, Drake suggested to Secretary of State Hamilton Fish, Turner's appointment "would give much satisfaction to the people of Missouri." Drake's letter was followed eight days later by one from the State Superintendent of Schools, Thomas A. Parker, the man whose name Turner continually invoked in his effort to establish schools for blacks in 1869. Parker acknowledged his acquaintance with Turner and described him as a man of "exemplary deportments and rare oratorical abilities. . . . No man in the whole country has

2. Information in this and the preceding paragraph is taken from William E. Parrish, "Reconstruction Politics in Missouri, 1865–1870"; Richard O. Curry, ed., *Radicalism, Racism, and Party Realignment: The Border States during Reconstruction*, 25–28.

given deeper study to the government and various relations of the Liberian Republic."[3]

Two days after the Parker letter was written, Missouri's Radical governor, Joseph W. McClurg, followed with his own endorsement of Turner, whom he described simply as "a citizen of African descent." In his letter to Pres. Ulysses S. Grant, McClurg told the president that Turner "is unquestionably a man of ability, sustains a fine moral character and would honor the position." Former Governor Thomas C. Fletcher, who was the brother-in-law of Madison Miller, the man whom Turner served as a body servant during the war, also joined the attempt to secure the ministership for him. Fletcher described Turner as an "intelligent and energetic young man and a true patriot" and said he believed Turner to be fully competent to serve as minister to Liberia, adding "in consideration of his past course he is deserving of such a mission. . . . I have personal knowledge of his integrity as a man and think him eminently an upright man." There was also a brief note from Carl Schurz, written on the back of Fletcher's letter, endorsing Turner's request. Schurz's support, however, ceased when the fight over reenfranchisement of rebels surfaced during the summer of 1870.[4]

Other letters from Missouri in support of Turner's attempt to gain the ministership came from State Treasurer William H. Dallmeyer, Secretary of State Francis Rushman, Attorney General Horace B. Johnson, and State Auditor Dan M. Draper. Draper's letter of April 30, 1869, was not followed by another until December 13, 1869. At that time, seven Missouri congressmen, along with the two Missouri senators, Drake and Schurz, forwarded a single letter to Grant. The letter called attention to Turner's desire to gain the Liberian ministership, adding, "Mr. Turner is a colored man of education, fine natural ability, and of unexceptionable character." In addition to Drake and Schurz, the following persons signed the letter: John F. Benjamin, representing Missouri's eighth congressional district; Joel F. Asper, from the seventh district; Gustavus A. Finkelnburg, from

3. C. D. Drake to Hamilton Fish, April 16, 1869; T. A. Parker to U. S. Grant, April 24, 1869, Applications and Recommendations for the Grant Administration.

4. J. W. McClurg to U. S. Grant, April 26, 1869; Thomas C. Fletcher to U. S. Grant, May 28, 1869, Applications and Recommendations for the Grant Administration. It is impossible to say whether Fletcher's "personal knowledge" of Turner's integrity referred to Turner's returning money to Fletcher's sister.

the second district; Sempronius H. Boyd, from the fourth district; David P. Dyer, from the ninth district; Robert T. Van Horn, from the sixth district; and Samuel S. Burdett, from the fifth district. Clearly, the endorsement of Turner seemed to party regulars to be a good political move. As Prof. William Parrish, a historian of Radicalism in Missouri, wrote, the list of Radicals supporting Turner "does not leave any party leader of significance out, except [B. Gratz] Brown who had retired." This, Parrish continued, was "quite an accomplishment."[5]

Unfortunately for Turner, however, Grant had already chosen Francis E. Dumas of Louisiana to serve as minister to Liberia. He received an appointment on April 21, 1869. However, Dumas declined the position on May 5, and the office remained vacant for nearly a year until James W. Mason was appointed on March 29, 1870. One can only speculate as to why Turner was not offered the position during this period. The only hint of an explanation comes in a letter from Carmen A. Newcombe to President Grant on January 28, 1871. Newcombe indicated that during the year after Turner's initial application, "it was not then known that Mr. Turner would accept the position if offered to him." Turner might have become so active in his work on behalf of black education for the Freedman's Bureau that he was thought to be no longer interested in the position. Additionally, he may have been optimistic about a Radical victory in the Missouri gubernatorial election of 1870 and, consequently, a position for himself somewhere in Missouri government.[6]

In any event, Turner was clearly a favorite of the Radicals. After his move to Jefferson City in March 1870 to raise funds for Lincoln Institute, his involvement with the Radicals became even more pronounced. In April 1870, he was a featured speaker at a St. Louis rally

5. William A. Dallmeyer to U. S. Grant, April 26, 1869; Francis Rushman to U. S. Grant, April 26, 1869; H. B. Johnson to U. S. Grant, April 30, 1869; Dan M. Draper to U. S. Grant, April 30, 1869; John F. Benjamin, Joel F. Asper, Gustavus A. Finkelnburg, Sempronius H. Boyd, Carl Schurz, Charles D. Drake, David P. Dyer, Robert T. Van Horn, Samuel S. Burdett to U. S. Grant, December 13, 1869, Applications and Recommendations for the Grant Administration; Gary R. Kremer, "Background to Apostasy: James Milton Turner and the Republican Party," 65. Professor Parrish made this written comment in the margin of an early draft of the article cited.

6. James A. Padgett, "Ministers to Liberia and Their Diplomacy," 57–59; C. A. Newcombe to U. S. Grant, January 28, 1871, Applications and Recommendations for the Grant Administration.

held to celebrate the adoption of the Fifteenth Amendment. That gathering was one of the most spectacular black demonstrations ever held in the city. The *Missouri Democrat* estimated the crowd assembled to be between eighteen and twenty thousand. Blacks formed a procession, extending for two miles to a "vast gathering at Yeager's Garden." Once at the hall those assembled were treated to a number of orations, the last of which was delivered by Turner. He spoke in bitter opposition to pending state amendments that proposed to lessen restrictions on former rebels. Indeed, concerned about the Liberals' increasing strength in the legislature, he said that the very fact that such amendments could be proposed by a so-called Radical legislature was evidence that some lawmakers had betrayed the Radical cause. He offered his own assessment of the amendments and bitterly attacked those who would "unhesitatingly place the loyal colored man's hope for eligibility to office in an amendment with the formerly disloyal white man, thereby insuring from the very outset the defeat of both proposals to hold office." Likewise, he criticized the proposed amendment that would remove racial barriers to officeholding because he considered it a ruse to reenfranchise rebels:

> By including negro suffrage these men thought to win the colored vote for the suffrage amendment, and by the help of Democrats who could have no possible objection voting for the enfranchisement of the already enfranchised colored men, they hoped to carry the proposition to enfranchise rebels, and thereby place these men in a position to vote two years from next fall for their own eligibility to office and to vote eternally against the loyal black man becoming an office-holder in this State.

He went on to criticize "this same Legislature" for its failure to make any provision for blacks to sit on juries. With black people being denied the privilege of serving on juries and of holding office, he indicated that he was not "in favor of enfranchising the disloyal men of Missouri." He recalled that many believed that the ratification of the Fifteenth Amendment ended the mission of the Republican party, but he did not share that view. "I contend the mission of the party will not be complete until the word white is stricken from the constitution of every State in this Union and all men placed on perfect equality before the law of the country."

Turner thought there was another immediate task facing black people. Blacks must be "thoroughly represented" in the next nominating convention, "and see that our influence be cast for only such candidates as have made a consistent record in the past." He said he had compiled a list of votes on matters of importance to black people, and he intended to campaign against "all such men as voted no when they should have voted aye." A truly Radical general assembly needed to be elected the following fall: "I much prefer trusting my cause to the hands of men who, in the face of all opposing influences, have carried the work thus far successfully, than depending on men who fought to make slavery the chief corner-stone of our beautiful structure."

In short, Turner concluded, picking up the familiar self-reliance theme, blacks must exercise greater control over their own destinies.

> The spirit of self-reliance is the gem of all real growth in the individual, and wherever discovered in the masses it forms collective strength and contributes largely to the intelligent development of natural resources. I think it for us a fortunate circumstance that we are thus made to depend upon our own merit for the status we shall hold in the future. For in reading history, I find that whenever men or classes have been taught to recline dependently upon others, they have invariably lost their stimulus for active, self-reliant industry, and inertia has invariably ensued. The abstract fact of voting cannot elevate us . . . I counsel individual improvement, personal effort to obtain education, wealth and every facility necessary to the citizen. I feel assured of success ultimately, provided we pursue this course.

Turner's lecture brought him much praise, but he was still criticized by both blacks and whites for his unwillingness to support rebel reenfranchisement.[7]

In May, the *Missouri Democrat* published a caustic critique of his actions. By that time, he had attended the planning meetings of the Radical state committee, which was making preparations for the state convention. According to the *Democrat,* he had "stated openly that he was making speeches and organizing the colored people to vote against the pending constitutional amendments." Consequently, the *Democrat* felt compelled to warn "people in every part of the State [to be] on their guard against this speaker." The newspaper admonished Turner, saying that if the amendments to the Constitution failed

7. Information in this and the preceding three paragraphs is taken from the *Missouri Democrat* and *Missouri Republican,* April 12, 1870.

to pass, "the colored men [of Missouri] can never hope to have any other rights extended to them beside those which the United States Constitution gives."

Many blacks opposed Turner's stand against the amendments because of their concern that he was jeopardizing future concessions to the black cause. Turner reacted strongly to such opposition. In fact, the *Democrat* reported, he publicly abused a number of black detractors at a gathering in May. According to the newspaper account, Turner became so angry with Charleton H. Tandy, one of his more vocal opponents, that he bit him. "Mr. Tandy," the paper reported, "showed the scar on his hand, caused by the teeth of Turner."[8]

Despite opposition from both blacks and whites, Turner continued in the same vein. A few days later in Columbia, Missouri, he delivered another speech commemorating the adoption of the Fifteenth Amendment. According to a local newspaper, the *Statesman,* he praised the American system of government and urged blacks to prepare themselves for full participation in it. Echoing the sentiments contained in resolutions adopted by the National Labor Union Convention of the previous year, he advised unemployed blacks living in towns and cities to move to the country, go to work on farms, presumably as hired laborers, and earn money to buy land. Indeed, he described money as a great power leading to respectability and importance in the community. He advised his black listeners to educate themselves and their children "at every cost, and learn how to depend upon themselves, as they could no longer lean for support upon the whites."

He counseled this audience also to vote against the proposed state constitutional amendments. He argued that blacks were under no obligation to disenfranchised whites who had done nothing for their advancement. His speech concluded, Turner turned over the podium to a black man named Cook who spoke "but a few minutes." Cook had come to Columbia specifically to counter Turner's arguments against the constitutional amendments. However, he changed his mind after hearing Turner's speech. Cook later invited Turner to travel with him to St. Charles, Missouri, to deliver an anti-amendment speech.[9]

Turner continued making speeches against the constitutional amendments throughout the summer of 1870. In late July, in fact, his

8. *Missouri Democrat,* May 13, 1870, reprinted in *People's Tribune,* May 18, 1870.
9. *Missouri Statesman,* May 20, 27, 1870.

campaigning gained him the criticism of several members of the Lincoln Institute Board of Trustees and Principal Richard B. Foster. Lincoln officials accused Turner of engaging in politics when he was supposed to be working as an agent for the school. Despite this pressure, Turner continued on as before. In early August he recounted for a St. Louis newspaper a conversation he said he had on a train with a white skeptic: "I met a man on the cars who asked, 'Do you think that your people ought to be allowed to hold office and vote?' I told him that I never honored the matter with a thought, and that I knew we ought." Turner added, "I believe with Thomas Jefferson that every man who pays taxes should be allowed to vote. But I believe also . . . that every man who commits treason should be hung dead by the neck."[10]

Everywhere he went Turner expressed hostility toward the "treasonous" rebels. Likewise, he continued to insist that blacks be given "fair" representation at the state nominating convention to be held in September. His position on those two issues placed him firmly in the camp of the Radical gubernatorial hopeful, the incumbent Governor Joseph W. McClurg, and against the more conciliatory Liberal faction, led by Carl Schurz and gubernatorial candidate B. Gratz Brown. The Radical State Executive Committee met at St. Louis in early May, with Turner appearing before it, reiterating his warning that the black vote would be cast for the Radical ticket only if blacks were given a fair share in its selection. The committee drafted a proposal for black representation, revised it and redrafted another proposal when it met again on August 2 to prepare for the convention. Turner rejected the committee's offer and was able to have his objections sustained, forcing the adoption of his recommendation for 180 black delegates out of a total of 797.

The Liberal followers of Schurz and Brown, already disenchanted with the autocratic machinations of the Radicals, were distressed over these concessions to Turner. They suspected, quite rightly, as it turned out, that his ability to have his way on the black representation issue was indicative of the McClurg faction's strength. The fight over re-enfranchisement of former rebels, combined with the quarrel over black representation, split the Republican party at the convention in September, with the Liberals nominating B. Gratz Brown for governor and the Radicals nominating Joseph W. McClurg. Both groups solicited the votes of Missouri's newly enfranchised blacks. Turner, con-

10. Dwight, "Black Suffrage in Missouri," 144, 124

vinced by the Radicals' stand against rebel reenfranchisement that they were truer friends of blacks than the Liberals, supported McClurg. Indeed, speaking in St. Joseph soon after the convention, Turner urged blacks to stand firm for McClurg and against the amendments, reminding them that they were no longer hewers of wood and drawers of water and that their numbers would more than offset the numbers of those who had bolted the party.[11]

Meanwhile, the Liberals attempted to win over the black voters by using the services of Charleton H. Tandy and George B. Wedley, both blacks from St. Louis. In mid-October, William Grosvenor, the editor of the *St. Louis Daily Democrat* and state chairman of the Liberal Republican party, even tried to bribe Turner into supporting the proposed amendments and the Liberal gubernatorial candidate Brown. Turner declined to do so and made public Grosvenor's offer of $2,500.[12]

As the November election drew closer, however, Radicals had second thoughts about their rigidity on the reenfranchisement issue. Finally realizing that winning the battle on that issue at the convention might lose him the war at the polls, McClurg signaled a Radical about-face when he indicated that he would no longer oppose the proposed constitutional amendments. On October 28, the day after McClurg's letter was written, Turner loyally but forlornly followed the party line by endorsing the passage of the same amendments. The *Missouri Democrat* responded immediately by castigating Turner for this "acrobatic feat" of reversing his earlier position. "No man," the *Democrat* reported, "can estimate the harm which he has done to the colored people who trusted his fluent talk." Likewise, the *Democrat* reacted with some shock at Turner's effrontery in announcing his own candidacy for a congressional seat from Missouri's second district. Turner even went so far, another newspaper charged, as to endorse the candidacy of certain Democrats, hoping to split the would-be Liberal vote, forcing Democrats and Liberals to neutralize each other. In that way, he attempted to stop the apostate Liberals from rising to power and restoring the old racist political and social order.[13]

11. *Missouri Democrat,* May 13 and August 4, 1870; *Missouri State Times,* May 27, 1870; Parrish, *Missouri under Radical Rule, 1865–1870,* 291; Dwight, "Black Suffrage in Missouri," 143.

12. Parrish, *Missouri under Radical Rule,* 301–2; Dwight, "Black Suffrage in Missouri," 143–44.

13. This announcement came in a letter from McClurg to a friend. The letter was subsequently published in newspapers throughout Missouri: *Missouri*

Such late-hour maneuvering was of little help to the Radicals. Despite these and other machinations, despite Turner's efforts and overwhelming black support, despite even the fact that President Grant endorsed the Radical candidates and condemned the bolters, the split in the party was too much to overcome, and a coalition of dissident Liberal Republicans and Democrats defeated the Radicals at the polls. The intensity and bitterness of the 1870 election in Missouri precluded any post-election rapprochement between Liberal Republicans and Radicals. Radicals could not count on patronage positions from the Liberals. As a result, many of them looked to the Grant administration as a source of federal appointments. One of those people who sought the special favor of the president was Turner. He renewed his effort of the previous year to gain appointment to the Liberian ministership.[14]

The facts surrounding the actual appointment are somewhat muddled. In 1933, a prominent St. Louis businessman, Rolla Wells, recalled in his memoirs that his father, Erastus Wells, had almost single-handedly obtained the ministership for Turner. He and his family were staying in the Willard Hotel in Washington, D.C., when his sister became ill. The father rushed to the hotel office trying to find someone to go for a doctor. Unfortunately, the distressed father was unable to find another soul awake in the hotel, since it was five o'clock in the morning. He rushed frantically onto Pennsylvania Avenue. Just then, a black man happened to come "sauntering along," recognized Mr. Wells as a St. Louisan, and asked if he could help. After being told that a child was quite ill, the black man raced off to locate a doctor, who "arrived in due time and all was well."

That black man from St. Louis was, of course, James Milton Turner. Several days later he returned to the hotel. Mr. Wells asked him what he was doing in Washington, and Turner replied that he had been trying unsuccessfully to gain the appointment to Liberia. He had, however, abandoned all hope for it and was trying to find a way to get back to St. Louis. Erastus Wells immediately told Turner that he would intercede with President Grant for him, asked him to

Statesman, November 4, 1870; Missouri Democrat, October 31, 1870; Missouri State Times, November 11, 1870. It seems unlikely that Turner saw himself as a serious candidate, given the fact that this announcement came only days before the election.

14. Parrish, Missouri under Radical Rule, 309–11.

stay in the city for a few days, and loaned him money "to tide him over."

Erastus Wells and Ulysses Grant were, according to son Rolla, "quite friendly, having known each other in the early days when Grant was living in St. Louis." Subsequently, Mr. Wells approached the president in the White House and asked him to appoint Turner to the Liberian ministership. Grant balked at the suggestion, however, claiming that the appointment of a black man to such a position was "unprecedented." The president's opposition to the appointment soon faded when he was told the story of "the supposedly dying infant daughter." The president, according to Wells, responded to the story by instructing his secretary to draw up a certificate of appointment for James Milton Turner as minister to Liberia. More than thirty years later, Turner endorsed Rolla Wells's candidacy when the latter was running for mayor of St. Louis in 1901. He told an audience at a large "Negro meeting" that Erastus Wells, the father of the Democratic candidate for mayor, had facilitated his appointment to the Liberian ministership.[15]

In an interview with a *St. Louis Post-Dispatch* reporter in 1898, Turner gave a somewhat different account of the appointment. He acknowledged that he had gone to Washington in search of a job shortly after the Radicals' defeat in the 1870 election. However, he did not acknowledge seeking a diplomatic post. In fact, he said he did not "aspire to anything higher than to be a messenger at $100 a month." Purportedly, he met with the president, told him of his intentions, and was turned down flat. The next day, he said, he chanced to meet the president, who was taking a morning walk in Lafayette Square. Again the two men talked, but Grant gave him no indication of a change of heart. By that time Turner admitted to thinking "very ill of General Grant" and being "mad all over." Later that day, en route by train to St. Louis, Turner was invited to join a "party of office-seekers" for dinner. He declined the invitation, and the group left him alone to sulk. While passing through Pittsburgh a few minutes later, these men suddenly burst into his car and congratulated him on being named a United States minister. His appointment to Liberia had been announced in the evening papers.[16]

Whatever truth there may be in either of these renditions of how the appointment occurred, both ignore the more important role of

15. The material in this and the preceding two paragraphs is drawn from Rolla Wells, *Episodes of My Life*, 20–23.
16. *St. Louis Post-Dispatch*, March 6, 1898.

Radical support in Turner's quest for office. Erastus Wells was not the major force behind Turner's appointment. Neither was Turner's visit with the president. In fact, Turner received the appointment because of another round of Radical support. Within days after the 1870 election, Grant again received pro-Turner letters from Missouri Radicals. Lame-duck Governor Joseph W. McClurg was the first to write, sending a letter dated November 10, 1870. McClurg emphasized that Turner could not expect anything from the party that had just come to power in Missouri, but insisted that Turner's ability was unquestioned and his qualifications for a high position undoubted. "I have carefully observed Mr. Turner during the canvass," he concluded, "and cannot hesitate to pronounce him a man of strict integrity."[17]

Two days later, E. S. Rowse, treasurer for the state Republican central committee, wrote a letter endorsing Turner's application. Rowse asserted that Turner's "great eloquence and power have rendered great aid to the national Republican cause in this state and his services should be recognized by all who have that cause at heart." He told the president that "no more efficient campaigner has worked in our cause and though we have not been successful our defeat has by no means been brought about for lack of earnest effort and one [of] the most efficient workers we had was Mr. Turner." Likewise, on November 12, the chairman of the state Republican committee, Isaac F. Shepards, endorsed Turner's candidacy. He acknowledged that Turner had worked as a canvasser for the state Republican committee, asserting that Turner was "an able speaker of intelligence and judgment, and an earnest devotee to Republican principles." He drew attention to the fact that Turner's "influence among the colored people has been very great," acknowledged that the black leader had been extensively criticized by the opposition press, but continued in an eloquent defense of Turner's character: "Where many white men of influence have faltered, he has stood firm; where personal friends of his own race have gone over to the bolters, he has maintained his integrity; and where pecuniary temptations have been proferred he has repelled them." Such a record, Shepards concluded, entitled him "to a full consideration for the service he has shown."[18]

17. J. W. McClurg to U. S. Grant, November 10, 1870, Applications and Recommendations for the Grant Administration.
18. E. S. Rowse to U. S. Grant; Isaac F. Shepards to U. S. Grant, November 12, 1870, ibid.

More than two months later, Turner was still without a position and eager for the appointment. In late January 1871, he traveled to Washington for an audience with Grant. He carried with him a letter of introduction, dated January 28, 1871, written by Carmen A. Newcombe, a party faithful and a personal friend of the president's. In his letter, Newcombe indicated that Turner stood "high in the esteem of the colored men of this State all of whom nearly to a man were faithful among the faithless" and was visiting Washington as an applicant for the Liberian ministership. Newcombe then went on to express the hope that "if [Turner] can go to Liberia for two years he will gain a National reputation which will make him the universally trusted leader of the colored men in the Campaign of '72." He continued: "It is highly important that the colored men of the nation be held together as a unit and in no way can this be better done than by recognizing their claims in an Executive appointment such as Mr. Turner seeks. He can come back in '72 and take his place as the chosen leader of his race and whose [sic] claims to leadership will not be disputed."[19]

Party faithfuls obviously viewed Turner as an actual political force in Missouri who had the potential to exert that same positive force on the national level, if he gained exposure. The president must have agreed with this analysis. Soon after Turner's visit, he reviewed Turner's dossier and made the following note on the back of one of the letters of recommendation: "If the Minister to Liberia does not accept, and leave for his post with but little delay, I am willing that this appt. be made. U. S. Grant." This note, dated February 2, 1871, also gives a ring of authenticity to Turner's 1898 account of the appointment. He reported then that during his conversation with the president, Grant told him that he had appointed an Arkansas man to serve as Liberian minister, but "he had delayed his departure and was not bowed down with gratitude." As Turner recounted the story, Grant then "rang his bell and instructed his secretary to notify this appointee that he must start that night or not at all." Less than two months after his visit with Grant, Turner received official notification of his nomination as Minister Resident and Consul General for the United States to the Republic of Liberia. On March 17, 1871, he wrote to Secretary of State Hamilton Fish, accepting "the exalted position thus tendered." After receiving senate confirmation, the new

19. C. A. Newcombe to U. S. Grant, January 28, 1871, ibid.

minister settled his personal affairs and sailed from New York on May 25, 1871. He arrived at his post on July 7, 1871.[20]

Turner's firsthand involvement in Missouri politics was over, at least for the time being. He had, by this time, become a formidable force. Julius Walsh, visiting St. Louis from Philadelphia in April 1871, expressed to his wife a sentiment that many who watched Turner's performances must have felt: "He is one of the best public speakers I have ever heard, his language & delivery would be creditable to a great many United States Senators."[21]

On May 17, 1871, the *Jefferson City People's Tribune,* often the black orator's foe, offered a sympathetic and generally accurate assessment of his political career in Missouri. The *Tribune* described him as "the connecting link between the black and white politicians." As such, he led a particularly precarious existence. "His luck has been like that of the flying fish who when acting as a bird gets the gull after him, and when he drops into the water finds the shark waiting to receive him." In short, Turner was criticized by both blacks and whites. "He became, as he claimed," the *Tribune* asserted, "the representative of 20,000 freedmen." That claim was disputed, of course, and Turner had numerous "quarrels on the stump, and everywhere with men of his own color. But," the paper continued, "he was triumphant."[22]

A speech Turner delivered at Jefferson City to a largely black audience shortly before leaving for Liberia offers a good illustration of how far, in his view, he had advanced. Indeed, he offered his own experience as evidence of how far a black man could advance, presumably in a Radical-run America. Turner spoke with great pride about how he appreciated his audience's confidence in his "ability to discharge the duties of this high and important mission to a foreign

20. Written on back of E. S. Rowse to U. S. Grant, November 12, 1870, ibid.; *St. Louis Post-Dispatch,* March 6, 1898; J. M. Turner to Hamilton Fish, March 17, 1871. These letters are filed with "Despatches from United States Ministers to Liberia, 1863–1906," roll 2, M170, vol. 2, October 24, 1868–January 24, 1872, National Archives, Washington, D.C. Hereafter referred to as "Despatches." J. M. Turner to Hamilton Fish, May 12, 1871, Despatch No. l, July 10, 1871, Despatches, vol. 2.

21. Julius S. Walsh to Mrs. Walsh, April 5, 1871, Walsh Collection, Missouri Historical Society, St. Louis, Missouri.

22. The material in this and the following three paragraphs is taken from *People's Tribune,* May 17, 1871.

port." He recounted how "a few short years since," he had been "a slave in this community." He continued, calling attention to the memory of white political heroes:

> But such has been the progress of your beauteous republic in the hands of men who learn well the lessons of Washington, Jefferson, Jay and that constellation of bright heroes who laid the foundation stone of our organic system; such has been the revolution accomplished under the auspices and control of their influence, that today instead of standing here a plodding slave I stand here the accredited representative to a foreign port.

He went on to promise those who had gathered to honor him that he would keep their trust. He indicated, in what was clearly a gross misrepresentation of the facts, that "the position has been thrust on me by popular opinion. It is not given to me of my seeking." That overdramatization of his appointment behind him, he went on to promise "to represent the whole United States, and the opinion of the American people . . . upon the sunny shores of Africa." He acknowledged, moreover, in a statement that clearly placed distance between himself and the black masses, that he had a special duty to remember "that heretofore despised class with which I hold my humble identity." He promised black people that he would "never no never, hazard your interests." He had been, he made clear, "born in your midst, one who has lived in this free republic from childhood, under auspicious circumstances, at risk of life and limb. . . . frequently opposed [to] the institution of slavery, [and] to-day. . . . the enemy of all legislation or law that would compromise any citizen of the republic."

Clearly, Turner saw his ministerial appointment as a vindication of his belief both in the Radical party and in America, the land of "organic government," where life was destined to get better and better for blacks. Not only had the Radicals gone to battle for black education and suffrage, they had even made him the official representative of all American people in a foreign land. What greater proof of sincerity and purity of motive could there be? All would be right with a Radical-run America. Radicalism would both carry through and preserve the revolution wrought by the Civil War.

Or so he thought. He could not anticipate the frustrations he would suffer subsequently in the face of a reinvigorated racism in the late seventies and beyond. He could not know that, within less than a decade, those same Radical Republicans would turn their backs on his own effort to be elected to a congressional seat from Missouri's third district; and that by the late eighties he would lead a movement of blacks away from Republicanism and toward Democracy and Independence. He could not foresee any of those events, so he left for Liberia with an optimism about his future and the future of the country that he would never experience again.

CHAPTER IV
The President's Man in a Savage Land

I am fully aware and highly appreciative of the importance of the position taken by the Administration in the presence of our entire country in elevating one like myself to a position of such great responsibility, trust, and confidence.

—James Milton Turner
March 30, 1872

James Milton Turner left New York City for Liberia on May 25, 1871. He had hoped to leave earlier but was detained, primarily by a desire to oversee the enrollment of his stepdaughter and an orphan niece in Oberlin College. His decision to send the two children under his care there is symbolically significant: it represented an attempt on his part to provide them with the same opportunity for growth and development that he had enjoyed.[1]

Indeed, it was that opportunity, in his view, combined with the responsiveness of the American political system, that allowed him to achieve so much in such a short time. He was flattered to be named the Minister Resident and Consul General to Liberia. He reveled in the irony surrounding the appointment. As a black man in Missouri little more than one year before, he had been unable to vote. Suddenly he had become the number-one American citizen in a foreign country, the official representative of the United States.

In his correspondence as minister, Turner exhibited a strong affection for the country that allowed his rise to a position of prominence. He also praised the Republican party for allowing virtuous

1. Turner to Hamilton Fish, March 12, 1871; Turner to Hamilton Fish, May 25, 1871, Despatches, vol. 2. M170, vol. 2, October 24, 1868–January 24, 1872, National Archives, Washington, D.C.

and hardworking men, whatever their skin color, to advance up the ladder of success. Because he found the Liberian life-style so inconsistent with values of hard work and self-reliance, he searched for ways to uplift what he continually referred to as "a barbaric people," hoping to become an instrument for progress and Americanization on the west coast of Africa. He reflected, in this effort, a desire similar to that of one of the best-known black missionaries to Liberia of the era, Alexander Crummell, who went to West Africa in 1853 and remained for twenty years. Crummell, like Turner, saw his role and that of other westernized blacks as "potential 'civilizers' of indigenous Africans."[2]

Unfortunately for Turner, however, his Liberian experience was destined to be smattered with disappointments. He found the Liberian social, political, economic, and religious ways of life highly resistant to change, and the Americo-blacks who had migrated there quite ineffective. Likewise, he never fully adjusted to the Liberian climate, succumbing frequently to bouts of malaria, several of them quite severe, throughout his seven years in Liberia. Finally, the drudgery of his day-to-day routine involved him in activities that he could hardly have anticipated when he wrote to Hamilton Fish, indicating that "after well matured deliberation I have determined to accept the exalted position thus tendered me by the government of my country."[3]

Turner arrived in Liberia unaware of what to expect, bereft of any detailed knowledge of West African culture, and armed only with the printed instructions given to all diplomatic agents of the United States. His instructions included a general if somewhat bland expression of confidence in his ability to do that which would be "conducive to the harmony and friendly relations existing between the governments of the two countries." At his official reception by the president of Liberia on July 19, 1871, he responded to his host's hospitality with a speech outlining what he hoped to accomplish as minister to Liberia. Relishing being the center of attention, he proclaimed his own closeness to power by emphasizing that he was carrying out the "expressed command" of President Grant in making known to the Republic of Liberia his country's desire to strengthen and perpetuate

2. Alfred Moss, "Alexander Crummell: Black Nationalist and Apostle of Western Civilization," in Litwack and Meier, eds., *Black Leaders of the Nineteenth Century*, 243; see also, Wilson Jeremiah Moses, *Alexander Crummell: A Study of Civilization and Discontent*.
3. Turner to Hamilton Fish, March 17, 1871, Despatches, vol. 2.

friendly relations between the two states. He congratulated the Liberian officials on the noble enterprise they were engaged in and revealed, in the process, both his own antipathy toward the "barbarism" of African culture and the means by which he believed Africa could be "saved." It would be, he said in tones reminiscent of his antebellum education, "the Christian religion" that would "debarbarize and benefit for almost immediate usefulness thousands of human beings whose intellects are today debased by the destructive potency of heathenish superstition."[4]

Sometime later Turner's wife wrote to a St. Louis friend of this occasion, telling her that "the President and Cabinet gave Mr. Turner a superb reception." She had been overwhelmed by the novelty of the proceedings. "Just to think," she wrote, "of generals and colonels in uniform, Cabinet officers, city councilmen, lawyers, doctors, other professional characters, authors, editors, poets, and other distinguished literary people, together with a live President and a bevy of ladies to correspond, and they, everyone, colored!"[5]

Another opportunity for similar festivities presented itself six months later when Joseph J. Roberts was installed as president. Turner attended the inauguration and was officially presented to President Roberts. He reassured Roberts of the United States' concern for the prosperity of Liberia and for the continued good relations between the two countries. He emphasized again that he had been "especially entrusted by His Excellency the President of the United States . . . with the responsible duty of contributing to the perpetuity of these important relations."[6]

State dinners such as one given by the Liberian president in March 1872 were common fare for the foreign minister. He enjoyed the opportunity to gather with other dignitaries, expressing delight at the number of distinguished persons present. On that particular occasion, Roberts offered a toast to President Grant, to which Turner felt it "a very pleasant duty to respond." Indeed, he rarely missed an

4. Instruction No. 1, March 10, 1871, "Diplomatic Instructions of the Department of State, 1801–1906," Liberia, March 16, 1863–July 1906, M77, roll 110, National Archives, Washington, D.C. Hereafter referred to as "Instructions." "Reception of the American Minister," *African Repository*, 47:309–13. For a handwritten version of this speech, see Enclosure 1, Dispatch No. 8, July 25, 1871, Despatches, vol. 2.

5. *African Repository*, 344.

6. Enclosure A, Dispatch No. 35, January 24, 1872, Despatches, vol. 2.

opportunity to praise publicly the president who had given him such a responsible job. Presumably, he saw Grant's willingness to appoint him to a high governmental position as one manifestation of the president's sensitivity to the problems of oppressed Americans. Unable to distinguish between his own success and the advancement of blacks generally, he wrote of his belief that Grant's major goal was "the utilization of every national capacity to the advancement, prosperity, and amelioration of the great-American masses." Only one other Republican, Charles Sumner, was fit to be ranked as Grant's peer. When Sumner died in 1874, still advocating the passage of a federal civil rights act, Turner wrote to W. H. Lynch, the secretary of an ad hoc committee formed to commemorate Sumner's passing. He praised Sumner as "America's most self-sacrificing humanitarian" and "her most eminent statesman," indicating that he identified Sumner's egalitarian attitude toward blacks as the standard by which all others should be judged.[7]

The country that Grant and Sumner served was no less blessed by Turner's tributes. Once, on the occasion of a Fourth of July celebration, he wrote to the administrative officers of the Republic of Liberia, informing them that his country's celebration of its independence "is to an American under any circumstances a proper occasion for the renewal of pledges to Democratic Institutions of Government." He went on to express the hope that those "same propitious institutions" could be made to work in Liberia, a place he identified as "the outpost of civilization in this unknown land."[8]

Even though state dinners, formal parties, and Fourth of July celebrations were important parts of the Liberian minister's job, they did not occupy most of his time. Nor were his more time-consuming duties always so pleasant. One of his most important tasks was to keep the State Department up-to-date on the internal politics of Liberia. That was no small task, considering the chaos of Liberia's domestic affairs when Turner arrived.

Turner's identification of Liberia as an "outpost of civilization" is a useful concept in trying to understand that country's avowed pur-

7. Dispatch No. 41, March 15, 1871, Despatches, vol. 3; Dispatch No. 106, January 1, 1874, Despatches, vol. 4; Turner to W. H. Lynch, June 20, 1874, Enclosure B, in Dispatch No. 130, June 20, 1874, Despatches, vol. 4.

8. Turner to J. J. Roberts, J. E. Moore, H. W. Dennis, and William M. Davis, July 4, 1874, Enclosure A, in Dispatch No. 136, July 8, 1874, Despatches, vol. 4.

pose in the 1870s. Liberia had been established in 1822 as the result of a movement begun by a private organization, the American Colonization Society, to establish a settlement for freed blacks of the United States on the west coast of Africa. The colony was named Liberia, after liberty, and its capital city, modeled after Washington, D.C., was named Monrovia after Pres. James Monroe. The political, legal, social, economic, and religious structures of the new settlement were determined by the American Colonization Society and modeled after that of the United States.

The task of carving out a new country in Africa was great. From the beginning, the black Americans who settled Liberia met fierce opposition from native Africans. That opposition, combined with the hostility of the climate to native Americans and the limited resources available to the settlers, made for a high level of tension and instability in the lives of the first generation of American blacks to go to Africa. Those obstacles were overcome sufficiently, however, to establish Liberia as a sovereign state after twenty-five years of existence, and in 1847 it elected its first president. By 1870 Liberia had become a successful commercial site for trade with Europe and the United States. Indeed, Liberia's increased production of sugarcane and coffee was at the heart of America's desire to maintain Liberia as a de facto colony. At this time, the country had 286 miles of coastland, but it stretched back from the coast only about forty-five miles. There were probably between seven and ten thousand Liberians of American origin in the country in 1870.

The first decade of Liberia's independence was dominated by Pres. Joseph J. Roberts, who was elected in 1847 and reelected every two years until 1855, when he was succeeded by his vice-president, Gen. Stephen A. Benson. Benson in turn served four terms (1856–1863). Daniel B. Warner served as president from 1864 to 1867 and James S. Payne from 1868 to 1869. All four of these men were members of the conservative Republican party, a group that represented the mulattoes of Liberia against the darker-skinned blacks, who were known as the Whigs. There were a number of issues on which the two parties differed. The Whigs wanted better-skilled and better-educated immigrants from the West Indies, while the Republicans, fearing that such people would challenge their power, wanted to encourage the less well educated blacks from the southern United States to emigrate. In addition, the blacks favored opening up the interior, while the mulattoes were fearful that new trade routes might mean a lessening of their grip on the commerce of the country.[9]

The black Whig candidate for president, Edward James Roye, won that position in 1870 after what historian Hollis Lynch has called "one of the most fiercely contested elections in Liberian history." He quickly committed his country to an expensive long-range plan of development. Roye, like Turner a former Oberlin College student, had been in Liberia since 1846. He and his Whig colleagues were determined to open the interior of Liberia to settlement and trade. Such a goal could be fulfilled most easily by means of a railroad. "I believe," he said in his inaugural address, "that erection of a railroad will have a wonderful influence in the civilization and elevation of the native tribes." He argued, "The barriers of heathenism and superstition will disappear before the railroad . . . as frost and snow will dissolve before a summer's rain." Such an undertaking would serve to increase Liberia's exports, while also providing the country with a potentially enormous market for finished goods. Unfortunately, however, such a program would be extremely expensive and burdensome for the country.[10]

Roye hoped to finance his scheme by securing a loan either in Europe or in the United States. David Chinery, Liberia's consul general to Great Britain, and William S. Anderson and William H. Johnson, Liberian financiers, quickly negotiated a loan for five hundred thousand dollars with a private corporation in London. Roye publicly supported the loan, even though its terms were usurious and the agents who arranged it stood to make windfall commissions. Immediate opposition to the loan arose among Republicans. They were further angered when President Roye declared the adoption of a constitutional amendment extending his term of office from two to four years. That was the last straw. The Republicans began a movement to depose Roye and his government. Turner kept the State Department

9. Information in this and the three preceding paragraphs is taken from Richard West, *Back to Africa: A History of Sierra Leone and Liberia,* 115, 224, 238; Benjamin Brawley, *A Social History of the American Negro,* 193. Problems faced by American settlers in Liberia are detailed in Tom Shick, *Behold the Promised Land: A History of Afro-American Settler Society in Nineteenth-Century Liberia.*

10. Hollis R. Lynch, *Edward Wilmot Blyden: Pan-Negro Patriot, 1832–1912,* 49; Abayomi C. Cassell, *Liberia: A History of the First African Republic,* 267, 272.

abreast of the events in Liberia, while maintaining close ties with both Roye's Whigs and the opposing Republicans. He hoped, however, to avoid taking sides. Unfortunately, the problem of adjusting to the Liberian climate led him to make a move that jeopardized the neutrality he was so intent upon preserving. Convinced that he needed some "trustworthy person" to help him during those periods when he was ill, he hired Henry DeWitt Brown to serve as his aide. He found Brown to be particularly competent and helpful, largely because Brown had recently retired as private secretary to the Liberian secretary of state.[11]

Turner quickly learned about the volatility of Liberian politics. In mid-August 1871, he received a letter from Liberia's acting secretary of state, Sydney Crummell, son of the American missionary Alexander Crummell, informing him that Brown was an enemy of the government and should be removed "from the responsibility of Secretary to the United States Legation." The American minister responded by informing Liberian officials that Brown had no official relationship with the United States government and, therefore, could not be removed from a position he did not hold. He explained that Brown was employed only to help him during his acclimation period, and that the Liberian citizen was not paid by the United States government, "but at my personal expense." He noted that his two immediate predecessors had done the same thing without objection being offered by the government of Liberia. He concluded by informing Liberian officials that if their government "feels still to request his dismissal and will place the matter in such terms as this legation can recognise, I promise to give the subject most earnest consideration." Crummell replied with an even stronger insistence that Brown resign, and he soon did so.[12]

The Brown incident was only one manifestation of the strong hostilities between Whigs and Republicans. Opposition to President Roye continued to grow. Turner indicated the impending coup when he wrote in September 1871 to notify the State Department of the assassination of Samuel S. G. Findlay, the postmaster general and

11. Cassell, *Liberia*, 272; see also Lynch, *Edward Wilmot Blyden*, 48–52; Brawley, *A Social History of the American Negro*, 195; West, *Back to Africa*, 240; Dispatch No. 10, August 26, 1871, Despatches, vol. 2.

12. Sydney G. Crummell to Turner, August 17, 1870, Enclosure A; Turner to Sydney G. Crummell, August 18, 1871, Enclosure B; Henry DeWitt Brown to Turner, August 19, 1871, Enclosure D, in Dispatch No. 10, Despatches, vol. 2.

collector of customs for the Liberian government. The assassination occurred near Turner's residence; as he told the story, "sixteen or twenty men lay in ambush until the return of the Post Master Genl. from his supper and fire[d] simultaneously upon him from his rear." The Whigs, according to Turner, described Findlay as an uncompromising supporter of the Roye administration while the Republicans declared that he was nothing more than a "desperado." The government's inability to arrest anyone for committing this crime led Turner to conclude in the letter that the Roye administration was in serious trouble.[13]

The coup finally came in late October 1871. On October 25, Turner wrote to the State Department, informing it that "a revolution exists in Liberia." The following day, the American minister was formally notified that Roye had been deposed and that a provisional government had been established. Two days later the provisional government arrested the deposed president, his secretary of state, and his secretary of the treasury. Turner attended a preliminary investigation and discovered that the president had been charged with pocketing seventy-five thousand dollars from the English loan.[14]

Turner waited only three days after the coup before extending official recognition to the new government. He assured the Chief Executive Committee that "the policy of strict neutrality with reference to any internal disturbance that may now exist within the Republic of Liberia, will be adhered to by the Government of the United States." That neutrality was threatened, however, by two separate requests made of Turner. On October 26 the citizens of Maryland County, Liberia, met in a mass meeting to express their opposition to the fall of the Roye administration. They were so displeased that they petitioned Turner to have the area in which they lived annexed to the United States. Turner responded that to extend protection to the secessionists would violate the pledge of neutrality that he was committed to uphold. Similarly, President Roye wrote to Turner, swearing an oath of allegiance to the United States and asking for the protection of that government from "mob action." The American minister de-

13. Dispatch No. 11, September 4, 1871, Despatches, vol. 2.
14. Dispatch No. 18, October 25, 1871, Despatches, vol. 2; U.S. Department of State, *Papers Relating to the Foreign Relations of the United States* (1872), 323. Hereafter referred to as *Foreign Relations*. Dispatch No. 19, October 30, 1871, Despatches, vol. 2; H. R. W. Johnson to Turner, October 28, 1871, Enclosure A, in Dispatch No. 20, November 1, 1871, Despatches, vol. 2.

nied Roye's request. Later, after several months of confinement in the
city jail, Roye managed to escape, only to be pursued by a group of
fifty men. According to Turner's account of what followed, Roye
leaped from the beach into the sea in an attempt to swim to the small
boat of an English vessel close to shore. He drowned in the process.
Exactly how is unclear. Turner wrote that he had talked with the
coroner who rendered the verdict of death by drowning, although he
also reported that an examining physician had reported a skull frac-
ture as well.[15]

The frenzy surrounding the 1871 revolution caused Turner great
personal discomfort, leading him to express increasingly hostile criticism of the Americo-Liberians. In February 1872 he wrote of his
displeasure with the "sensitiveness of the people of this country as
relates to real or supposed interference by foreigners," adding that
this "renders my position both official and social exceedingly delicate." In short, the image-conscious Turner experienced a drop in
prestige during the period of the revolution because of the prevailing
suspicion of foreigners, and he was quite unhappy about his declining
status.[16]

Six weeks later he offered a concrete example of the lack of respect that the Liberians showed him. Liberian officials had been
searching for the fifteen-thousand-dollar first installment of the English loan for some time. They believed it was stolen by former President Roye. The search for the money, Turner wrote, "had been diligent and persistent, and so eager does this government seem for the
capture of said monies, that its eagerness apparently gives assurances
to the citizens of this country to reciprocally suspicion each other and
especially to suspect foreigners." He went on to explain that his wife's
recent illness had forced both of them to move temporarily outside
the city of Monrovia. He had left most of his possessions in the house
of his landlord. Prior to this, he had been trying to accumulate "some

15. Turner to H. W. B. Johnson, October 30, 1871, Enclosure B, in Dispatch No. 20, November 1, 1871, Despatches, vol. 2; Foreign Relations, 1872,
327–28; H. W. Erskene to Turner, October 26, 1871, Enclosure A, and Turner
to H. W. Erskene, October 26, 1871, Enclosure B, in Dispatch No. 21, November 1, 1871, Despatches, vol. 2.
16. E. J. Roye to Turner, October 23, 1871, Enclosure A, and Turner to
E. J. Roye, October 26, 1871, Enclosure B, in Dispatch No. 22, November 1,
1871, Despatches, vol. 2; Dispatch No. 39, February 14, 1872, Despatches,
vol. 3.

English gold coin" with which to finance his sick wife's return to the United States. As it happened, Mrs. Roye gave Turner two hundred pounds in return for his personal draft. Soon after she carried the money to him, Turner's landlord witnessed the exchange and concluded that the money given to Turner was part of the fifteen-thousand-dollar installment. The landlord and his wife entered Turner's room while he was out of the city, searched his belongings, and found the money tied in a red shawl. The Liberian immediately concluded that Turner was party to the theft.

Subsequently, Turner overheard his landlord criticizing him to a friend. The words stung Turner's pride. The landlord called him a "nigger" and a "black thieve" and complained that "we have enough [of that type] here without getting more from America." Accustomed to the United States sending white diplomats to his country, the landlord went on to say that he did not understand why a "nigger" had been sent to Liberia to serve as minister, concluding with the assertion that "we can't respect no nigger as Minister." It was this last statement that particularly offended Turner, and his response ironically revealed his own distinct class biases. Certain that his education, background, and experience had allowed him to escape any identification with a lower class, he complained bitterly to the State Department that the repeated personal indignities he suffered had led him to the conclusion that "the policy of our President in appointing a negro citizen of the U.S. to this country is not fully appreciated." Even if others did not understand, he was "fully aware and highly appreciative of the importance of the position taken by the Administration in the presence of our entire country in elevating one like myself to a position of such great responsibility, trust, and confidence." Indeed, he continued, it was the very importance of his position that led him to feel a responsibility toward the United States government, and also to the people of Liberia, "an immature state," he noted, "which is composed of men with whom I am identified by blood and race."[17]

17. Dispatch No. 40, March 30, 1872, Despatches, vol. 3; Turner to H. W. B. Johnson, March 9, 1872, Enclosure A; H. W. B. Johnson to Turner, March 13, 1872, Enclosure B; Turner to H. W. B. Johnson, March 14, 1872, Enclosure C, in Dispatch No. 40, March 30, 1872, Despatches, vol. 3. Upon learning of the accusations against him, Turner went to the Executive Mansion and protested to President Roberts. He offered to allow his baggage to be searched, but the president assured him that the American minister was above suspicion. Later the Liberian secretary of state wrote to Turner assuring him that he was not a suspect.

Regardless of the insults that had been inflicted upon him, he still felt obligated to play a role in the advancement of civilization, both among the native Africans and the Liberians. Consequently, in May 1872 he forwarded an optimistic four-thousand-word dispatch, assessing the "national capacities, present condition, and future prospects of Liberia," as a means by which to enlighten that country as to the route it must travel. He began by emphasizing the vast potential of the small republic. Liberia, he wrote, was "better adapted to the rapid progress of civilization than any African territory." It had good harbors and was blessed with an abundance of streams and rivers. Its soil, he wrote, was "inexhaustibly productive." In short, he said, "the liberality of nature . . . is quite sufficient for the purposes of Christianity . . . [and] no country better compensates industry, especially the labor of the farmer, than does Liberia."

Indeed, Turner believed it was for the "purposes of Christianity" that the little republic existed. He spoke with approving affection and unrestrained paternalism of the Americo-Liberians who had left their country behind so that they might spread "among their still benighted brethren the softening influences of Christian light and love." Like many other contemporary black elitists, most noticeably Crummell and Martin Delany, Turner believed that Liberia's mission was to establish a Christian commonwealth that would serve as a "radiating force . . . in the civilizing and Christianizing [of] Africa." To accomplish that goal, Turner continued, Liberia needed men, education, and wealth. Those three elements would provide "the beginning of civilization," but the completion of the task would be left to the native Africans. In keeping with the self-reliance rhetoric he had employed on the campaign trail in 1870, Turner urged the Liberian government to adopt a policy of taking aborigines out of the hinterlands of Africa and sending them to Christian countries for education. "In the adoption of such a policy," he wrote, "lies Liberia's most direct route of developed nationality; her grandest prospects for the future." The ultimate success of such a plan was assured, Turner concluded naively, because it was God's will. God would not have endowed Liberia and Africa generally with such rich natural resources had he not intended "the evangelization of Africa."[18]

18. Dispatch No. 45, May 25, 1872, Despatches, vol. 3; *Foreign Relations, 1872,* 330–37. For Delany's position, see Painter, "Martin R. Delany: Elitism and Black Nationalism," in Litwack and Meier, eds. *Black Leaders of*

Turner carried this paternalistic attitude of superiority over into his relations with the aborigines. Nowhere is his feeling of cultural and class superiority more evident than in the account he gave of an 1874 visit by a group of natives of the Vey tribe who "serenaded" him. He wrote to the State Department that their music and instruments reminded him of the customs of the still primitive North American Indians. He relished the opportunity to meet with them in his "official capacity" and felt certain that he had persuaded them of the United States government's desire to see "the elevation and civilization of the aboriginal tribes of Africa." He was impressed by the Vey and suggested that they would be prime candidates for civilization. They already had a language, he wrote, which had been "found susceptible of, and reduced to grammar." Likewise, he continued, they had shown "indications of inventive genius, general teachableness, [a] desire to be advanced and to learn and adopt the ways of civilization." Hence, it seemed reasonable for him to assume that the Vey would play an important part in the future expansion and maturation of the Liberian state.[19]

Liberia's primitiveness led Turner continually to express the hope that the government would somehow be able to harness effectively the country's natural resources. On December 31, 1873, he reported to the Fifth Auditor of the United States Treasury that the Liberian legislature was considering several proposals to locate and develop the country's mineral resources. Such proposals, if enacted, would have a salutary effect on the country, for they would put many people to work, people "now unemployed and aimless," and would channel them "to the soil,—the only real source of commercial greatness."[20]

The country's inability to pull itself out of financial trouble placed Turner in a delicate position in 1873, when the State Department instructed him to collect a debt due the United States. In October 1869 the Republic of Liberia purchased "arms and munitions of war" totaling $38,684.14 from the United States. The debt was to be paid by October 19, 1872. When that date passed without any money changing hands, Turner was instructed to collect. On April 19, 1873, he presented an account of indebtedness to the Liberian government

the Nineteenth Century, 159–61.
    19. Dispatch No. 143, August 22, 1874, Despatches, vol. 4. It should be recalled that it was the Vey tribe from which Turner claimed in 1911 to be descended.
    20. Turner to Fifth Auditor, United States Treasury Department, December 31, 1873, Enclosure A, in Dispatch No. 105, December 31, 1873, Despatches, vol. 3.

and followed it with a personal audience with President Roberts, who had been reinstated after the coup, during which he asked for payment on the account. Roberts expressed the conviction that "the Government of the United States will probably, in view of Liberia's embarrassed financial condition, forgive the debt without payment thereof." On May 17, 1873, the Liberian secretary of state penned a formal response to Turner's request for payment. He apologized for his government's failure to respond earlier and laid the blame for that negligence on the political troubles that had surrounded the revolution of 1871. The embarrassing financial situation of his government was referred to again, and he asked Turner to inform the United States of the country's financial condition. He expressed the belief that the amount was so small a sum for such a great country as the United States that the latter would cancel the debt.[21]

A week later Turner wrote Hamilton Fish offering his assessment of the situation. He reported that he was fully satisfied "of the inability of Liberia to pay this or any other one of her several foreign debts." Indeed, he doubted that the Liberians could afford to pay even the interest due. He knew, he wrote, "of no fact more strikingly apparent to the most casual observation than the general absence of money throughout the Republic of Liberia." This predicament was due largely to unskilled management of financial affairs. Liberia's financial problems were hard to understand, particularly when one contemplated "the untiring willingness of the soil to liberally remunerate the labor of the farmer." Hence, Turner returned to a familiar theme, arguing that "the impoverished condition of the masses" in Liberia was due to the failure of the government "to make the cultivation of the soil the principal industry of their country." Coffee, he wrote, could easily become the most profitable agricultural product of the country, if only some attention would be given to its growth. That was not being done, however, because of a widespread tendency in the country to indulge in "continued consumption without adequate production." He warned that unless the people broke out of their lethargy, Liberian finances would remain "impotent" and the

21. Dispatch No. 74, April 25, 1873, Despatches, vol. 3; Turner to H. R. W. Johnson, April 19, 1873, Enclosure A, in Dispatch No. 74; H. R. W. Johnson to Turner, May 7, 1873, Enclosure A, in Dispatch No. 74. Note an error in lettering the enclosures, for both this enclosure and Turner's letter to Johnson are marked "Enclosure A."

independence that could result from self-reliance would continue to escape the country. On October 1, 1873, Turner reported his government's decision to Liberian Secretary of State Johnson. He informed Johnson that President Grant accepted the problems of Liberia as sufficient justification for the past delay in paying the debt, but that the president wanted the interest of $9,168.13 paid as soon as possible. The interest was finally paid in August 1874.[22]

Not all of Turner's time in Liberia was spent reporting on Liberian politics, offering philosophical assessments of the country's potential, or collecting old debts. A good deal of it was spent in performing routine, clerical chores. The most routine of all his tasks was that of simply acknowledging receipt of the instructions sent to him by the State Department. In addition, there was always the task of keeping an adequate amount of supplies in the legation. When he first arrived in Liberia, Turner surveyed the consulate's inventory and discovered that he did not possess the consular arms or an American flag, both of which he quickly ordered. He also found that he needed more than a dozen different kinds of blank forms to carry out his bureaucratic chores.[23]

Likewise, he had to make quarterly and annual reports to the State Department. The quarterly report included a list of all official letters sent from the Liberian consulate, along with a brief notation of the contents of those letters, an indication of the number of enclosures forwarded with each letter, and the amount of postage required by each piece of correspondence. Also, each letter received at the consulate had to be recorded. Since Liberia was seen as a de facto

22. Dispatch No. 74, May 14, 1873, Despatches, vol. 3. Note that there are two dispatches marked "No. 74," one dated April 25, the other May 14. Turner to H. R. W. Johnson, October 1, 1874, Enclosure A, in Dispatch No. 88, October 20, 1873, Despatches, vol. 3; Dispatch No. 112, March 4, 1874, Despatches, vol. 4; Dispatch No. 141, August 10, 1874, Despatches, vol. 4; Dispatch No. 144, August 22, 1874, Despatches, vol. 4.

23. Nearly 21 percent of the 306 dispatches sent by Turner during his Liberian career was devoted primarily to acknowledging receipt of instructions. Dispatch No. 6, July 12, 1871, Despatches, vol. 2; "Inventory of the Archives of the U.S. Legation at Monrovia," July 13, 1871, Dispatch No. 7, Despatches, vol. 2; Dispatch No. 16, September 30, 1871, Despatches, vol. 2. The following dispatches have to do primarily with ordering or receiving supplies for the legation: No. 1, July 12, 1871, vol. 2; No. 15, September 30, 1871, vol. 2; No. 38, February 6, 1872, vol. 3; No. 86, September 30, 1873, vol. 3; No. 122, April 29, 1874, vol.4; No. 135, July 7, 1874, vol. 4; No. 283, December 1, 1877, vol. 7.

economic colony, the State Department expected a record of every American vessel either arriving in or leaving from Liberia. The report had to indicate the month and the day that the ship arrived or departed, its class, name, and tonnage. It had to provide the name of the port from which the ship had set sail, when it was built, where it was built, where its home base was, where it was bound, the name of its owners, and the name of its master. Each quarterly report had to include statements about the ship's cargo, such as where it was produced, where it was manufactured, a general description of the cargo, its quantity, and an assessment of its value. Next, the report required a listing of any deceased American citizens in Liberia, along with an estimation of the value of the deceased person's belongings left with the consulate and an accounting of the disposition of those belongings. That list also had to include the permanent place of residence of the deceased, where he or she died, and what vessel he belonged to if a seaman.[24]

As the official representative of the United States, Turner found himself attending to a wide variety of requests made upon his government. In December 1872, for example, he became the caretaker of an American seaman who had been discharged from the ship *Albert* while it stood in the harbor of Monrovia. Turner reported that he attempted to convince the seaman, John H. Myers, to leave Liberia for England, "but he did not seem inclined to leave, his appearance [and] manner proclaim him to be a man of reckless habits." Some days later, word was brought to Turner that Myers had fallen desperately ill with malaria. Turner immediately dispatched his personal physician to care for the stricken seaman, but the effort was in vain.

24. "Quarterly Report for the Quarter Ending September 30, 1871," Dispatch No. 14, September 30, 1871, Despatches, vol. 2. The following dispatches contain quarterly or annual reports: No. 14, September 30, 1871, vol. 2; No. 36, January 24, 1872, vol. 2; No. 42, March 31, 1872, vol. 3; No. 50, June 30, 1872, vol. 3; No. 66, November 5, 1872, vol. 3; No. 68, December 31, 1872, vol. 3; No. 78, June 30, 1873, vol. 3; No. 85, September 30, 1872, vol. 3; No. 104, December 31, 1873, vol. 3; No. 117, March 31, 1874, vol. 4; No. 13, June 30, 1874, vol. 4; No. 149, September 30, 1874, vol. 4; No. 159, April 16, 1875, vol. 4. In April 1875, Turner was instructed to separate future diplomatic and consular correspondences forwarded to the State Department. Consequently, the quarterly and annual reports for the remainder of his term in Liberia are contained in "Despatches from United States Consuls in Monrovia, Liberia, 1852–1906," M169, vol. 3, April 15, 1875–August 11, 1882, National Archives, Washington, D.C. Turner filed thirty-six consular reports.

Turner reported that after Myers's death he discovered that the deceased "wasted his money most reckless[ly] by buying whole cases of Gin, and making extravagant presents." As a result, Myers died penniless, and Turner felt obliged to pay the balance due on his board bill and to cover the seaman's funeral expenses.[25]

On another occasion, in 1873, Turner suddenly found himself trying to care for three orphaned children. The children's mother had died suddenly, so Turner was left with the responsibility of returning them safely to relatives in the United States. Locating relatives who were willing and able to pay the children's way to America and to care for them once they were there was not easy. In the meantime, someone had to look after them. Two of the children had some semblance of temporary care, although in the case of "little Anthony," Turner remarked, the poverty of the aged widow who cared for him "vies in many respects with that of the child." The oldest of the three, Clarence, had no one to turn to, and he received the American minister's personal sympathy. "The result is," Turner wrote, "that . . . notwithstanding my financial inability long to continue such a course, [Clarence] is now with me at Monrovia, an attendant upon the school of this place, and undergoing treatment for a horrid ulcer upon his left ankle, of more than eighteen months standing."[26]

Another of Turner's responsibilities was to facilitate the development of American business interests in Liberia. In 1873, for example, the State Department instructed him to contact D. C. Perrin and Company, a manufacturing firm of Boston, Massachusetts. Perrin and Company had been given a sample bale of something they labeled "bamboo fibre" by two merchants named Lewis, also of Boston. The Lewises obtained the material in Liberia and hoped to sell it to Perrin on a regular basis. The company was much impressed with palm fiber. "It is," the spokesman wrote, "very tough [and] colors easily, and thus becomes an excellent material for us to weave with a cotton warp to manufacture as banding for cheap hats, to take the place of cotton ribbons, which are imported from England and Germany." Consequently, Perrin had a number of questions to ask about the fiber, all of which its representative addressed to Turner "at the suggestion of Hon. Hamilton Fish." Perrin wanted to know how

25. Dispatch No. 28, December 22, 1871, Despatches, vol. 2.
26. Dispatch No. 59, September 6, 1872, Despatches, vol. 3; Dispatch No. 79, August 1, 1873, Despatches, vol. 3.

cheaply the fiber could be purchased and whether it could "be pre-pared for the looms to the best advantage in Liberia, where labor is cheap." Perrin even suggested that if it could be bought cheaply enough, the company would consider establishing a branch of its business in Liberia. He added in a postscript, "For reasons that will be obvious to you, we should prefer that you would be independent of the Mess. Lewis agent." Subsequently, Turner referred Perrin's re-quest to a firm known as B. P. Yates and Sons of Monrovia, Liberia, and arranged a meeting between the two businesses. The Yates firm promised to become a supplier of palm fiber to Perrin. Turner assured Perrin that Yates could be trusted, explaining, "I am personally ac-quainted with both the partners of B. P. Yates and son and feel confi-dent you may rely upon their statement."[27]

It was more than a routine duty that Turner performed when he encouraged American businessmen to invest in Liberia. Given his perception of the country's continued consumption without adequate production—its inefficiency and aimlessness—he became increasing-ly convinced that Liberia would be prosperous only if it had present on its soil American capitalists who could serve both as models and as prods to Liberian business. It was in that spirit of needed training that he promoted another business venture in May 1874. Edward S. Mor-ris of Philadelphia and his business associates wrote to Turner ex-pressing the desire "to build up in a substantial manner, between Liberia and this city in particular a substantial trade." He informed Turner that the Liberian government had granted them five "Letters Patent," two for hulling coffee and three for manufacturing indigo, and asked Turner to let him know if the minister became aware of any infringements of the contract. Turner responded with an expression of appreciation for Morris's letter and added his prediction that if the venture was given the proper care, it would be virtually impossible for it to fail. He expressed the desire to help in any way he could and also took the opportunity to tell Morris how grateful he was for what the latter was doing. The letter's effusive language and clear message warrant its quotation at length. Turner told Morris that he wanted

27. D. C. Perrin and Company to Turner, February 20, 1873, Enclosure A, in Dispatch No. 98, December 30, 1873, Despatches, vol. 3; Turner to D. C. Perrin and Company, no date, Enclosure B, Dispatch No. 98, December 30, 1873, Despatches, vol. 2; see also, B. P. Yates to D. C. Perrin and Company, December 20, 1873, Enclosure C, in Dispatch No. 98, Despatches, vol. 3.

to express to you both my gratitude for your persistent effort and determination to aid in the grand work of evangelizing and civilizing Africa, and my high apreciation of your apparent comprehension of the means needed to remove the wants of this Republic. Your philanthropic effort to spread the sunshine of modern progress in the shadowy places of this mighty, but unknown land, unlike the great majority, does not pause to spend its strength in fruitless endeavor upon the Americo-Liberian, but goes directly to the native African or aborigine—the only real hope for this country's future. . . . Your valuable machine is not only an economy to the coffee planter, but the native African, by contact therewith, shall find it not only capable of utilizing his labor, but of educating, elevating, and advancing him toward civilization.

While Turner held out the hope that American capitalists would eventually uplift the African natives, he was less certain about his own ability to persevere in Liberia. Perhaps his greatest difficulty in that country was his inability to adjust to its climate. He had been in Africa for less than a month when he was stricken with what he described as a "severe illness."[28]

Turner was suffering from malaria, which he contracted soon after he arrived. Presumably he was affected by the disease in the way that many other nineteenth-century victims were. At times his symptoms were so severe that he was confined to bed with a high fever and general debilitation. Other times he was able to function at a near normal capacity, with little or no fever and only a slight lessening in strength. Unquestionably the disease had a general enervating effect on him, which must have been very frustrating for one who had a few years earlier demonstrated such vigor and energy.

By May 30, 1872, the American diplomat still could not get well. He wrote to the State Department, informing Secretary Fish that he had been suffering from malaria for much of the previous year. He noted that his physician had repeatedly suggested that he leave Liberia temporarily. Although he had thus far declined to leave his post of duty, his weakened condition caused him to reconsider that decision,

28. Dispatch No. 125, May 19, 1874, Despatches, vol. 4; Edward S. Morris, Esq., to Turner, March 10, 1874, Enclosure A, in Dispatch No. 125; Turner to Edward S. Morris, Esq., May 19, 1874, Enclosure B, in Dispatch No. 125; Turner to Sydney G. Crummell, July 28, 1871, Enclosure C, in Dispatch No. 9, July 31, 1871, Despatches, vol. 2.

and he requested a leave of absence "until such time as I shall be able to recruit strength to endure the severity of this climate." He enclosed a doctor's statement, attesting to his illness and his need for a change of climate. The leave was granted, although Turner was unable to depart until the middle of August. He chose Professor Martin Henry Freeman of Liberia College to perform his duties while he was gone. Turner noted in a dispatch to the State Department that in view of the fact that the department would offer no compensation to Professor Freeman, he would pay the professor himself.[29]

Turner made his quarterly report from his home in St. Louis on November 6, 1872. On November 22, 1872, he wrote to Hamilton Fish, indicating that his address had been changed from St. Louis to New Richmond, Ohio. He also requested a twenty-five-day extension of his leave. Turner was granted the additional days but was still unready to return to Liberia by mid-January 1873, so he requested another extension of his leave. He explained to the State Department, "Much of my leave of absence was used by me in observing the general condition of my own people in the Southern States." As a result, he found himself in Vicksburg, Mississippi, waiting for his baggage and papers to be shipped to him by rail. "I will be forced to remain here some days or loose personal effects of greater value than I am monetarily able at present to replace." He did not return to his post of duty until April 17, 1873, more than six months after he had left.[30]

During the next year Turner had frequent, although milder, attacks of malaria. On April 30, 1874, he again wrote to Hamilton Fish, informing the secretary that he had been suffering from the disease for an extended period. The illness had been particularly severe during a three-month period prior to his writing, forcing him to be confined to his room instead of going to the legation. Again he

29. Dispatch No. 46, May 30, 1872, Despatches, vol. 3. Dispatch No. 57, August 15, 1872, Despatches, vol. 3.
30. Turner to Hamilton Fish, November 6, 22, 1872, filed with Dispatch No. 66, November 5, 1872, Despatches, vol. 3. Presumably, Turner's wife had gone to Ohio when she left Liberia. Her daughter later testified that Mrs. Turner had been from the Cincinnati area. New Richmond is only a short distance from Cincinnati. Testimony of Lillie B. Mason, *Charles W. Turner et al. v. Miltonia Turner Hill et al.*, Case No. 2884B; Turner to Hamilton Fish, January 14, 1873, filed with Dispatch No. 68, Despatches, vol. 3; Dispatch No. 71, April 18, 1873, Despatches, vol. 3.

reported that his physician had told him to leave Liberia for sixty days, advice that he had ignored because he wanted to stay at his post. He could stand it no longer, however, and again he asked the State Department for a leave of absence. The second leave was granted, and Turner left Liberia on October 25, 1874. He arrived in Washington, D.C., on November 28 and reached his home in St. Louis on November 30. From St. Louis, he went again to New Richmond, Ohio.[31]

Four days before his leave expired, Turner wrote to the State Department requesting an extension. He indicated that he had "discovered that it is necessary for me to wait until about the last days of next month for direct transit from the United States to my post in Africa." Therefore, he "reluctantly" requested the department to extend his leave twenty-six days. He concluded by informing the department that if it consented to extend his leave, he planned "to spend a portion of that time, in making an informative visit of very general nature, to several citizens of the more eastern cities, who bestow and direct much of the philanthropy now going from the United States to Liberia." He finally arrived back in Liberia on April 12, 1875.[32]

He had, by that time, been the Liberian minister for nearly four years. Liberia had not yet reached that state of "debarbarization" that Turner had looked forward to upon his arrival in 1871. If anything, his tenure in that West African country had further convinced him of the seriousness of the Liberian problem. The ministership had not given him the kind of life that he had expected. Many things had happened over the four years that he could hardly have anticipated. The 1871 civil war had introduced him to the intense political animosity and instability in the country. Although he retained an exalted view of his position and responsibilities, he recognized that he was not universally admired in Liberia. Indeed, he must have at least wondered whether anyone else took his position as seriously as he did. He often participated in gala affairs open only to those in the country's political inner sanctum, but he spent more time filling out forms and processing often depressingly mundane requests for his services.

31. Dispatch No. 123, April 30, 1874, Despatches, vol. 4; Dispatch No. 152, October 25, 1874, Despatches, vol. 4; Turner to Hamilton Fish, January 21, 1875, filed with Dispatch No. 154, December 31, 1874, Despatches, vol. 4.

32. Turner to Hamilton Fish, January 26, 1875, filed with Dispatch No. 154, December 31, 1874, Despatches, vol. 4. Dispatch No. 155, April 12, 1875, Despatches, vol. 4.

Even had all else about the ministership been totally rewarding, his poor health would have prevented full enjoyment.

Still, his notion of what Liberia needed to help it pass into the modern age remained unshaken. Little wonder, then, that he should seek the financial support of American philanthropists upon his return to the United States. If anything, he had become increasingly eager to help American businessmen and philanthropists export capitalism and Christianity to Liberia. He continued to think of himself as an instrument of education and progress in Africa. Despite all of the problems, therefore, he was not ready to remain in America for good, and so, he returned to the outpost of civilization that he had left six months before. There was still work to be done.

CHAPTER V
The Preservation of a Noble Experiment

We are a great and powerful Christian nation . . . pledged by our very origin and the richness of the legacy of our principles to the promotion of international friendliness and unity. . . . I have, in consideration of that grand fact . . . striven to have the United States always occupy the highest ground in her effort to extend the moral influence of her friendship to Liberia.

—James Milton Turner
April 15, 1878

James Milton Turner returned to Liberia in April 1875 and within six months was confronted with the difficult situation of another civil war in Liberia. In this instance, the rebellion was led by the Grebo tribe against the black Americo-Liberians who made up the central government of the nation. Turner, fearful for the safety of Americans in Liberia and for the survival of the Liberian republic, sided with the government in spite of his previously harsh criticism of its mistakes. Ultimately he facilitated armed intervention into the war by the United States: maintaining an admittedly inept group of westernized blacks in power seemed more palatable to him than returning the country to savagery.

The Grebo War was not, however, the only problem Turner faced. He regarded it as simply symptomatic of the sorry state of Liberian internal affairs. The black diplomat became increasingly disillusioned with what he considered to be the Liberian government's pursuit of self-defeating policies—particularly its hostility toward American business interests, which, Turner believed, were the single most important instruments for progress. He retained the conviction that American entrepreneurs, by bringing their businesses to Liberia, could provide a model of industrialized civilization. Liberia would

then become the prototype of self-sufficiency and republican government for all of Africa. But the Americo-Liberian government resisted
adopting these principles and insisted on pursuing shortsighted policies that jeopardized the achievement of that goal. In Turner's view,
the government did not know how to treat the native Africans in
Liberia, and that led to a running battle between aborigines and the
more civilized settlers.[1]

Turner had been given no specific diplomatic instructions upon
assuming his position as minister to Liberia. The handling of the
Grebo War was as much the product of his own notions about how
the matter should be dealt with as it was the result of State Department directives. His career fits comfortably into what diplomatic historian Robert L. Beisner has defined as "Old Paradigm" diplomacy.
Beisner argues that from the end of the Civil War to at least the advent
of the Harrison administration in 1889, guidance offered to American diplomats sent abroad was "minimal and vague." That was due
primarily to what Beisner calls "the core assumption of the Old Paradigm—that the United States was safe, her security threatened in no
way by anyone." Consequently, it was not unusual for policy proposals to flow from the field to the State Department rather than the
other way around.[2]

Turner first mentioned the problems with the Grebo tribe in a
dispatch written on September 7, 1875. He informed the State Department that the Grebos had declared war against the Liberian government "and are under arms and strongly entrenched in Cape Palmas and
along the Cavalla River, a distance of thirteen miles southeast by east
from Cape Palmas." The Grebos, according to Turner, numbered
approximately thirty thousand. Their complaint against the Liberian
government was that it had sanctioned the theft of land from them by
a group of American-born blacks at Cape Palmas under the auspices
of the Maryland Colonization Society.[3]

Grebo–Liberian government conflict had existed since the found-

1. Helpful discussions of Liberia's problems during these years are Harrison
Ola Abingbade, "The Settler-African Conflicts: The Case of the Maryland Colonists and the Grebo 1840–1900," 93–109, and Tom Shick, "The Social and Economic History of Afro-American Settlers in Liberia, 1820–1900, and *Behold the
Promised Land.*

2. Robert L. Beisner, *From the Old Diplomacy to the New, 1865–1900,* 39.

3. Dispatch No. 178, September 7, 1875, Despatches, vol. 5; *Foreign Relations, 1875,* 831.

ing of the Cape Palmas colony in 1857. Repeated efforts at reconcilia-
tion had been unsuccessful. Moreover, the Grebo tribesmen were
feared as potentially powerful foes. According to Turner, there was a
widespread conviction in the country that the Grebos had been taught
to use firearms in the American Episcopal mission school at Cape
Palmas. The American minister acknowledged the seriousness of the
problem but typically laid most of the blame on the Liberian government. The leaders of the small republic, he argued, had not made the
proper efforts to forestall such a crisis. If the Liberian experiment was
to prove successful, Turner argued, then the Americo-Liberians needed
to elevate the African aborigines and move them into the mainstream
of the civilized world, not antagonize them. Turner was especially
galled because the Liberians had found it impossible to avoid an
armed conflict even with the Grebos, "the only tribe of aboriginal
Liberians upon which schools, and the influence of civilization have
made any considerable impression." It was plain to see, he argued,
that the government's policy toward the natives was a "downright
failure." The government was failing in its responsibility of assimilat-
ing the natives into the civilized business and social activities of the
country. The natives could not be ignored or simply dismissed as an
inferior class; they had to be educated and their skills used if the
Liberian state was to prosper.[4]

Turner's view of the missionaries' role in bringing about democracy, especially the Methodists and Episcopalians, was best summed
up in his assertion that "the aggression of Christian missionaries
upon heathenism is always the harbinger of the highest civilization."
Had the Liberian government used the missionaries' schools more
effectively, Turner argued, they could have induced the aborigines "to
enter and become an integral part of the sovereign state of Liberia."
In language echoing one of the most famous black missionaries to
Liberia of the era, Alexander Crummell, Turner argued that those
two American churches represented a direct assault upon "mahom-
adanism and upon the superstitious traditions and fetish worship of
the African tribes who dwell in this quarter." The efforts of the missionaries, however, had been negated by the faulty decision-making
and general insensitivity of the Liberian government, so assimilation
did not take place. As a result, violence could not be forestalled and

4. *Foreign Relations, 1875,* 833; Dispatch No. 189, November 3, 1875,
Despatches, vol. 5.

the first major battle of the Grebo War occurred on September 8, 1875. A party of Grebo tribesmen, "armed with excellent Snyder rifles," attacked Cape Palmas. The attack was repelled, but only after six Liberians were killed and an undetermined number were wounded. Turner grimly proclaimed his belief that the Grebos might fight on indefinitely, in view of the fact that they were struggling for the land that had always been their home.[5]

The implications of the war for Americans in Liberia became apparent soon after the actual fighting started. On September 20, 1875, William Allen Fair of the American Protestant Episcopal Church mission informed Turner that two members of the mission at Cavalla, in Maryland County, as well as the American property there, were "in danger in consequence of the war between the natives and the Liberians." Communications with the missionaries had been cut off, Fair wrote, and he expressed the view that "the only way they can be gotten out from there is by means of an American 'Man of War.'"[6]

The American minister responded to Fair's request on October 7. He indicated that his inquiries had led him to believe that the missionaries in question were British subjects, not American citizens. He had, however, asked the Liberian government to do what it could to insure the safety of both. He explained that for the moment he could not even extend protection to American property in the area. The Liberian government was obligated by treaty to protect such property and he could not interfere without a formal governmental request. Meanwhile, he explained, as the representative of the United States he was bound to take a stand of strict neutrality.[7]

The government's request came quickly, however. Within four days of his letter to Fair, Turner telegrammed Secretary of State Hamilton Fish that the Liberian government had informed him of its inability to protect Americans or American property. Furthermore, the government wanted Americans removed from the native towns for their own protection. In consideration of those dire circumstances,

5. Dispatch No. 178, September 7, 1875, Despatches, vol. 5; *Foreign Relations, 1875,* 834; Dispatch No. 296, February 15, 1878, Despatches, vol.7; Moses, *Alexander Crummell,* 183–85. Dispatch No. 178, September 7, 1875, Despatches, vol. 5; *Foreign Relations, 1875,* 835.

6. William A. Fair to Turner, September 20, 1875, Enclosure A, in Dispatch No. 183, October 7, 1875, Despatches, vol. 5.

7. Turner to William A. Fair, Dispatch No. 183, October 7, 1875, Despatches, vol. 5.

Turner suggested that an American warship be sent immediately to Cape Palmas. He followed with a lengthy letter to the State Department on October 11, 1875, clarifying the problem and arguing for United States intervention in the Grebo War. He then set forth the argument that Liberia would be "incalcuably benefited" by American assistance in her effort to put down the Grebo rebellion. The government's army, he reported, numbered only one thousand men and its supplies were meager. By contrast, he explained, the Grebos had a population numbering more than twice the civilized population of Liberia. Moreover, they were capable of enduring the hardships of a war in a tropical climate. In addition, Turner emphasized, "two thirds of the American [business] interests in Liberia are situated in Maryland County."[8]

Just as important, Turner argued, the rebellion threatened to inflame other aboriginal tribes, which would render Monrovia, the nation's capital, defenseless. Americans living in Liberia were unanimous in their view of the need for the presence of a United States man-of-war on Liberia's coast. Logistically, he explained, the impact of the ship could be maximized quite easily since the Grebos were, in most cases, congregated close to the seashore and could, therefore, offer little resistance. In fact, Turner argued, "one ship-of-war could disable their campaign in a few hours, by destroying their towns, and demolishing their works." The very presence of such a ship might by itself be sufficient to restore peace and "create for Liberia a moral influence with the tribes now so generally restive."[9]

The day after forwarding this letter, Turner sent another dispatch to the State Department, reiterating his request for a ship and offering additional evidence supporting the wisdom of that action. He enclosed two letters from the director of the domestic and foreign missionary society of the United States, the Reverend T. H. Eddy, which emphasized the serious danger in which the Protestant Episcopal Church Mission in Liberia found itself and pleaded with Turner to see to it that "an armed vessel of the Navy of the United States" was

8. Turner to Hamilton Fish, n. d., filed with Dispatch No. 184, October 11, 1875, Despatches, vol. 5.
9. Ibid.; Dispatch No. 184, October 11, 1875, Despatches, vol. 5. See also, S. B. King to Turner, October 8, 1875, Enclosure A; J. E. Moore to Turner, September 28, 1875, Enclosure B; Turner to S. B. King, October 8, 1875, Enclosure C; Turner to Jasper Smith, October 11, 1875, Enclosure D, in Dispatch No. 184.

sent to Cape Palmas. Turner's hastily scribbled note to the State Department, written on the street as he made his way to a steamer bound for Cape Palmas, came just after he received word that the Liberian forces there had suffered heavy losses in an important battle. Eight or nine government soldiers had been killed, about thirty-five wounded, and three brass pieces of artillery captured. Again he expressed the hope that "the Department will see fit to order a Man-of-War to Palmas immediately."[10]

The American minister arrived at Cape Palmas on October 19, 1875. He quickly discovered that the Grebo forces controlled most of the towns in which American businesses were located. He informed the department that he had taken steps to secure the lives and property of American citizens but again expressed the fear that it would be a long war "the severe afflictions of which will be of small import compared with the almost sure disaster which must sooner or later befall [Liberia's] institutions of government . . . should the 'Grebo' tribe succeed in their . . . efforts to drive Liberians from this country." The war took an even more serious turn in late November 1875. The fear that the Grebo rebellion might touch off a revolt among other tribes intensified when two German vessels were captured off the coast of Liberia and five crew members were murdered. According to Turner, the tribe that perpetrated this "outrage" was the Kroo, who "strongly sympathize with the 'Grebo cause', and have for some time threatened Liberia with hostilities, of which it is thought this deed is the beginning."[11]

By December, the Liberian government had become impatient for a response to its request for a man-of-war. It forwarded a letter to Turner and asked him if he had received a reply to the request. He had not, he answered, but he did send the Liberians' note to the State Department. Later, when Turner met with Pres. Joseph Roberts to discuss the seriousness of the Grebo revolt, the president again spoke of his eagerness to determine the intentions of the United States. Liberia's survival demanded the assistance of a foreign power, and alluding to the recent capture of the German boats, Roberts expressed

10. Eddy to Turner, October 9, 1875, Enclosure A; Eddy to Turner, October 12, 1875, Enclosure B; Turner to Eddy, October 12, Enclosure C. in Dispatch No. 185, October 14, 1875, Despatches, vol. 5.

11. Dispatch No. 187, October 19, 1875, Despatches, vol. 5; Dispatch No. 196, December 2, 1875, Despatches, vol. 5.

"the conviction that all interests on the Liberian coast will be insecure unless Liberia issues victorious from her present troubles." He told Turner that he was confident of receiving help from England, should he request it, but emphasized his bias toward the United States. Turner transmitted the president's concerns to the State Department along with his own dire warning of impending doom, explaining that "the situation at Cape Palmas grows each day more appalling for the interest of Liberia."[12]

Neither Turner nor the Liberians needed to be concerned about the American government's willingness to provide a man-of-war to assist in quelling the Grebo rebellion. Turner's request to Fish for an American ship reached the State Department on October 27, 1875. Although Turner would not know it for more than a month, Fish wrote to the secretary of the navy that same day and requisitioned a man-of-war. The decision to intervene was heartily supported by the American Colonization Society, the organization that had been responsible for the founding of Liberia. The society indicated its belief that the public generally had been gratified by the announcement that the USS *Alaska* had been ordered to Cape Palmas. In fact, the society called for a continued American military presence in Liberia, adding that "the interests of humanity, religion, science, legitimate commerce, and duty require this service." Indeed, the society expressed the hope that Liberia would become "the mart where American manufactures could be exchanged for the products of Western and Central Africa," thereby making African trade "one of the most important branches of American commerce."[13]

The *New York Times* was no less ebullient in its support of the use of American force to preserve in power the Liberian government. In an editorial closely paralleling Turner's own attitude toward the West African nation, the *Times* offered the following argument on November 28, 1875:

12. J. E. Moore to Turner, December 3, 1875, Enclosure A; Turner to J. E. Moore, December 3, 1875, Enclosure B; J. E. Moore to Turner, December 4, 1875, Enclosure C in Dispatch No. 199, December 6, 1875, Despatches, vol. 5. Dispatch No. 200, December 6, 1875, Despatches, vol. 5.

13. Instruction No. 104, November 15, 1875; Instruction No. 103, October 27, 1875, Instructions; *African Repository* 52 (January 1876): 7. For additional information on the attitude of the American Colonization Society toward the Grebo War, see *African Repository* 52 (April 1876): 40–42, 59–60; *African Repository* 52 (July 1876): 80–82, 90; *African Repository* 53 (April 1877): 40–41.

We have planted the Liberian Republic, and we can hardly permit it to be destroyed. It is true that it is not altogether as successful a State as we could wish it to be. What with the coast fever on one end, the wild Africans on the other, and the constitutional reluctance of the colonists to do any unnecessary work, Liberia has had great difficulties to contend with. Still, a Christian and civilized African State has been established, and it may yet prosper and exert a civilizing influence upon the African Continent which will be worth infinitely more than Liberia has hitherto cost. If the colonists are really in danger of being overwhelmed by the savage tribes, by all means let us protect them. It will not do to let the experiment of an African republic be suddenly brought to a violent and bloody end.

Turner received notification from the State Department in mid-December 1875 that a man-of-war was on its way. Subsequently, he forwarded a lengthy dispatch in which he offered an assessment of the role he believed the United States should play in ending the fighting and establishing amiable postwar relations between the Grebos and the Liberians. He began by enumerating several lingering difficulties. He noted that morale was low among supporters of the government, largely because the government did not have enough money to purchase arms and provisions necessary to keep an army in the field. But even if that obstacle was overcome and the Grebos were actually defeated, the natives could still continue to conduct a guerrilla war indefinitely. If that happened, it would be difficult for the Liberian government to maintain control over Cape Palmas "without . . . the constant maintenance throughout several years upon that part of this coast . . . of a force sufficiently strong to hold the natives in awe." Despite the fact that many Liberians hoped that the United States would maintain a military presence in Liberia after the Grebo revolt had been put down, Turner argued that the expense of such an undertaking made it highly unlikely. Alternatively, he suggested the natives had to be convinced that "the presence of the Republic of Liberia on the coast of Africa is intended to evangelize, civilize and bring the tribes . . . into closer and more happy commercial relations with the modern world and not to terrorize or treat those tribes unjustly." Hence, Turner saw a simple show of force as being adequate to chasten the Grebos. After all, he noted, if that did not work there would always be sufficient time to subdue the tribe by force of arms.[14]

14. *New York Times,* November 28, 1875. See also *New York Times,* Octo-

The USS *Alaska* arrived in Monrovia on February 3, 1876. Capt. Alexander A. Semmes contacted Turner immediately and was briefed by the latter. Turner wrote to the State Department that he was happy to see that Semmes agreed with Turner's "show of force" plan. Subsequently, the *Alaska* embarked for Cape Palmas with Pres. James Payne, who had recently succeeded President Roberts, on board and with a view toward avoiding actual hostilities if possible. Turner noted that Liberia was pervaded "by a universal gratitude" for the United States' decision to send a man-of-war. Indeed, the Liberians were so pleased that Turner felt compelled to write of his hope that they would not interpret the action of the United States in the wrong light. He wanted the Liberians to understand that the United States sent the man-of-war only because of a dire emergency, and he expressed the fear that such "gratuitous aid" furnished upon such a large scale might further handicap Liberia's development of an attitude of independence and national self-reliance.[15]

Semmes minced no words in his dealings with the African aborigines. He gathered the leaders of the rebellion together and told them that the United States government was prepared to use the full extent of its power to subdue them. When the rebels complained that the amount they had received for land cessions was too small, Semmes contemptuously told them, "That's more than we gave the Indians for their land." The pressure imposed by Semmes was enough—the Grebos signed a peace treaty on March 1, 1876. The next day, Captain Semmes wrote to Turner informing him that the Grebo rebellion against the Liberian government was over and a peace treaty signed. The Liberian officials felt very comfortable with the terms of the

ber 8, 12, 22; November 2, 25, 26, 27; December 1, 3, 22, 28, 29, 1875. Dispatch No. 203, December 13, 1875, Dispatch No. 204, December 13, 1875, Dispatch No. 211, January 29, 1876, Despatches, vol. 5; Turner to J. E. Moore, December 11, 1875, Enclosure in Dispatch No. 204, December 13, 1875, Despatches, vol. 5.

15. Dispatch No. 214, February 11, 1876, Dispatch No. 215, February 14, 1876, Despatches, vol. 5. See also the following enclosures with Dispatch No. 215: Turner to J. E. Moore, February 4, 1876, Enclosure A; J. E. Moore to Turner, February 4, 1876, Enclosure B; J. E. Moore to Turner, February 4, 1876, Enclosure C; A. A. Semmes to Turner, February 4, 1876, Enclosure D; "Protocol," Enclosure E; Turner to J. E. Moore, February 7, 1876, Enclosure F; A. A. Semmes to president of Liberia, February 4, 1876, Enclosure G; J. E. Moore to Turner, February 9, 1876, Enclosure H; J. E. Moore to A. A. Semmes, February 9, 1876, Enclosure I; Turner to A. A. Semmes, February 11, 1876, Enclosure J.

peace treaty. The Grebos agreed, among other things, "to fully and unequivocably . . . acknowledge the Supremacy of the Government of Liberia and agree to submit to its laws."[16]

The self-destructive policies that had gotten the Liberian government involved in the Grebo War in the first place also caused mistreatment of actual and potential capital investors from other countries. In addition to abusing African aborigines, Turner maintained, the Liberians pursued policies that antagonized the very people who held the key to the survival of the Liberian experiment: the businessmen who were willing to transport their civilizing capitalism to the shores of Africa. In May 1875 Turner offered the State Department the example of the problems encountered by the firm of Edward S. Morris and Company of Philadelphia, which he had helped to establish in Liberia barely one year before. The firm used steam machinery to hull coffee and process indigo. In the spring of 1875, Turner was approached by John O'Neale Stockham, a representative of the firm. According to Turner, Stockham "complained to me that he experienced great annoyance and embarrassment on account of the persistent disposition of Liberians to intimidate, if not to obstruct his business operations on the St. Paul's River." Stockham said that legal proceedings against him had been threatened because he was operating a business away from a port of entry.[17]

Turner investigated the complaint made by Stockham and reported that the chief opposition to the American merchant was his establishment of a place of business approximately thirteen miles from coastal Monrovia. Stockham was intercepting customers on their way to the capital city and selling goods to them at cut-rate prices. Irritated that Stockham was taking business away from them, Liberian merchants responded with retaliatory measures. The "Port of Entry" law was a typical ruse to antagonize foreigners: "The property of foreigners investing capital in Liberia has come to be looked upon as subject to whatever inconvenience of obstruction Liberians

16. Abingbade, "The Settler-African Conflicts," 102; "The War of 1875–1876 between the Liberian Government and the . . . Tribes Composing the 'Grebo Reunited Kingdom'"; Records of the Department of State Relating to Internal Affairs of Liberia, 1910–1929, Record Group 59, National Archives, M613, roll 3; Dispatch No. 220, March 8, 1876, Despatches, vol. 5; J. E. Moore to Turner, April 8, 1876, Enclosure B, and "Treaty of Peace," Enclosure C, in Dispatch No. 226, May 31, 1876, Despatches, vol. 5.

17. Dispatch No. 164, May 7, 1875, Despatches, vol. 4.

in their more capricious moments, may feel inclined to expose such property to."[18]

The harassment of Stockham continued when he was sued for damages by a man who had been found guilty of stealing merchandise from Stockham's store. The man claimed that Stockham's binding and delivering of him to the local magistrate entitled him to a compensation of one thousand dollars. Moreover, the writ was not served on Stockham until he was preparing to leave on an important business trip to the United States, and the hearing for the case was set for June despite Stockham's repeated requests that it be postponed until after his return from the United States. Turner appealed unsuccessfully to the Liberian attorney general to have the case postponed. Annoyed over the incident, he informed the State Department of his belief "that this entire matter is a conspiracy, upon an unwarrantable pretext, to intimidate and discourage Mr. Stockham's firm in their business in Liberia." He explained that there existed in Monrovia "a strong prejudicial feeling against anyone who prefers to do business on the river upon a scale sufficiently large to attract trade that would otherwise push its way to Monrovia." As a result of the Liberian government's "morbid tendency to inconvenience foreigners," Turner looked to the State Department to establish a precedent for protecting American citizens who invested their capital in Liberia. He asked for instructions that would "unequivocally" articulate the intention of the United States government "to protect the interests of Americans and their property in Liberia." Second, Turner asked that the indignity imposed by the Liberian attorney general on the United States in the Stockham case "be not passed unnoticed." Still feeling the slights he had been subjected to over the years of his stay in Liberia, Turner pleaded that something be done to prompt the Liberians to offer his legation the respect that it deserved.[19]

On June 28, 1876, Turner apprised the State Department of another "Port of Entry" victim. Osceola Jackson was a United States

18. Ibid.; see also, the following enclosures with Dispatch No. 164: Turner to Secretary of State J. E. Moore, April 15, 1875, Enclosure A; J. E. Moore to Turner, May 6, 1875, Enclosure B; Attorney General W. M. Davis to J. E. Moore, April 30, 1875, Enclosure C; "An Act Confining and Restricting Foreign Vessels to Ports of Entry," Enclosure D.

19. Dispatch No. 167, May 28, 1875, Despatches, vol. 4; Affidavit of John O'Neale Stockholm, May 25, 1875, Enclosure A, in Dispatch No. 167; Dispatch No. 167, May 28, 1875, Despatches, vol. 4.

citizen doing business at Buchanan, in Grand Bassa County, for the firm of Gates and Porterfield of New York City. The case began in February 1876 when Jackson forwarded a letter to Turner complaining of the Liberian law that prohibited foreigners from trading at any points other than "the so called 'Ports of Entry.'" The result of that law, Jackson explained, was that Liberian merchants monopolized trade. Jackson hinted that it was possible to bypass the law, but only by paying fees that amounted to extortion. He argued that in view of the fact that the Liberian government had asked for American support during the Grebo War, the State Department should be made aware of Liberia's mistreatment of foreigners. Jackson closed by expressing disappointment at having found that "an american [sic] if his skin was white could neither own land, or enter into business, except under such restrictions as placed him at the mercy of rival Liberian Houses." Turner followed with a letter to Liberian Secretary of State J. E. Moore, informing him of Jackson's complaint and indicating his belief that the "Ports of Entry" law was discriminatory. He argued that such a policy unjustly subjected American citizens doing business in Liberia to unequal burdens before the law.[20]

It took Moore six months to reply to Turner. When a reply finally came it contained a flat denial that any discrimination against foreigners was taking place. This response caused Turner to hold out little hope for the progress of a nation that not only refused to reverse antiforeign business policies, but denied that they even existed. The same logic that led Turner to endorse the use of an American man-of-war to put down a native rebellion and to protest the antiforeign policies of the Liberian government led the American minister to develop an increasingly cynical attitude toward the wisdom of the colonization of American blacks in Liberia. He came to this realization slowly. During his first year as a foreign minister he had spoken with nothing but praise for those "expatriated Americans" who had chosen Liberia "for the purpose of planting upon these shores of Fatherland the banner of untrammeled manhood, and of spreading among their still benighted brethren the softening influences of Christian light and love."[21]

20. Osceola Jackson to Turner, February 1, 1876, Enclosure A; Turner to J. E. Moore, February 29, 1876, Enclosure B, in Dispatch No. 233, June 28, 1876, Despatches, vol. 6.
21. J. E. Moore to Turner, June 28, 1876, Enclosure H, in Dispatch No. 233, June 28, 1876, Despatches, vol. 6. For a general discussion of the post-Reconstruction movement of southern blacks to Liberia, see George B. Tindall,

The improved postwar conditions of blacks in America, however, raised serious questions, as far as Turner was concerned, about the wisdom of continued migration of blacks to Liberia. "While none would discourage such a desire to leave the United States for Liberia," he wrote in 1872, "all must concede that the number who desire to leave is comparatively small, and of a class whose degraded manhood and absolute dependence but ill adapts them to the wants of the primary economy of a young and aspiring democratic government." Many of the blacks who came to Liberia, he explained, were lured there by what he considered to be impossible dreams. He wrote of a group that arrived in Liberia in December 1871. Within five months 45 to 50 of the original 243 persons had died. Of the remaining number, he explained, "Many are acclimating, thirty-five or forty are intending to return, the remaining are quite despondent, and those who remain here will be little else than a burden to the country."[22]

Turner's position as Minister Resident forced him to deal directly with disenchanted and frustrated blacks who had been disappointed in their search for a better life in Liberia. Such was the case when John H. Adams and Sandy Garroway requested his help on behalf of a group that claimed it had been duped. The persons Adams and Garroway represented professed to be citizens of the United States and wanted help in returning to their homes. The group had arrived in Liberia with the help of the American Colonization Society, hoping "by their labor [to acquire] comfortable homes and spend useful lives" in Africa. Instead, they had spent their entire time in Liberia in "the Receptacle," a house located near Cape Palmas, established to provide new immigrants a home for the first six months after their arrival. There were sixty-four persons in all. They had been told by Liberians that they had forfeited their American citizenship by going to Liberia. After a round of questioning, Turner gave them a tentative reply, suggesting to them that they were still American citizens unless they had expressly denied their citizenship. He did, however, caution them that he knew of no statutory provisions that would allow the United States government to pay for their return trip to America.

"The Liberian Exodus of 1878," 133, and Lenwood G. Davis, "Black American Images of Liberia, 1877–1914," 53–72. Dispatch No. 45, May 25, 1872, Despatches, vol. 3. For the published version of this dispatch, see *Foreign Relations, 1872, 333.*

22. *Foreign Relations, 1872, 337.*

This group of immigrants was typical, "composed from among that class of American freedmen whose wealth of inexperience is equaled only by their incomparable credulity." They were well-meaning, upright people, he wrote, but they should have stayed home. Had they remained in the United States, he suggested, they would have been among familiar people whose customs they shared. Likewise, they would have been able at least to fulfill their basic needs by performing the task "in which of all others they were at present most useful, 'to wit,' that of laborer upon the southern farms."[23]

Turner was quiet on the colonization issue through much of his tenure in Liberia, but he finally took a strong stand against such activities in 1877. The intensity of colonizationist activities increased dramatically in that year, in the wake of Pres. Rutherford B. Hayes's withdrawal of federal troops from the south as part of the 1877 Compromise. The removal of federal troops from the South left blacks unprotected in their effort to exercise basic political and civil rights. The American Colonization Society made widespread appeals to American blacks to leave the United States. Turner quietly observed the society's efforts until August 1877, when a rumor circulated that J. B. Finney, "a prominent and enthusiastic advocate of the emigration of negro citizens of the United States to Liberia, has been named . . . Minister to Liberia, with a view of facilitating that emigration scheme." Such a policy, Turner pointed out, was inconsistent with the stand of a government that "has never announced any policy with the view to facilitate the emigration of any class of her citizens." These rather innocuous statements about colonization schemes were followed a few days later by a frontal assault on those forces that conspired to remove black Americans from the United States to Liberia. Turner's opposition against black emigration to Africa placed him firmly in line with the vast majority of other conservative black leaders of the era.

On September 3, 1877, Turner forwarded a lengthy dispatch to the State Department, parts of which were published in American newspapers, offering his assessment of the Colonization Society's proposals. The American minister called attention to newspaper publicity being received by the advocates of colonization. In view of the popularity of emigration schemes, he said, he felt compelled to speak out. He wanted to protect American blacks, particularly those

23. Dispatch No. 81, August 12, 1873, Despatches, vol. 3.

who had no idea of what Africa was like. They were leaving the southern United States, where they were in demand as laborers and where they lived in "comparative comfort." They had very little hope of succeeding in Africa—indeed, nine out of ten would not even be able to make enough money to return to the United States. That being the case, Turner felt obligated to detail his reasons for opposing the movement of American blacks to Liberia.

First of all, he argued, although the African soil was quite fertile, the tools used for tilling it were primitive, and the climate was so harsh that it was "almost impossible for anyone except a native to work." And even though the soil was fertile and the mineral wealth of the country great, he emphasized that the Liberian government had not yet learned to take advantage of those blessings. As a result, Liberia's economy was entirely colonial, the country having "never been independent to loose herself from other countries enough to produce food sufficient for her daily home consumption." Thus, a commodity such as rice that could be easily and profitably produced at home was imported from England and purchased for four dollars a bushel. Such a situation made it difficult for American immigrants to survive because most of the goods they consumed had to be imported, making their cash outlay very high. By contrast, Turner wrote, "the native is strong and hardy, with a very few wants, and able, at fifty cents per day, to perform the labor usually assigned to horses in other countries."

Even if the immigrants could find ways to sustain life on the west coast of Africa, Turner argued, its quality would be quite low. They would be cut off from family and friends back in the states, without knowledge of African customs, and would probably suffer from malaria or mourn the loss of family members who had succumbed to the unhealthy climate. There was little wonder, he remarked, that most American blacks who arrived in Africa soon wanted to return home. For every vessel that returned to America, he received "a dozen applications to be sent back." Another of Liberia's shortcomings was the absence of a public school system. The only roads in existence were "footpaths cut by the natives," and the only way of transporting goods was on the heads or backs of natives.

In short, Turner argued, neither Liberia nor Africa was any place for American blacks. He categorically rejected the contention "that the negro of America, after three centuries of absence from Africa, the long weary years of which were not altogether devoted to training him in the things which pertain to the higher walks of knowledge, is better prepared than any other foreigners, physically or otherwise to carry civilization to this unfortunate people." Thus Turner, far from seeing black Americans as potential participants in a pan-African brotherhood of the oppressed, saw them as citizens of the United States whose futures were tied to the growth and development of that country. "In fine," he wrote, "my experience has been that when the American negro is brought face to face in contact with this work, he is, for all practical purposes, as much a foreigner as any other people, and can only extend to the barbarous African the same philanthropic sympathy." Even if they could adjust to the rigors of Liberian life, their dream of "evangelizing, civilizing, and colonizing Africa" was destined to fail. "After sixty years," he wrote, "we find that those who have remained with praiseworthy determination . . . have not assimilated a single tribe of native Africans."

In view of the fact that the migration of blacks from America to Africa was not achieving its desired purpose, Turner called for it to stop. That was not to say that he thought efforts to civilize Africa should end. Rather, he suggested, Americans should adopt a policy like that employed by other enlightened countries. The Europeans, for example, saw the necessity of "supplying light from without Africa; but . . . they trust the continuation, indeed the completion, of the work to the indigenous inhabitant himself." The best procedure, Turner argued, would be to establish schools and colleges where the natives could acquire an education without having to leave Africa. Expressing the sentiment of a host of nineteenth-century black leaders, from John Berry Meachum to Booker T. Washington, Turner called for the establishment of "Manual-labor schools" that would "supply the class of men needed in this country." He suggested that the Vey tribe, because of its members' desire to learn and their "inventive genius," would be "the best vehicle for the propagation of civilization to the interior tribes of Africa." The money that was being spent on transporting American blacks to Liberia would be better spent in educating the Vey.[24]

Such a move should be made quickly, however, for Christian evan-

24. Dispatch No. 272, August 30, 1877, Despatches, vol. 6. Although Turner feared that Finney would replace him, the latter was never appointed to the ministership. Information in this and the preceding five paragraphs is drawn from Dispatch No. 273, September 3, 1877, Despatches, vol. 6. For a published version of this dispatch, see *Foreign Relations, 1877,* 370–75.

gelists who procrastinated were in danger of losing the battle for souls to Moslems. Hence, he warned,

> If Christian philanthropists loiter much longer in manipulating this chiliahedronic idea into shape, the Mandingoes, who as Moham-medans, are indefatigable missionaries will probably very soon dis-seminate the dogmas of their religion among this desirable people, and thus place their evangelization at least another half century far-ther into the future.

Given all the problems that the Liberians faced, Turner was not at all certain that the Liberian experiment could survive. Fearful that it might not, he closed this lengthy dispatch with the assertion, "Wheth-er Liberia succeeds or fails, she cannot be accepted as a fair test of the negro's capacity or incapacity for self-government."[25]

Turner's stand on the emigration issue was a controversial one that drew the wrath of opponents. Initially, the State Department issued a statement critical of Liberian emigration, abstracting Tur-ner's arguments but not indicating the name of the author. Members of the executive committee of the American Colonization Society, upon seeing this statement, met in a special meeting to draft a rebuttal. The committee responded by offering testimonials from persons "whose knowledge and opinions formed from personal observations in Libe-ria, constitute them impartial and unbiased witnesses." Supporting statements were offered by the Reverend Abraham Hanson, former Minister Resident of the United States to Liberia; Comdr. R. W. Shu-feldt, who had twice visited Liberia; and Bishop Gilbert Haven, who had only recently returned from an official examination of the Meth-odist Episcopal Church mission in western Africa. Once the source of the anti-emigration statements became known, excerpts from Tur-ner's dispatch appeared in newspapers throughout the country. Again, the American Colonization Society offered a rebuttal, this time di-rected at the American minister. The Reverend Thomas S. Malcom, who wrote the essay on behalf of the society, called Turner's state-ments "self-contradictory." He repeated Turner's litany of Liberian shortcomings, countered it with his own list of that country's attri-butes, and concluded with an expression of hope that the "Christian civilization may eventually penetrate the Dark Continent, enlighten-

25. *Foreign Relations, 1877,* 374–75.

ing it, redeeming it and transforming it into the arena of a new and splended history."[26]

Opposition to Turner's criticisms of Liberian colonization was not confined to the shores of the United States. Indeed, resistance was even more intense in Liberia, prompting Turner to forward a lengthy dispatch on April 15, 1878, explaining that his opposition to colonization had resulted in "a series of unfriendly behavior and indeed downright mistreatment directed against me during the last past two or three months by Liberians high in official station in their country." Turner explained that the supporters of the Colonization Society in the United States exercised a good deal of influence over Liberian affairs, and that ever since the publication of his Dispatch No. 273, society spokesmen had been encouraging Liberian officials to harass him. His dispatch had, he continued, touched off a debate that was still raging, for in addition to discouraging potential black emigrants from leaving the United States, his comments had also discouraged would-be philanthropists from contributing to the cause. In fact, he believed that colonization agents in the United States were already writing to Liberian officials, working to have him removed from office. While Turner could offer no tangible proof that those letters existed, he explained that he was inclined to believe they did because of a host of "collateral occurrences." Numerous little incidents of harassment had become commonplace, "such as taking away the halliards from my flagstaff several times by night, significant but disguised expressions and innuendoes concerning my despatch, and other such things."

Conditions worsened, however, following the distribution among Liberian officials of a *St. Louis Republican* commentary upon extracts from the dispatch. The article, he wrote, was taken "from house to house" and shown to "gathering knots of persons," and even exhibited "in the streets of Monrovia with excited recommendations that summary vengeance be wreaked upon me." At about the same time, the American minister reported, "the Secretary of the Treasury of Liberia abused me in the street publicly." Later the same day, the secretary again directed "abusive and indecent language" against

26. William A. Coppinger, "Liberia, A Statement," *African Repository* 54 (January 1878): 21–23; see also, G. W. Samson, "Liberia Defended," *African Repository* 54 (April 1878): 54–59; Rev. Thomas S. Malcom, "Is It Suitable for Emigrants?" *African Repository* 55 (January 1879): 19–22.

him. Simultaneously, word spread erroneously that Turner had told a group of recent emigrants that they had forfeited their American citizenship. The dissemination of that rumor increased the number of people unhappy with Turner, and added to their displeasure. "That and the following night," he wrote, "rocks were thrown against the door of the Legation." There was even considerable sentiment to mob him, although that idea was discarded "on account of the harm which might befall the state."

In the midst of this hostile atmosphere, Turner received instructions from the State Department to try to collect the 1869 debt owed to the United States government. Many people in Liberia, Turner explained, felt that he had "managed or manipulated in some mysterious ways to prevent the Government from canceling that indebtedness by making a bestowal of it upon Liberia." At the same time, the Liberian secretary of the treasury tried to tax, unjustly the American minister maintained, an American vessel stopping at Liberia on a nontrading mission. Turner was incensed by such "incivility" and closed this dispatch with a statement that reveals the depth of his annoyance and disappointment over the Liberian government's failure to appreciate adequately either his own efforts or those of the government he represented. He had, he said, always been aware

> that we are a great and powerful Christian nation recognizing and morally defending the confraternity of the nations, and pledged by our very origin and the richness of the legacy of our principles to the promotion of international friendliness and unity, and to the universal brotherhood and amity of man, I have, in consideration of that grand fact, as well as the origin of the people composing this far off and struggling Republic, striven to have the United States always occupy the highest ground in her effort to extend the moral influence of her friendship to Liberia.

Turner had had his fill of being unappreciated. He was gone from Africa almost before his dispatch of April 15 had a chance to arrive at the State Department. He left Monrovia for good on May 20, 1878, his continuing health problems causing him to overcome whatever hesitancies he had about leaving.[27]

27. Dispatch No. 302, April 15, 1878, Despatches, vol. 7. For Turner's request to be recalled, see Dispatch No. 266, July 14, 1877, Despatches, vol. 6. For accounts of Turner's health during the latter years of his stay in Liberia, see

There was no reason for him to stay. He had gone to Liberia initially feeling important, convinced that he would be respected as the valued representative of the government of the United States. He had hoped to be instrumental in the furtherance of Christian institutions in that country so that Liberia could become, in turn, a civilizing force throughout the west coast of Africa. But it had not worked out the way he had hoped. He was sick most of the time, and even when he was well he had to sit by and watch the Liberian government do things that he knew were inimical to the future growth of the country. Moreover, when he tried to point out to the officials the error of their ways, he found them to be totally unappreciative. In fact, they were downright disrespectful of his position and his authority. Instead of the universal gratitude he expected for the tasks he performed in Liberia, he was increasingly criticized during the latter years of his stay there. Grossly limited in vision by his own ethnocentrism, by his class biases, and by his internalization of Western, and especially American, notions of progress, Turner saw the problems in Africa as insurmountable. He was unwilling to accept the integrity of any part of African culture; Africans and their culture must become westernized, a task that the Liberians demonstrated an incapacity to perform. It was time for him to go back to the United States.

Dispatch No. 202, December 18, 1875, Despatches, vol. 6; Dispatch No. 220, March 8, 1876, Despatches, vol. 5; Dispatch No. 249, September 8, 1877, Despatches, vol. 6; Dispatch No. 266, July 14, 1877, Despatches, vol. 6; Dispatch No. 292, January 26, 1873, Despatches, vol. 7; Dispatch No. 306, April 24, 1878, Despatches, vol. 7.

CHAPTER VI
In Search of Power Back Home

I saw that we were restive and discontented because of this lack of
honorable recognition, and that we . . . had determined to throw
ourselves in the breach, and test the professions of the Republican
party. . . . If the Republican party is sincere, then it won't reject a
man simply because his skin is black.

—James Milton Turner
August 8, 1878

James Milton Turner returned to Missouri early in the summer of
1878. The status, power, and wealth that he equated with success
had eluded him in Liberia, so he renewed the search back home.
Turner still regarded the Republican party as a suitable vehicle for
collective and individual black upward mobility. As the violations of
black rights associated with the restoration of white southern home
rule became more apparent to him, however, his attitude began to
change. He initially had misgivings about black migration from the
South but came to be an active supporter of the exodus—as long as it
did not mean migration abroad. He also became increasingly annoyed with the Republican party's unwillingness to fight racism,
either within the country generally or within its own ranks specifically. By 1882, after four years of firsthand experience with the Republicans' resistance to countering southern white violence and oppression, he counseled blacks to end their support of Republicans
who perpetuated racism in the country.

Not all of Turner's frustrations were the result of white oppression. The black leader who had united black voters in 1870 sought
unsuccessfully to regain the status he had held in the Missouri black
community earlier in the decade. He failed in that effort because the
old charge of opportunism resurfaced, because he alienated many of

his would-be followers by criticizing their way of life, and because jealousy and factionalism arose among other black leaders.

Turner's eagerness to leave Liberia became apparent during the winter of 1876–1877 when he used much of his last leave of absence trying to find a better position for himself in America. He set his sights high and wrote a letter in March 1877 to Blanche K. Bruce, the black senator from Mississippi with whom he had visited while on leave, and whom he had known through their work together with the Missouri Equal Rights League. Bruce was one of the leading black persons in the country whom Pres. Rutherford B. Hayes turned to in making patronage decisions.[1]

Turner began his letter to Bruce with a vague reference to the atmosphere of uncertainty that surrounded the election of President Hayes, presumably wondering whether the resulting decline in southern black political participation might adversely affect his fortunes. He indicated that he had already written "to the three or four Republican members [of congress] from Missouri" informing them that "while the 800,000 negro voters are not unappreciative, . . . the present political exigencies require that every element of our party, to its utmost fibrous capacity should be attracted—not dispelled—contracted not scattered." Black people, Turner informed the Missouri congressmen, expected "substantial recognition of their power with the party." In Turner's view, that recognition should take the form of appointing "elite" blacks such as himself to positions of authority and responsibility. Moreover, the experience already gained by "negro gentlemen in responsible stations" should not be lost. Therefore, he requested "their advice and endorsement for either a promotion in the Foreign Corps or for the post of Governor of one of the territories."

Turner indicated to Bruce that if he continued to work for the State Department he wanted to be sent "to the Central American states, vix: Costa Rica, Guatemala, Hondurus, Nicaragua and Salvador, as Minister Resident, or in the same capacity to Hawaii." He explained, "Either of these positions are of more importance in our Foreign relations than the one of which I am at present the incumbent, and of more distinguishing grade as they do not in their Archives of Legation, include the duties and title of Consul General." If

1. Howard N. Rabinowitz, "Three Reconstruction Leaders: Blanche K. Bruce, Robert Brown Elliott, and Holland Thompson" in Litwack and Meier, eds., *Black Leaders of the Nineteenth Century*, 199.

his services were needed more in the United States, and if "it should be thought impolitic to request that a negro gentleman be entrusted with the gubernatorial authority over one of the territories, then, though differing with that opinion, I would be willing to accept such position as my partisan friends in their judgement might pronounce the most advisable." Whatever happened, Turner concluded, it was "of first importance to our cause, that some distinguished negro gentleman be accredited by the new administration to some other than a negro Court." Not to press the point at the present, Turner proposed, would be to demonstrate that "we had in some sense given a kind of tacit acquiescence in the policy of sending negro gentlemen as diplomatic officers only to negro Courts."[2]

Turner's desire to continue his public service career in a highly visible position foreshadowed his activities upon his return to the United States. He could hardly have been home more than a few weeks when a movement to elect him to a congressional seat developed within the black community. Whether or not that movement was initiated by Turner is hard to say. On July 18, 1878, the weekly *St. Louis Globe-Democrat* carried an open letter from six clergymen, "and others," asking Turner's permission "to use your name before the Republican Nominating Convention as a fit and proper person to be Representative from the Third Congressional District of the State of Missouri." The letter writers indicated both their regard for Turner as an "exponent of the fixed and settled principles of the Republican party of Missouri" and their belief that those principles were "in a sense essential to insure prosperity and revive the prostrate condition of the industries of the country." The clergymen recalled Turner's record of "distinguished services" and asked to place his name before the Republican nominating convention.[3]

The clergymen's appeal was only a preliminary to the "Rousing Meeting" held in early August by the Independent Republican Club. "A big turnout of the colored folks" gathered at the corner of Eleventh and Christy avenues in St. Louis on August 7, 1878. The purpose of the meeting was to propose Turner as a candidate, although the latter

2. Turner to Blanche K. Bruce, March 12, 1877, Blanche K. Bruce Papers, Moorland-Spingarn Research Center. Bruce's response, if he made one, is not extant.

3. *St. Louis Globe-Democrat,* July 18, 1878. The Missouri *Statesman* carried a notification of Turner's candidacy the next day.

claimed to be there because the gathering was "to protest against the domination of the Post Office ring in the Republican party."[4]

Turner was asked by a reporter just before the meeting began whether he thought he could get the nomination, despite the fact that "Mr. Filley" was opposed to him. Chauncey Filley, a white Republican, served as the Radical mayor of St. Louis in the 1860s and as the St. Louis postmaster in the 1870s. Filley was a leading strategist of the Missouri Republican party after the Civil War and remained active in St. Louis politics until at least 1909. Turner identified him as part of "the Post Office ring" and blamed him for the party's failure to give blacks more meaningful patronage jobs. Turner told the reporter that he could win the nomination "if the Republicans outside the ring stand together." He argued that most of Filley's power in Washington was due to the erroneous belief that the Republican leader controlled the black St. Louis vote. That was simply not true, Turner insisted, and informed the reporter that he had "just returned from Washington" and had "enlightened President Hayes on the subject."[5]

The conversation between the journalist and the aspiring congressman was cut short as speeches endorsing Turner's candidacy began. John Little gave the first speech, an oration that must have stirred fond memories of the early days of the decade when the black vote was being courted by both factions of Republicans as well as by the Democrats. He complained that the Republican party had been guilty of using the black vote for "self-aggrandizement," without rewarding blacks for their support. He emphasized that there were seven thousand black votes to be had in St. Louis, and "if they were properly organized they would be the balance of power." James Milton Turner, he asserted, "was a demonstration that a black man had not only the right to vote, but the right to be voted for." Indeed, John Little believed it unlikely that any man placed on the Republican ticket would be mentally superior to Turner.

William R. Lawton, a Democrat turned Republican, spoke next. Black people, he explained, simply sought justice. They wanted someone who could and would represent their interests in Washington. "If

4. *St. Louis Globe-Democrat,* August 8, 1878.

5. Lawrence O. Christensen, "Black St. Louis: A Study in Race Relations 1865–1916," 208–9. For Filley's relationship with blacks in later Missouri politics, see Larry H. Grothaus, "The Negro in Missouri Politics, 1890–1941," 1–7. *St. Louis Globe-Democrat,* August 8, 1878.

Mr. Turner were placed in the Congressional chair," he said, "he would display intelligence which would eclipse that of any of the present Representatives, and when he came back the people would not need to ask him to show his papers to see whether or not he had been to Congress." Three other men followed with similar speeches, including Charles W. Scheutzel, described by the *Globe-Democrat* as "one of the old time Republicans, and the only white man who spoke."

The preliminary speeches out of the way, Turner arose to address the meeting of his admirers. He began by recounting a conversation he had a few days earlier with President Hayes. He had complained to the president, "The negro vote of the state of Missouri had been ever faithful to Republican principles without receiving . . . that degree of political recognition which other classes of voters in the Republican party has received." He had pointed out that even though blacks held the balance of power among the Republicans in St. Louis, and even though blacks were "diligent and untiring" members of the Republican party, "they had never yet had the happiness of receiving from the National Administration, the elevation of a single one of their race to an executive office where patronage to their own people could be dispensed." Indeed, he exclaimed to a loudly cheering audience, blacks had thus far had to be content with "the position of messenger at the Post Office or as boot-black to the Collector of Customs and to United States Marshals."[6]

The black orator's candidacy for political office was an effort to reverse that situation. He had decided to run, he said, because "I saw that we were restive and discontented because of this lack of honorable recognition, and that we the Third District had determined to throw ourselves in the breach, and test the professions of the Republican party." The matter was an easy one to resolve, and he knew he was well qualified for the office. Hence, it seemed clear to him that "if the Republican party is sincere, then it won't reject a man simply because his skin is black." Rejection of his candidacy, he reasoned, would be obvious evidence of insincerity. Even should the Republicans demonstrate their insincerity by turning their backs on his candidacy, Turner resolved not to leave the Republican party. His audience again cheered loudly as he emphasized that instead of leaving the party, blacks should "organize and show it that we are the balance of power." Victory would ultimately go to blacks, he argued, because

6. *St. Louis Globe-Democrat,* August 8, 1878.

the party would eventually return to the same high principles to which it had been committed during the Grant years. "I know from my travelings between here and New York and the Capitol," he proclaimed, "that the Grant campaign is 'booming' in the hearts of all true Republicans." He closed his speech by asking his audience to "look forward to the Presidential candidate for 1880, and proclaim yourselves Grant men fearlessly, and then you will be on the side of right in the time of danger."[7]

Despite strong black support for Turner, he did not gain the nomination at the fall convention. In fact, newspaper accounts of the convention do not mention his name as a candidate. He seems to have had no support from anyone other than blacks. With all the former rebels reenfranchised in the state, and with a profoundly conservative mood dominating Missouri politics, the Republicans were much less solicitous of the black vote than they had been in 1870. Turner and Moses Dickson were elected to the Republican Central Committee only after a Boone County delegate made "a strong appeal on behalf of the colored people of his region, saying that they had always been faithful to the party, yet had never been represented in the state central committee." Although the convention was willing to tolerate the token number of two black members on the state central committee, a motion to add four blacks instead of two met with strong opposition.[8]

Turner's unsuccessful candidacy in 1878 marked the third time in the decade that he had failed in a bid for an elective office. He had declared himself a candidate for a congressional seat from Missouri's Second District only days before the election in 1870. He followed that short-lived and unsuccessful effort with an attempt at a position in the Missouri House in 1872, while on one of his leaves of absence from Liberia. Arriving in St. Louis on October 1, 1872, just a month before the fall election, Turner had received a hero's welcome when met at the train station by a large reception committee that included the Reverend John Turner, George B. Wedley, Charleton H. Tandy, and the Reverend Moses Dickson. His carriage was pulled through the downtown streets and along the wharf where a large crowd of

7. The *Colored Citizen* of Topeka, Kansas, counseled St. Louis blacks to "'show no quarter' in the coming campaign. . . . If the Republicans refuse to nominate him," it continued, "he should run as an independent candidate. No need of mincing matters. If unprejudiced, white Republicans will vote for him—if prejudiced, the colored voters should vote against them." *Colored Citizen*, August 30, 1878.

8. *Missouri Statesman,* October 18, 1878.

people cheered his presence. Turner, introduced to the crowd as "Africa's Burke," delivered a speech to a large assembly of his followers from the balcony of a friend's house. On that occasion, and throughout the 1872 election, his rhetoric was reminiscent of his 1870 campaign speeches: "he enjoin[ed] the colored people to remain steadfast in their fealty to the Republican Party," and "warned [them] not to trust the Democratic party which was trying to re-enslave them."[9]

Two days after that impressive mass meeting, blacks of the Eighth Ward in St. Louis circulated a petition to have Turner's name placed on the ballot for state representative. The petition, sent to the state Republican party, argued that blacks "needed at least one representative in the state legislature who would introduce legislation conducive to their advancement and educational interest." But, according to Margaret Dwight, "Jealousy among prominent black leaders soon arose and ended in a violent attack upon Turner."[10]

On October 9, 1872, Turner ran afoul of one of his old political foes from the 1870 election, George B. Wedley. The *Missouri Statesman* of October 25, 1872, reported that Wedley was one of Turner's most outspoken opponents in his effort to be elected to the Missouri House. According to the newspaper, the two men met at a reception for Turner and the latter "denounced Wedley in strong terms." Early the next morning, Wedley left his home with a colleague for a political meeting and encountered Turner on the street outside his house. This time it was Wedley's turn: he reproached Turner for his insulting behavior of the day before. Turner's response was direct and unequivocal: he "knocked him down three times," whereupon Wedley "drew a pen-knife and thrust it into the lower part of Turner's left lung." That fracas left Turner critically wounded and probably had a great deal to do with his inordinately long absence from Liberia until April 1873. He did not mention the stabbing in any of his correspondences with the State Department. Martin H. Freeman, his temporary substitute in Liberia, however, noted in December 1872 that the "mail of 26 November . . . brought newspaper accounts that Hon. J. Milton Turner had been stabbed as supposed fatally."[11]

9. *Missouri Democrat,* October 31, 1870, and October 2, 3, 1872.

10. *St. Louis Daily Democrat,* October 6, 1872; Dwight, "Black Suffrage in Missouri," 168–69.

11. *Missouri Democrat,* October 31, 1870; Dispatch No. 67, December 17, 1872, Despatches, vol. 3.

Following his recovery from the attack, Turner campaigned throughout the state, urging blacks to vote for Grant and a solidly Republican
ticket. Turner never received the party's nomination for a seat in the
legislature and, although Grant was reelected, the president did not
carry Missouri. Indeed, Republicans fared poorly in Missouri, with
the Democrat Silas Woodson defeating his Republican opponent for
governor, John Henderson, by more than thirty thousand votes.[12]
Turner's failure to gain elective political office either in 1872 or in
1878 was only a symptom of the decline in black power in the former
slave states. The question of black rights became much less important
to the country generally after the election of Pres. Rutherford B.
Hayes. Turner's absence from the United States during most of the
1870s had kept him from experiencing firsthand the most serious
manifestations of this reaction. Undoubtedly, he read about them and
made an effort, on at least one of his leaves of absence, to travel
through the South and assess the condition of blacks, although he left
no account of his response to what he saw. He had even had his own
brush with overt racial discrimination early in 1877 when he was
refused a room at the Astor House in New York City. Turner sued the
proprietors of the hotel, contending that they had violated the 1875
Civil Rights Act. He acknowledged to the court that the actual damages he suffered amounted to only two dollars, the amount he said
that he had to pay a porter for taking his luggage to another hotel.
Still, there was a principle of law at stake. There is no evidence as to
the outcome of his suit.[13]

Whatever the degree of his immediate awareness of the crimes
against black people in the South during the period following the
Compromise of 1877, Turner was soon to get a firsthand view of the
freedmen's plight. Political terrorism and "bulldozing" were so bad
by 1878 that many blacks began to flee the South for "the promised

12. Dwight, "Black Suffrage in Missouri," 169, 173.
13. For a general discussion of black life in post-Reconstruction America,
see Logan, *The Betrayal of the Negro*. In 1875, Turner indicated his desire to
receive, at government expense, the Washington daily newspapers, *Republican*
and *Chronicle*. Dispatch No. 151, October 16, 1875, and Dispatch No. 156,
April 15, 1875. He also asked to receive the *New York Daily Evening Post*. Turner
justified his request for an extended leave of absence in 1873 on the grounds that
he spent much of his time "observing the general condition of my own people in
the Southern States." Dispatch No. 68, Despatches, vol. 3; *New York Times*,
January 17, 1877.

land" of Kansas. St. Louis, located as it was at a critical juncture on the Mississippi River, near the mouth of the Missouri, became a way station for the pilgrimage to the West. By early March 1879, the first of the more than six thousand blacks who would come to St. Louis during the next four months, en route to Kansas, arrived. The sheer numbers of these people, known contemporaneously as "exodusters," not to mention their generally destitute condition, had a profound effect on Turner and other black leaders.[14]

The problems faced by the exodusters were legion. The first obstacle they had to overcome was to secure money for boat fare up the Mississippi. It cost from three to four dollars per adult to travel from the vicinity of Vicksburg, Mississippi, to St. Louis. Children under ten years of age were transported for half price, and a small amount of baggage was carried free of charge. Consequently, a family of five needed from ten to fifteen dollars just to get up the river, an amount that, in many cases, blacks had to raise by a hasty and unprofitable sale of most of their household goods.[15]

They arrived in St. Louis with their money spent and no way to secure passage to Kansas. They were in desperate need of immediate relief, and the black community of St. Louis was quick to respond. The first attempt to extend aid to the black emigrants from the South was organized by Charleton H. Tandy. Approximately two hundred and eighty men, women, and children arrived in St. Louis on March 11, 1879, in a condition of "utter want." When the news of their arrival reached Tandy, he tried to find jobs for a few of the men and to arrange impromptu shelter for the entire group. He made an unsuccessful effort to obtain financial help from a white organization known as the Mullanphy Emigrant Relief Board. This was an asso-

14. Nell Irvin Painter, *Exodusters: Black Migration to Kansas after Reconstruction*, 10. The term *bulldozing* referred to the night-riding violence of white vigilantes. Painter's book is the best account of the 1879 exodus movement nationally. The most detailed account of the exodus as it related to St. Louis remains Robert G. Athearn, *In Search of Canaan: Black Migration to Kansas, 1879–1880*, particularly his chapter "The Spirit of St. Louis." Also important is Glen Schwendemann's "Negro Exodus to Kansas: First Phase, March–July, 1879."

15. These figures are based on testimony offered before the Select Committee of the United States Senate to Investigate the Causes of the Removal of the Negroes from the Southern States to the Northern States and quoted in Schwendemann, "Exodus to Kansas," 39–40.

ciation established under the provisions of the will of Bryan Mullanphy of St. Louis to help emigrants moving West.[16]

Failing to get adequate help for the emigrants from the Mullanphy Board, Tandy concentrated on the St. Louis black community for
a relief effort. He issued a call to blacks of the city on March 14,
1879, asking them to come together to consider the plight of the
exodusters. Three days later a mass meeting of blacks was held in
St. Paul's Chapel. Tandy was elected president; J. T. Smith and J. W.
Grant, vice-presidents; Charles E. Starkes, treasurer; and Robert
Kimbrough and J. B. Dyson, secretaries. After considerable discussion, the gathering resolved to create a committee of fifteen persons
who were charged with the responsibility of seeing to the needs of the
emigrants, including the arrangement and supervision of their transportation to Kansas.[17]

The black churches of the city were the focus of relief activity, all
of them having opened their doors to the emigrants. On March 18,
the day after the mass meeting, the members of the Committee of
Fifteen met at St. Paul's Church and decided that there was so much
work to be done that they needed to expand their group to become a
Committee of Twenty-Five. Turner was selected as one of the ten new
members. The Committee of Twenty-Five divided into subcommit-
tees on Finance, Resolutions, Reception, Entertainment, and Com-
missary. Since all of the other activities were possible only if there was
money, the finance subcommittee's task was the most urgent. Turner's name was added to that subcommittee's membership sometime
prior to March 26, 1879.[18]

On the same day that the Committee of Twenty-Five was created,
the number of black exodusters in the city rose to fourteen hundred.
Once again it seemed necessary to call a mass meeting, this time for
the evening of March 20. Tandy again presided and asked the Reverend John Turner, chairman of the Committee of Twenty-Five, to
report on the group's progress. Turner responded with an informal

16. *St. Louis Globe-Democrat*, March 12, 13, 14, 1879. For a detailed
account of Tandy's attempt to solicit funds from the Mullanphy Board, see
Schwendemann, "Negro Exodus to Kansas," 40–46.

17. *St. Louis Globe-Democrat*, March 14, 18, 1879; Schwendemann,
"Negro Exodus to Kansas," 46, 55.

18. *Missouri Republican*, March 19, 1879; *St. Louis Globe-Democrat*,
March 21, 26, 1879; April 26, 1879; Schwendemann, "Negro Exodus," 59.

report, explaining that he had not had time to prepare a written statement. His report was followed by an attempt by Albert Carter to
persuade the gathering to endorse what the *Missouri Republican*
called "a series of bitter resolutions indorsing [*sic*] the emigration
from the South upon the ground that the colored people were too
much abused and maltreated by the whites of the South." Carter
wanted a standing committee appointed "whose duty [would] be to
encourage emigration from those Southern states from which these
people come; to distribute circulars among them, and if need be go
down in person and urge them to quit the land of oppression to move
to a more genial clime."[19]

Turner interrupted Carter's speech on at least two occasions and
made it clear that he did not support the resolutions proposed by
Carter. After the latter had finished, John W. Wheeler, publisher of a
local black newspaper, responded to the Carter proposal angrily,
warning that "the colored people . . . could not afford to array themselves against the white population and that was what the adoption of
Carter's resolutions meant." A heated debate followed Wheeler's remarks with the more moderate members prevailing upon the group
to pass a resolution that recounted the crimes of violence against
black people in the South, offering them as justification for the black
exodus. Turner, ever the believer in direct appeals to the federal government, got through an amendment requiring the resolution to be
forwarded to the president of the United States. Clearly, despite the
1877 Compromise, he still hoped for federal intervention to protect
black political and civil rights.[20]

Turner addressed at length the question of the exodus two days
later in a letter to the editor of the *St. Louis Globe-Democrat*. He
acknowledged that the presence of hundreds of blacks in the city fleeing from the South made it necessary to consider "the vexed question
of the negroes' condition in that section of our country." He asserted
that even the most incredulous person had to be convinced "that rifle
clubs and other political organizations have worked the persecution,
perils and death of hundreds, not to say thousands of negroes at the
South." He had little sympathy for the opinion that blacks were leaving the South because they had been persuaded to do so by political

19. *Missouri Republican,* March 21, 1879.
20. *St. Louis Globe-Democrat,* March 21, 1879; *Missouri Republican,*
March 21, 1879; Schwendemann, 62–65.

demagogues. Rather, he insisted, they were leaving "because of ostracism and persecution . . . and downright race prejudice." Nor did they leave because of a naive conviction that they would receive "that imaginary 'mules and forty acres.'" It took more than that to remove people "from places on which many of them were born and have grown to old age," and who weren't particularly well informed of what lay ahead for them. In a sentence reminiscent of Turner's comments about the Liberian exodus movement, he pronounced the blacks fleeing the South to be "inexperienced and ignorant of the outside world and its way." Still, he wrote, the fact "that a people so ignorant as these emigrants would start upon a long and uncertain journey without clothes, food, money or other necessary preparation, argues more than resentment or despair." In fact, he continued, "it argues desperation."

Ultimately, Turner maintained, it would be to the South's own detriment to maintain blacks in such a condition of destitution and frustration. "The political and race prejudice of the white man," he wrote "have so blinded him to his own interest in the case that he has allowed the relations of labor and capital at the South to become utterly disrupted." Recounting a theme that had become central to his vision of postwar America, he went on to explain that he thought whites should be training blacks to become respectable landowners. But if he was critical of the white South, he was also dissatisfied with the life-style of the southern black masses. In language mirroring his comments about native Africans, he wrote that southern blacks needed to be taught self-reliance:

> Where the negro or laborer is improvident and a spendthrift, the white man or capitalist is so prejudiced that his own interests would be to teach the laborer frugal and provident habits. Many of those people who were reared in the south have never been twenty miles from home, and have always been accustomed to depend on others. It is not surprising, therefore, that in numerous instances they are without frugal habits and in their new estate of freedom remind one more of grown up children than of persons of mature mind.

Turner continued to write approvingly of the paternalistic way in which one planter in Arkansas had taught his black field hands how to keep "their expenditure within their income." The result was, he declared, "Gilliland's people are prosperous and contented. The Gilliland place is not for sale, nor would the laborers leave that place, much less the South."

Turner concluded the letter by declaring his belief in the need for an "adjustment of the relations between labor and capital at the South." In the absence of such an adjustment, and with blacks leaving the South, Turner thought it possible that "our great cotton-growing sections" could be destroyed. Blacks leaving would also deprive grain farmers of the North and West of "a considerable home market" for cereal products. Moreover, he was suspicious of the black laborer's ability to adjust "to the climate, habits and farm customs of our Western section." Despite these reservations, however, Turner encouraged black workers to leave the South "in numbers sufficiently large until his emigration shall prove a corrective to the haughty, domineering, selfish, landholder and capitalist of the South, solving forever the vexed question of the relations of the capitalist and contributor to the nation's material wealth in those parts."[21]

Within a few days after Turner's letter appeared in the *Globe-Democrat,* the number of black emigrants in the city rose to twenty-five hundred, and more had to be done to offer them temporary relief while they awaited transportation to Kansas. On March 26, the *Globe-Democrat* published a notice issued by the Committee of Twenty-Five, asking for assistance for the refugees. It encouraged all "charity-loving people of St. Louis" to send "provisions and clothing," part of which would be used to sustain the emigrants in St. Louis, with the remainder helping to defray the cost of sending a number of blacks on to a colony at Wyandotte, Kansas.[22]

Despite the fact that he was a member of the committee coordinating relief activities for the refugees, Turner still had reservations "as to the propriety of the action of the congregations in giving food, shelter and transportation to the immigrants." He was concerned that the aid provided to black emigrants would only serve to encourage destitute southern blacks to move North, decrease their ability to help themselves, and add to the relief rolls. Blacks, he explained, "would be emboldened to spend all they possessed for passage to this city, and trust to persons here for assistance." He mustered still another argument against the black exodus: blacks, by leaving the South, were forfeiting any possibility of Republican victory there, and they

21. Information in this and the preceding two paragraphs is from Turner to the Editor of the *Globe-Democrat,* March 22, 1879. *St. Louis Globe-Democrat,* March 23, 1879.
22. Ibid., March 26, 1879.

were moving to Kansas, a state that was already indisputably Republican, a reality that would give them little political influence. Those reservations aside, however, Turner took the position that inasmuch as a relief program "had been begun . . . it was necessary to continue it."[23]

The arrival of black emigrants in St. Louis continued unabated into April. The black community of the city, unable to generate sufficient relief funds in St. Louis, sent Charleton H. Tandy on a fundraising trip east. Tandy arrived in Washington, D.C., with a memorial to be presented to the Congress and signed by, among others, former Missouri Congressmen Lyne S. Metcalfe and Nathan Cole, former Sen. John B. Henderson, former Gov. Thomas B. Fletcher, and James Milton Turner. The memorial included a protest against the conditions that had led to the exodus, asked for an investigation into the treatment of southern blacks, and closed with an appeal to "enforce law and order" below the Mason-Dixon Line.[24]

Turner's support of the exodus grew as the number of southern blacks moving into St. Louis increased. By April, his explanation of the exodus included the following "basic causes": the partial failure of crops the year before, black overpopulation in the cotton states, and "adverse political pressure." The exodus, he now argued, would help to ease the overpopulation problem in the South, to the advantage of both blacks and whites remaining there. Moreover, it would have the effect of improving race relations in the South because the blacks who remained would be encouraged to become more self-sufficient. According to Turner, the exodus

> would necessitate more industry among the colored people [who remained], give them better social organization and more steady remunerative employment. Beyond doubt the indolent and airless lives of many of the Southern blacks, their improvidence and slothfulness, have the effect of promoting and maintaining a strong aversion between the two races, and constant discord and more or less intimidation is the result.

As his interest in the exodus increased, so too did his dissatisfaction with the work being done by the Committee of Twenty-Five, and in mid-April 1879 Turner headed a movement to create a new organiza-

23. Ibid.
24. *New York Daily Tribune*, April 8, 1879.

tion to take its place. The *Globe-Democrat* on April 18 carried the announcement that an organization, known as the Colored Emigration Aid Association, had been formed. Turner was one of eight charter members.[25]

In contrast to the all-black Committee of Twenty-Five, the membership of the new organization included three prominent white politicians: Jacob E. Merrell, William Alexander Scudder, and Edward S. Rowse. Those three men were invited to serve as members of the board of directors of the society in order to establish a "permanent organization" that would offer relief to "the 196 families now camped upon the Levee, and such others as come along." There was another, more fundamental difference between Turner's group and the Committee of Twenty-Five. Turner proposed to do more than simply meet the immediate needs of blacks en route to Kansas. He hoped, through his organization, to establish settlements in Kansas and elsewhere that would instill into the black emigrants responsible work habits, so they would not become "paupers in the land whither they journey."[26]

Turner's Colored Emigration Aid Association met on April 19, 1879, with Turner serving as president. He announced early in the meeting that he had received letters from various parts of the country, expressing sympathy with the relief efforts and offering to provide money when it was needed. He also explained that his group was an organization established to supplant the loosely structured Committee of Twenty-Five, which "had done its business in a very random and irresponsible way" and had become "wholly disorganized and could not be got together."

The association president went on to predict that the migration from the South would continue. He reiterated a familiar theme when he explained that, although there were many reasons for the exodus, "the principal [one] was the conflict between capital and labor" and "the extravagance both of the white planter and the colored laborer." He was particularly critical of thriftless black workers who, he said, "ran up large grocery bills for cove oysters and candy." He did not

25. Ibid., April 7, 1879; Painter, *Exodusters,* 244; *St. Louis Globe-Democrat,* April 18, 1879.
26. *St. Louis Globe-Democrat,* April 18, 20, 1879; U.S. Congress, Senate, *Report and Testimony of the Select Committee of the United States Senate to Investigate the Causes of the Removal of the Negroes from the Southern States to the Northern States,* 120–21.

ignore the fact that besides these improvident habits "the colored man was practically ostracized, bulldozed, shot, hung."

According to Turner, the Committee of Twenty-Five had gotten into debt because of its inefficiency and was eager "to turn over their liabilities to the present organization." He argued that bringing respectable white citizens such as Merrell, Scudder, and Rowse into the society would serve "to place the organization above suspicion." The Committee of Twenty-Five, however, was not about to turn anything over to the new organization. Indeed, discussion at the April 19 meeting made it clear that the committee would not cooperate with Turner's group: "There was the green eyed jealousy existing between the two bodies, and . . . nothing could be done to bring about harmony."[27]

Two days after Turner's society met, the members of the original Committee of Twenty-Five gathered to establish a counter "permanent aid association." There was little effort made to conceal the committee's ill-feeling toward James Milton Turner. The Reverend Moses Dickson, with whom Turner had worked closely on behalf of black education during the immediate postwar period, insinuated that Turner had misused funds collected for the refugees and expressed his opinion that "Milton Turner . . . had not treated the other members with courtesy." John Wheeler labeled Turner as "the Judas of the committee" for having created a separate organization, arguing that Turner had betrayed them and that they did not want anything more to do with him. "The unanimous feeling," according to the Globe-Democrat, "was that no attention should be paid to the society led by J. Milton Turner." The Reverend John Turner, president of the committee, wanted it clearly understood that "he was a distinct person from J. Milton Turner." Apparently, James Milton Turner tried to impress his brethren with the righteousness of his position by reminding them that he had previously held a high governmental office, for the Reverend John Turner sarcastically emphasized that "he was not of the 'diplomatic corps.'" Meanwhile, Turner's group met in another part of the city, although with a considerably smaller attendance, and stoked the fires of discord by accusing the Committee of Twenty-Five with the same misuse of money and general irresponsibility with which it was being charged.[28]

Turner was grossly offended by the sudden upsurge of animosity

27. St. Louis Globe-Democrat, April 20, 1879.
28. Ibid., April 22, 1879.

toward him, and on April 24, 1879, he addressed a letter to the editor
of the *Globe-Democrat,* indicating his intention to "henceforth treat
with contemptuous silence all innuendoes levelled at me." In a phrase
that offers insight into the condescension that must have grated his
opponents, Turner remarked that he would in the future ignore the
criticisms of men "who are scarcely known beyond their own family
circle, and who, through a spirit of envy, jealousy or malice, belabor
themselves to pervert my motives and endeavors in behalf of my poor
afflicted people, and to detract from my well-earned reputation and
character in this country." He defended the idea of the Colored Emigration Aid Association as "a grand conception," arguing that the
men who composed it were determined to carry out its mission. As to
allegations that he was dishonest, Turner remarked, "I have only to
point the people of the country to my public record." He continued
to sing his own praises in a passage much like the speech he had given
in Jefferson City just before leaving for Liberia. He pointed

> with especial pride to the fact that, born on these streets, in remote
> and humble circumstances, I have had a somewhat, at least, con-
> spicuous public experience, and it is my especial pride to-day to be
> able to defy any man in or out of this country, living or dead, to
> place a finger on the point of my infidelity to the interest of the
> elevation of my unfortunate people.

He closed his letter by defying "any living man or any dead man's
history" to make "any direct and definite assault upon my good name
and honest character."[29]

Two days later a mass meeting called by Turner attracted two
hundred black citizens. According to the *Globe-Democrat,* at least
two-thirds of those present were dissatisfied with and critical of the
Committee of Twenty-Five, particularly with regard to its failure to
turn any funds over to the group headed by James Milton Turner. On
April 28, the Reverend John Turner's faction again met, with the Reverend Mr. Turner labeling Turner's mass meeting "a disgrace to the
colored people." Charges of the latter's misuse of funds were reiterated. Ultimately, the Reverend Turner's committee was more successful in raising money for the cause. Perhaps it was more representative
of and appealing to both the black St. Louis community and the black

29. Turner to the Editor of the *Globe-Democrat,* April 24, 1879.

emigrants. Unquestionably, Turner's paternalism rankled potential grass-roots supporters. He had difficulty viewing the exodus as the life-and-death struggle that it was for the emigrants. To them, the exodus meant an opportunity to live the kind of life that had been denied them in the South—an end in itself. To Turner it was, first of all, a way of changing that life-style and, second, a concrete way of demonstrating black power in the South—both means to an end. The sole concrete contribution of the group headed by the former minister to Liberia consisted of two hundred and fifty dollars in cash, turned over to the Reverend Mr. Turner's Colored Relief Board in midsummer. By contrast, the Reverend Mr. Turner's group provided nearly three thousand dollars of goods and services between March 17 and April 22 alone.[30]

The confusion over two seemingly identical black relief organizations operating within the same community handicapped the Relief Board's efforts to secure financial assistance outside the St. Louis community. An editorial comment in Kansas's *Atchison Globe* best summed up the wariness of potential contributors: "The colored preachers of St. Louis are making a great deal of money out of the exodus doners. There are two societies, and each one accuses the other of gross irregularities, which are nothing short of thefts."[31]

In May 1879 a meeting was called at the Eighth Street Baptist Church in St. Louis to hear Charleton Tandy's report on his generally unsuccessful visit east "on a mission in the interest of the refugees." Tandy criticized Frederick Douglass, a fierce opponent of the exodus, indicating that Douglass had treated him coldly and had refused to assist. At that point, John W. Taylor arose to offer a resolution "comdemning Fred Douglass and declaring him a traitor to his race." James Milton Turner, who by this time knew what it was like to be labeled a "traitor," came to Douglass's defense. As the motion was about to be voted upon, Turner jumped from his seat and rushed to the platform shouting, "My Friends, dear friends; hold on, just think first what this means!" The chairman of the meeting ruled Turner out of order, but, according to the *Missouri Republican,* he "persisted in speaking, and a motion carried to allow debate."

Turner argued, "Fred Douglass ha[s] done more than any living

30. *St. Louis Globe-Democrat,* April 26, 29, 1879; July 22, 26, 27, 1879; August 5, 1879; Painter, *Exodusters,* 227; Schwendemann, "Negro Exodus," 82; Senate Report 693, part 2, 121–22.

31. *Atchison* [Kansas] *Globe,* May 19, 1879.

man for his race and it would be a shame and scandal on St. Louis colored people to declare him a traitor without an investigation into the charges preferred against him." The resolution of condemnation was withdrawn by acclamation following Turner's speech, to which he responded, "This is the happiest moment of my life, this prevention of a wrong to Douglass and the colored race." As Nell Irvin Painter has pointed out, the St. Louis Colored Relief Board "limped along" for the remainder of the year and continued into 1880, even though "the public had lost interest in the Exodus, and contributions were negligible."[32]

James Milton Turner's interest switched from relief back to politics as the 1880 election drew near. Presumably eager to become a power broker the way that he had been a decade earlier, he laid the groundwork in March of that year for his appointment to a federal position. First he gathered all of the letters of recommendation filed with the State Department in 1870–1871 in support of his application for appointment to the Liberian ministership. Less than a month later he headed a delegation of Missouri blacks, a group known as the Missouri Republican Union, that traveled to Washington and called upon President Hayes. The group explained to the president, "The negro vote of the State of Missouri is entirely unrepresented in official positions." That was unfortunate, the members argued in an exaggeration of their power, since "the negro vote amounted to 40,000, and controls two, if not three, Congressional districts of St. Louis." They further urged "that if the President would elevate a colored man to a responsible official position in Missouri it would reunite the colored people, who are now disaffected on account of having to carry the burdens of the party without charge or emoluments."[33]

A sentiment of disenchantment was growing among prominent

32. *Missouri Republican,* May 16, 1879. For a similar account, see the *St. Louis Globe-Democrat,* May 16, 1879. Painter, *Exodusters,* 229–30.

33. Turner to the State Department, State Department Registers of Miscellaneous Communications Received, M17, roll 63, vol. 139, 90, NA. James Milton Turner file, Applications and Recommendations During the Hayes Administration, R.G. 59, NA. This was the second time since his return from Liberia that Turner made an overt attempt at securing a federal position. In the summer of 1878 he had applied for the position of "Appraiser of Customs" at St. Louis but had withdrawn in favor of someone else, perhaps because he wanted to devote more time to his candidacy for a congressional seat. *St. Louis Post-Dispatch,* March 6, 1898. Turner claimed in 1898 that under "Gen. Arthur he had an easy berth as special agent of the Customs Department," a grossly erroneous claim. *New York Times,* April 2, 1880; Athearn, *In Search of Canaan,* 283n, 12.

black leaders throughout the nation, and it threatened to increase after James A. Garfield's election to the presidency in 1880—if Garfield did not become more responsive to his black constituency. Black leaders expected two things. One was the placing of prominent blacks in important patronage positions controlled by the Republicans, the kind of thing that Turner and the Missouri Republican Union had declared a necessity in April 1880. In addition, black leaders wanted some federal action to be taken to protect the civil rights of blacks in the South. One month after the election of Garfield, Turner presided over another meeting of the Missouri Republican Union. Again trying to employ strategies that dated from the years of Radical rule and relative black power, the group called for a national black convention to be held in Washington, D.C., as a preliminary step to making political demands on the Republican administration.[34]

The call began with the assertion that "the Negro has reached a significant juncture in citizenship." It proclaimed the "truth" that Garfield's victory could not have occurred without the black vote. The black vote, it declared, was "an indispensable factor. It can grant triumph or secure defeat." With that principle in mind, it followed logically that the black vote "should receive the respect due its power." Anything less, the call proclaimed, "is not the dignity of citizenship; whatever is less than citizenship is peonage and serfdom." The Missouri Republican Union addressed itself specifically to the plight of black people in the South, where "the new amendments [to the Constitution] are practically abrogated; labor is unremunerated; life and property insecure; [and] terrorism prostrates the American ballot, and retards development." The seriousness of these matters prompted the Union to "request the patriotic and public spirited negro men to assemble in council in the city of Washington, D.C., March 3, 1881."[35]

34. Elizabeth Caldwell Beatty, "The Political Response of Black Americans, 1876–1896," 35–38, 47–48. Nationally, the demands focused on the appointment of a black person to a cabinet position. Frederick Douglass, Blanche K. Bruce, John M. Langston, Robert Elliott, Robert Devaux, and William Wells Brown were among those thought by the black press to be best suited for such a position. *Tribune* [Topeka, Kansas], December 25, 1880.

35. Turner's role in the nomination and election of Garfield is unclear. He did attend the 1880 Republican convention, one of many prominent black leaders who did so. He was one of a group of people specifically mentioned by Edward W. Blyden, president of Liberia College and Liberian minister of the interior, with whom Blyden was invited to dine. The other "leading colored men" mentioned by Blyden were Frederick Douglass, Blanche K. Bruce, Dr. Robert

The March conference never materialized. The *Washington, D.C.*, *People's Advocate* summed up the attitude toward the proposed convention when it reminded its readers how singularly unsuccessful such movements had been since 1873. The *Advocate* spoke against the gathering simply because it believed that such a meeting would not be effective. It suggested an alternative "way to secure recognition" by "local conferences and local organization." Whether as a direct response to this suggestion or not, Turner turned his efforts back toward Missouri early in 1881. In February, the month before the proposed national conference was to have been held, he and Joseph H. Murray of St. Louis visited the Missouri capitol in support of proposed changes in the school law that would have provided better facilities for black education. The two men met with Democratic Gov. Thomas T. Crittenden, who presumably endorsed an end to segregated education. Crittenden informed them that, although he would support "any action to advance the objects sought by the colored representatives," he "thought it would not be wise to disturb the present law so far as it provides for the separation of the colored and white scholars." In part, Crittenden's response may well have been tempered by the conservative 1875 constitution's dismantling of the Radical's educational reforms and the return of control over educational matters to local school boards. While in Jefferson City, Turner tried to gain access to the hall of the House of Representatives "to lecture upon the political condition of the country," presumably much in the same way that he had done in early 1870. Rep. Richard M. Wray of St. Louis moved the adoption of a resolution offering the House facilities for the occasion, but the resolution did not come to a vote, and there is no evidence that Turner made his speech.[36]

Nearly one and a half years after the aborted national conference was to have been held in Washington, Turner presided over a state convention held in Missouri's capital city. Much of the convention

---

Purvis, and Robert B. Elliott. Hollis R. Lynch, *Edward Wilmot Blyden,* 111; *Tribune* [Topeka, Kansas], December 25, 1880; see also, *Louisianian* [New Orleans], December 25, 1880, and the *New York Times,* December 16, 1880.

36. *People's Advocate,* January 8, 1881; *Louisianian,* January 15, 1881; *Missouri Statesman* [Columbia], February 4, 1881, reported that Turner's request was denied. The House *Journal,* however, indicates that a motion to table the Wray resolution was defeated 113 to 11 but shows no vote on the resolution itself. *Journal of the House of Representatives of the Thirty-first General Assembly of the State of Missouri,* 244.

was a reiteration of what had become a familiar Turner theme: emphasis on self-reliance and the preparatory tool of education. Turner's long-since-dead mentor, John Berry Meachum, would have been pleased with the gathering. More than thirty years before, he had proclaimed the need for education among blacks to prepare them for the eventual day when freedom would come. In particular, he had placed emphasis on vocational education, which, he believed, offered the best hope for the unity and eventual advancement of blacks. Now Turner, committed to the belief that the acquisition of skills would lead to economic self-sufficiency, which would lead to status and political power, modified the message to apply to the post-emancipation era. Turner began the proceedings with a brief but "earnest" speech in which he "stated the object of the council to be for the purpose of discussing the subject of the establishment of a mechanical or industrial school in which colored boys and girls may be taught the skilled trades and arts." Subsequently, the convention passed resolutions endorsing the creation of kindergartens for blacks and the establishment of compulsory education for black youths.

While much of the meeting was a rehash of Turner's by now familiar emphasis on the need for black people to make adjustments in their lives to put themselves in tune with the mainstream of white society, and while much of it was consistent with his long-existing optimism that blacks would one day be assimilated into American society, there was another side to the proceedings. The gathering carried with it an element of the politics of confrontation that had led Turner and the Missouri Republican Union to call for a national convention two years earlier. It was a defiant and even angry meeting of persons who were quite dissatisfied with their lack of political power. In Turner's case, it was a clear example of how far Republican racism had driven him away from the hallowed sanctuary of the party of Grant and moved him down the path toward political apostasy.

The convention, with Turner presiding first as temporary and later as permanent chairman, passed a resolution endorsing "every movement whose purpose shall be the emancipation of the negro race from the thraldom of political demagogues." It acknowledged "with profound gratitude the efforts of the Republican party in behalf of our race." It even acknowledged that the Republicans' "platform of principles as announced at every convention is the most practical, progressive, and safe to all the elements of our composite nationality." Nevertheless, Turner remarked, the black people of Missouri attending this meeting were sufficiently disillusioned with the Republican party that they felt compelled to "announce as the new Monroe Doctrine of the era of emancipation that the negro voter in the United States shall not henceforth consider himself a subject for colonization and appropriation for any political party, but that the individual['s] right to think, speak, and act for himself shall be untrammeled by party chains." The convention went on to endorse a specific way of dealing with an unresponsive Republican party. It encouraged black Missourians to adhere to the following policy in the next election: "That whenever a colored man has been nominated on the Republican ticket and been beaten, while the other part of the ticket was elected, we recommend them to vote independently and without regard to party."[37]

That position was a far cry from the party line that Turner had endorsed throughout the previous decade. Perhaps he would have come to it sooner had he not been out of the country during the period that the South and his own state were retreating from the gains of Reconstruction. As it was, his faith in the Republican party did not wane until he saw the effects of unrestrained southern racism in the exodus movement and witnessed, along with other black leaders, the unwillingness of Republican leaders to extend important patronage positions to the best of his race.

His return to America had been an enlightening, if not altogether pleasant, experience. Despite what he considered to be his superior qualifications to lead black people, he had been overtly rejected by many St. Louis blacks who did not share his views about what needed to be done to help southern exodusters. Moreover, his earlier view of the Republican party's commitment to egalitarian principles was seriously called into question. Still, he retained the view that black people were important politically and that a properly organized black coalition could wield considerable power. But if that overall strategy was sound, perhaps the tactics needed to be reconsidered.

37. *New York Times,* August 26, 1882; *The People's Tribune,* August 30, 1882. Subsequently, there came out of this conference a "memorial" presented to the state legislature at the beginning of the 1883 session, "praying for the establishment . . . of an industrial school for the education and training of the colored youth," along with a better, and compulsory educational system for blacks. The memorial was referred to the Committee on Education which reported back two days later, concluding that members "have considered the same and recommend that no action be taken." *Journal of the House of Representatives of the Thirty-second General Assembly of the State of Missouri,* 179, 195.

Thomas C. Fletcher, Radical Governor of Missouri at the end of the Civil War, signed the proclamation freeing Missouri's slaves on January 11, 1865. He was the brother-in-law of Col. Madison Miller whom Turner served as a body-servant during the war. Courtesy of the State Historical Society of Missouri.

A Congregationalist minister from New Hampshire, Foster was an officer with the Sixty-Second U.S. Colored Infantry during the Civil War. He served as the first principal of Lincoln Institute and employed Turner in early 1870 as a fund-raiser. Courtesy of the State Historical Society of Missouri. From the *Thirty-Second Annual Catalogue of Lincoln Institute,* Jefferson City, Missouri, 1903–1904. Courtesy of the State Historical Society of Missouri.

Lincoln Institute was founded in 1866, the product of the vision of black Missouri soldiers who made up the Sixty-Second and Sixty-Fifth U.S. Colored infantries during the Civil War. As a result of Turner's efforts, the school received its first state appropriation in 1870. Courtesy of the State Historical Society of Missouri.

Masonic Home near Hannibal, Missouri, established for indigent masons, their widows and orphans. James Milton Turner was a principal supporter of the home. From the *Official Proceedings M. W. Grand Lodge, 1908–.* Courtesy of the State Historical Society of Missouri.

James Milton Turner as he appeared at the height of his power, in approximately 1870. From Lincoln University, Jefferson City, Missouri. Courtesy of State Historical Society of Missouri.

Office of
State Superintendent Public Schools.

City of Jefferson, Aug 27 1869

J. Milton Turner
Agt. B. R. F. & A L,
Boonville
Cooper Co
Mo

Saml. Peterson
Co. Spt. Public Schools
Fredericktown
Mo

My Dear Sir

Prof. Parker requested me to ask you if the proper officers have taken any steps toward opening colored School this ensuing term, at Fredricktown & Mine lamotte. I wish also to know if the men have done anything toward building their School House

Very Truly
J. Milton Turner

State Superintendent of Public Schools letterhead. Turner wrote many letters as he traveled across southeast Missouri to enforce compliance with an earlier directive to establish schools for blacks. Courtesy of the Missouri State Archives.

Robert L. Owen was Indian agent at the Union Agency in Indian Territory during the controversial 1887 election, when Turner was accused of interfering in Cherokee politics. Turner's opponents pleaded with Owen for the black lawyer's removal from Indian Territory. Courtesy of Archives and Manuscripts Division of the Oklahoma Historical Society.

Joseph W. McClurg was elected Missouri's Radical governor in November 1868. He supported Turner's appointment as Minister Resident and Consul General to Liberia. Courtesy of the State Historical Society of Missouri.

Elias C. Boudinot, a Cherokee Indian who encouraged Cherokee freedmen to hire Turner as their attorney. Boudinot subsequently claimed that Turner owed him money for introducing the black attorney to the freedmen's case. Courtesy of Archives and Manuscripts Division of the Oklahoma Historical Society.

John W. Noble was the secretary of the interior during the period after the passage of the Cherokee Freedmen's Act (1888), when a controversy ensued over identifying the freedmen who were entitled to share in the benefits of the legislation. Courtesy of Archives and Manuscripts Division of the Oklahoma Historical Society.

Undated photograph, taken in Washington, D.C., of James Milton Turner in late life. Courtesy of the Kingdom of Callaway Historical Society.

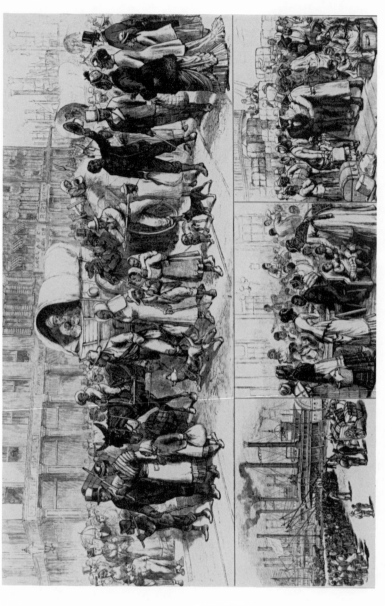

Artist's rendering of black Exodusters from the South as they gathered along the levee in the spring of 1879 in St. Louis. Courtesy of the Western Historical Manuscript Collection at the University of Missouri–St. Louis.

CHAPTER VII
For Justice and a Fee

I will say to our Republican friends who are so solicitous about us, that we are not being enticed away from the Republican fold. We are simply coolly and deliberately walking away.

—James Milton Turner
July 26, 1888

James Milton Turner's Colored Emigration Aid Association was a colossal failure with regard to its avowed goal of providing relief and direction to black exodusters. It did, however, have one important long-range effect: it introduced Turner to the Oklahoma Territory and to the former black slaves of Indians who remained there after the Civil War. In the process of trying to help southern blacks find a place to move, he became aware of what he considered to be a gross violation of the civil rights of the freedmen living in Indian Territory: the denial of their tribal rights among the Indians who had enslaved them. Consequently, in 1883 he sought legislative and judicial remedies to their problems.

Turner encountered difficulties almost from the beginning. He lobbied for five years on behalf of a bill to give the freedmen full tribal rights. Ultimately, he was able to secure passage of that bill, but only with the help of the Democratic party, which a few years before he had considered to be the bane of the American political system. Mindful of the help of his benefactors, he committed the ultimate act of political apostasy—he switched party affiliations. After years of vitriolic criticism of Democrats, he became one of them. A new era in Turner's struggle for status and power had begun.

The Cherokee freedmen's case was tailor-made for Turner. Here was an opportunity to combine his own interests with the interests of the people he hoped to serve. The fees he collected from the Cherokee freedmen would help him escape the financial problems he had experienced for more than a decade. He, in turn, could help them achieve what was rightfully theirs. Ironically, the criticism of Turner increased in proportion to the intensity of his machinations on behalf of the freedmen. He was labeled an opportunist, a manipulator, and even a fraud. He eventually achieved the legislative goal he sought, but his reputation was seriously damaged by the aura of suspicion emanating from the tactics he used.[1]

Turner's Colored Emigration Aid Association had declared in May 1879 that it was in favor of black emigration. It did not "favor that the immigration should be confined to Kansas, but to such sections of the country, Kansas included, as will receive and protect them in the exercise of the rights which the Constitution guarantees alike to all citizens." Presumably, the society had in mind the Oklahoma Territory, for there was a growing tendency around the turn of the decade for black leaders to view that region as a land of promise for the freedmen. Black newspapers, in particular, advocated opening the Oklahoma Territory to blacks.[2]

Although Turner's society failed miserably in 1879, he rebounded in 1881 with a plan to settle southern blacks in Oklahoma by means of a new organization called the Freedmen's Oklahoma Association. The association planned to facilitate the acquisition by blacks of one-hundred-sixty-acre tracts of land in the Oklahoma Territory, charging a fee for its services. The association distributed handbills to blacks in early spring, "promising 160 acres of land to every signed freedman who will go and occupy the public lands of Oklahoma." Turner was the president of the association, a relationship, the *Jefferson City Daily Tribune* noted, that made the success of the venture

1. Turner had been plagued by money problems throughout his stay in Liberia and made repeated efforts to have his salary of four thousand dollars a year raised. His financial condition had been so unstable in 1871 that he had to borrow money to go to the West African country. He lost an undisclosed sum when a New York bank where he had money crashed during the 1873 Panic. Kremer, "Biography of James Milton Turner," 186.

2. *St. Louis Globe-Democrat,* May 15, 1879; Beatty, "Political Response," 59. A resolution was offered at the 1883 National Negro Editors' Convention, held in St. Louis, to ask the secretary of the interior to appropriate five thousand dollars for the support of black schools in Indian Territory. The resolution was tabled. *New York Times,* July 14, 1883.

very unlikely. Obviously, the negative publicity surrounding Turner's Colored Emigration Aid Association had damaged his reputation statewide. The *Tribune* went on to note that "of late the Hon. J. Milton Turner has been rendering himself unpopular with his own people, and they look with suspicion on any proposition coming from him." The suspicion apparently was that Turner would swindle the potential settlers, although the manner in which he would attempt this was not speculated upon.[3]

The association failed to last more than a few months. The assertion of Acting Commissioner of Indian Affairs C. W. Holcomb, in a letter to Secretary of the Interior Kirkwood, that "there are no lands in the Indian Territory open to settlement or entry by freedmen, or by any other persons, under any of the public land laws of the United States" sealed its fate. That view was given judicial sanction in the May 1881 case of the *United States* v. *Payne,* in which the district court of Arkansas ruled, "Colored persons who were never held as slaves in the Indian country, but who may have been slaves elsewhere, are like other citizens of the United States, and have no more rights in the Indian country than other citizens of the United States."[4]

Presumably that meant the end of Turner's attempts to settle southern blacks in Indian Territory, although the *Indian Chieftain,* a weekly newspaper published in Vinita, Indian Territory, carried an announcement in September 1883 indicating that "J. Milton Turner, the colored orator and politician of St. Louis," had been in Indian Territory and was "working up a scheme to locate a colored colony on the strip of country called Oklahoma." The *Chieftain* noted that Turner had been a frequent "visitor to Vinita and other points in the territory within a few months." If Turner was still interested in a black colony in 1883, it is likely that he hoped to establish a settlement in Oklahoma Territory populated by black men and women who had formerly been slaves of the Indians. As early as 1881, he had written to the office of the commissioner of Indian affairs in an attempt to ascertain the legal status of freedmen within the Choctaw and Creek nations. Unfortunately, the original letter written by Tur-

3. U.S. Congress, Senate, *Senate Executive Documents,* 2–4; *Daily Tribune,* April 15, 1881.

4. C. W. Holcomb to S. J. Kirkwood, *Senate Executive Documents,* 2–4; Thomas F. Andrews, "Freedmen in Indian Territory: A Post–Civil War Dilemma," 373.

ner has long since disappeared, making it impossible to determine exactly what he asked.

The September 1883 edition of the *Chieftain,* which carried the announcement that Turner was in the territory, also begrudgingly acknowledged that there was unhappiness among black freedmen in Indian Territory, particularly in the Cherokee Nation. However, the *Chieftain* took the position that insofar as the Cherokee Nation was concerned, "the obligations she voluntarily assumed towards her colored citizens have been carried out in good faith and there is no portion of the race . . . within the limits of the United States whose condition is so good or privileges so extensive and valuable."5

The Cherokee freedmen took a different view of their condition. They argued that the Cherokee Nation systematically and illegally deprived them of the full tribal and political rights to which they were entitled. That difference in perception of the status of the freedmen cannot be understood without reference to the previous twenty years or more of Cherokee-black relations. It had its origins in the antebellum days of black slaves and Indian masters, the Civil War, and the Reconstruction Treaty of 1866.

The Cherokee Nation had been split into northern and southern factions since the 1830s. Most of the slaves lived among the southern Cherokees, and that faction aligned itself with the Confederacy during the Civil War. The war proved disastrous for both sides. All of the

5. *Indian Chieftain,* September 14, 1883. In the spring of 1883, Turner had attempted to get a federal appointment as a "special agent of the Department of the Interior . . . with the view of facilitating the investigation of fraudulent entries of portions of the public lands." John M. Hamilton to Secretary of the Interior H. M. Teller, April 27, 1883; Turner to H. M. Teller, May 3, 1883; Department of the Interior, Appointment Division, File No. 784, December 1883, NA. Morris L. Wardell, *A Political History of the Cherokee Nation 1838–1907* (Norman: University of Oklahoma Press, 1938), 231. Only a brief abstract of the 1881 letter remains; the original letter was H. C. Carter and Turner to the Justice Department, March 22, 1881, Letters Received, Land Division, Bureau of Indian Affairs, Record Group 75, National Archives, Washington, D.C. Hereafter cited as L.D., BIA, R.G. 76, NA. Turner recalled in 1889 that in 1881 and 1882, "I was representing the Freedmen of the Choctaw Nation before the Department of the Interior," but no specifics were given; affidavit filed by Turner, Enclosure, Turner to secretary of the interior, September 10, 1889, File 298, Special Files of the Office of Indian Affairs, 1807–1904, National Archives M574, roll 81, frame 0238. Hereafter cited as Special File 298.

bitter animosities displayed on the larger scene between North and South were played out in microcosm within the Cherokee Nation. Homes were burned, fences and farm implements destroyed, livestock slaughtered, and human blood shed. So bitter was the hatred, in fact, that the loyal Cherokees confiscated the land of the less numerous Confederate members of the tribe so that the southern Cherokees had no homes to return to at the end of the war.[6]

The federal government moved in to restore order in the Cherokee Nation in late 1865. On September 1 of that year a meeting was called to draw up a Reconstruction Treaty. The commissioner of Indian affairs, unwittingly serving as a protagonist rather than a conciliator, began the first session by accusing all Cherokees of being traitors to the United States during the Civil War. He refused to distinguish between the minority southern party that had joined the Confederacy and the majority northern party that had remained loyal to the Union. The commissioner's charge set the stage for a debate that lasted more than ten months, until, on July 19, 1866, the Cherokee Nation became the last of the Five Civilized Tribes to sign a Reconstruction treaty.

While the major issue had been whether or not to divide the Cherokee Nation permanently into northern and southern factions, the question of what to do with blacks within the territory also proved important. Southern faction representatives Stand Watie and Elias C. Boudinot argued that the federal government should remove all blacks from Cherokee Territory at government expense. The northern faction, first headed by John Ross and then, after Ross's death, by Lewis Downing, argued for a section of land to be set aside within Cherokee Territory for the exclusive use of black freedmen. Ultimately, both sides agreed to the government's compromise that allowed former slaves of Cherokee masters still living in the Cherokee Nation in 1866, as well as former slaves who had fled during the Civil War years but who returned within six months after the date of the treaty, to enjoy all the rights and privileges of full-blooded Cherokees. That six-month provision and the confusion it created over

6. Hanna P. Warren, "Reconstruction in the Cherokee Nation," 180; Walt Wilson, "Freedmen in Indian Territory," *Chronicles of Oklahoma,* 230; the definitive work on the topic of the freedmen in the Cherokee Nation is Daniel F. Littlefield, Jr., *The Cherokee Freedmen: From Emancipation to American Citizenship.*

who did and who did not have legal status posed problems for the Cherokee Nation for nearly fifty years.[7]

The treaty provision granting a narrowly defined group of freedmen unspecified equal political and civil rights was the focal point for controversy in which James Milton Turner became involved in the 1880s. In 1883 the United States Congress ordered that the Cherokee Nation be reimbursed three hundred thousand dollars for the cession of several millions of acres of land west of the Arkansas River. The money was to be distributed among members of the Cherokee Nation as its council saw fit. Problems arose, however, when the council voted to limit the distribution of money to full-blooded Cherokees, thus excluding black freedmen. Cherokee Chief Bushyhead vetoed the act, but it passed over his objection.[8]

The Cherokees advanced a twofold argument in defense of their action. They reasoned that the dispersal of the money was an internal matter in which no outside party had a right to interfere. Land, they maintained, was a commodity held in common by the Cherokee people. No individual had a right to buy or sell land within the nation or, for that matter, to derive any personal benefit from the sale of land by the nation. Money received from land cessions went into a common fund and was distributed by the Cherokee Council according to need. There were, as far as the Cherokees were concerned, no inherent individual rights or claims to the material bounty of the nation. The Cherokee Council used money in the common fund to provide social services such as educational facilities and poor relief whenever it deemed those services necessary. The black freedmen, it argued, had not contributed toward the expansion of the common fund and, therefore, were not entitled to share in the 1883 appropriation. Almost as an afterthought, the Cherokees also pointed out that no other reconstructed state had been forced to share its financial resources with black freedmen.[9]

The freedmen viewed the situation differently. They immediately

7. Warren, "Reconstruction in the Cherokee Nation," 181–89; Wilson, "Freedmen in Indian Territory," 233; Paul F. Lambert, "The Reconstruction Treaty of 1866," 474, 488–89.

8. Wardell, *Political History of the Cherokee Nation, 1838–1907*, 235. For a concise chronology of the case, see Turner to Pres. Grover Cleveland, June 14, 1886, Letter No. 15802, Letters Received, L.D., BIA, R.G. 75, NA.

9. H.R. 1345, 48th Congress, first session, 1883, Special File 298, roll 81, frames 664–72.

expressed their dissatisfaction with the council's decision and agitated for its reversal. During the early summer of 1883, an annual "Emancipation Day" fair became a forum for a discussion of ways to force the Cherokees to share the three hundred thousand dollars. The freedmen decided to send two black members of the tribe to Washington, D.C., to plead their case. On June 2, 1883, Lewis Daniels and Ike Rogers arrived in the capital. On June 9 they met with Secretary of the Interior Henry M. Teller, who listened to the story of their plight but declined to become involved in the imbroglio. Ten days later Daniels and Rogers were back in Indian Territory planning to pursue the matter by means of a mass meeting of all freedmen in the Cherokee Nation.[10]

Two mass meetings were held in December of 1883: the first on December 6, at Lightning Creek in Indian Territory, and the second on December 11, at Fort Gibson. Out of those meetings evolved a committee empowered to select an agent to represent the freedmen in their claims against the Cherokee Nation. Daniels and Rogers's experience with the secretary of the interior convinced the freedmen that the success of their cause depended upon their ability to solicit the support of a prestigious spokesman to intervene on their behalf. Turner's ministerial experience seemed to qualify him for that role. In addition, his efforts to facilitate black migration into Oklahoma had made him a well-known figure in Indian Territory. Hence, the ad hoc committee of freedmen approached Turner about the job and, upon his acceptance, granted him the power of attorney for the entire group.[11]

Turner's assumption of the role as an "attorney" is one of the many mystifying incidents in his life. Although many late nineteenth-century Americans "read" law before practicing the profession, there is no evidence that Turner formally apprenticed or was ever admitted

10. Lewis Daniels, Affidavit filed with the commissioner of Indian affairs, September 28, 1889, Special File 298, frames 299–303; David Martin and Andrew Norwood, Affidavits filed with the commissioner of Indian affairs, September 19, 1889, Special File 298, frames 269–70.

11. Minutes of the meeting of the freedmen held at Lightning Creek, December 6, 1883, Special File 298, frames 397–99; Letter from Lightning Creek Committee to Permanent Committee, December 14, 1883, Special File 298, frames 414–17; Minutes of the meeting of the Permanent Committee held at Four Mile Creek, December 20 and 21, 1883, Special File 298, frames 409–13; Special Contract of Turner, Special File 298, frames 51–53.

to the bar association. In spite of this, he listed his occupation as "law-yer" or "attorney" for fifteen of the thirty-five years that his name appears in *Gould's St. Louis Directory* between 1877 and 1915. In 1916, Charleton H. Tandy offered testimony before the St. Louis Cir-cuit Court in a trial aimed at the disposition of Turner's estate. Tandy, who had known Turner from 1857 until the latter's death in 1915, was asked directly, "Was Milton Turner a lawyer?" Tandy's response: "Not to my knowledge. I don't think he was ever admitted to the practice of law." Tandy did go on to note, however, "I really think he was a better lawyer than one half of the men that are at the Bar."[12]

The first reference to Turner as a lawyer appears in the account of his January 1877 discrimination suit against the Astor House in New York City. The newspaper identified him as "quite a linguist and an able lawyer" but noted that he had employed legal counsel to pros-ecute his claim. One can only speculate why Turner identified him-self as an attorney at that early date. Clearly, he had no idea at that time of being involved in the Cherokee freedmen's case. But given Turner's apparent desire to reenter politics in 1878 and his continual search for status, it may be assumed that he thought his identification as a lawyer would be personally gratifying as well as politically help-ful. There is another, admittedly more speculative, but perhaps more important, reason that Turner began to call himself a lawyer. His actions during this time are those of a man who believed that the law was his friend and that familiarity with the law would assist him in his quest for maximum participation in the promise of America. His efforts to force compliance with Missouri school laws in the 1860s, the wrangling over constitutional amendments later, and the interna-tional intrigue of his Liberian years all suggest a constant, continuing interest in law. Quite simply, Turner studied law, used it, and even-tually came to identify with the profession that practiced it.[13]

Whatever Turner's original motives for calling himself a lawyer, his ability to play the role of an attorney was crucial to the success or failure of his efforts on behalf of the Cherokee freedmen. His attempts at colonization had led him to a realization of the problems confront-ing blacks in Indian Territory. By 1883, he had developed singularly negative feelings toward the Indians. In June of that year he wrote to

12. *Gould's St. Louis Directory;* testimony of Charleton H. Tandy, Case No. 2884B.
13. *New York Times,* January 17, 1877.

Missouri Republican Congressman James H. McLean about how "Indians discriminate against [blacks] on account of color." Blacks, he told McLean, were trying to become industrious and "to materially build up themselves and their children and obtain a substantial ownership of the soil." Hence, he saw blacks as being at least nascent capitalists. "While the Indian goes down showing no longevity to withstand civilization," he continued, "the Negro . . . shows a desire for the text books and takes to the ways of civilized life." He concluded by noting, "Whatever else may be said upon this subject, it is true that the Negro is in no sense advanced or improved by contact with the Indians."[14]

Turner made it clear, however, that not all of the blame should fall on the Indians. The federal government, which had been dominated by Republicans since the Civil War, was also at fault for creating an atmosphere that was conducive to the violation of black rights. Turner thought the government had been too mild toward all former slave states. The Cherokees had freed their slaves and made concessions to blacks in the 1866 Reconstruction Treaty only because they feared governmental reprisals—much like opponents to black education had feared being reported to State Superintendent of Schools Parker in the late 1860s. However the Turner scenario went, as the post-Grant federal government became more and more permissive of racist actions against blacks, the Cherokee Nation embarked on a program of "debarring the black freedmen from their rights."[15]

To reverse that trend, Turner accepted the position of attorney for the freedmen and launched a campaign in support of their rights. His motives were not confined to the benefits he believed he could gain for his downtrodden black brethren. He clearly entered the case with the hope of personal gain, indicating, according to a man whose aid he solicited, "There is a lot of money to be made in this thing." When he signed the "Power of Attorney Agreement" drawn up on December 20, 1883, he also signed a contract that promised him 25 percent of the gross amount to be paid by the United States, in addition to a sum equal to "all necessary expenses in the prosecution of this claim."[16]

14. Turner to James H. McLean, June 2, 1883, Letter No. 10546, Letters Received Relating to Choctaw and Other Freedmen, L.D., BIA, R.G. 69, NA.

15. Enclosure No. 2, Turner to commissioner of Indian affairs, June 8, 1887, Letter No. 14942, Letters Received, L.D., BIA, R.G. 75, NA.

16. Henry E. Cuney to Secretary of the Interior John W. Noble, August 16, 1889, Special File 298, frame 146; Special Contract, Special File 298, frames 51–54.

After signing the contract on December 20, 1883, Turner left for Washington, "in company with Joseph Brown, a Cherokee freedman, and a regularly authorized representative of the Cherokee freedmen." In either February or March 1884, he and Brown presented their claim to the commissioner of Indian affairs, who, according to Turner, "prepared a bill which was argued . . . before the Indian Committee of both the Senate and the House of Representatives." The Senate Committee on Indian Affairs subsequently recommended that money be appropriated to send a special subcommittee on a fact-finding trip to Indian Territory. Although the Senate endorsed that procedure, the subcommittee did not begin its work until May 1885. In the meantime, Turner, who, along with Joseph Brown, had lobbied more than nine months in Washington already, returned to St. Louis. From there he traveled to Muskogee and Vinita in Indian Territory for a two months' stay, came back to St. Louis late in 1884, and returned again to Washington in January 1885.

Prior to the special Senate subcommittee's May trip into Indian Territory, Turner was instructed by the chairman of the group, Sen. Henry Dawes, to gather witnesses at Vinita where their testimony would be taken around May 20, 1885. Turner complied with the chairman's request and assembled twenty-nine witnesses at the appointed time. Abruptly, however, the subcommittee changed course and decided instead to meet at Muskogee rather than Vinita. Turner transported the twenty-nine freedmen to Muskogee at his own expense—$169.65 for transportation costs and an additional $50 for food and lodging. Fifteen of the twenty-nine persons presented by Turner testified before the subcommittee.[17]

In addition to his work in Indian Territory, Turner had begun to lobby among congressmen in an effort to convince them to support the freedmen's claim to seventy-five thousand dollars as their share of the 1883 settlement. Realizing that he needed help in Washington, he sought to employ someone acquainted with the legislative process who could introduce him to those persons whose friendship would be valuable in his attempt to get a freedmen's bill passed. Shortly after his arrival in Washington, the attorney for the freedmen contacted Henry Cuney, described by Capital observers as a man who was em-

17. Turner to Secretary of the Interior William F. Vilas, undated, received in the Department of the Interior December 12, 1888, Special File 298, frames 0034–42.

ployed intermittently in the House and Senate. Cuney agreed to assist him in the case. Subsequently, Turner and Cuney visited, among others, the following congressmen: Samuel West Peel, a Democrat from Arkansas and chairman of the House Committee on Indian Affairs; David Browning Culberson, a Democrat from Texas; Constantine B. Kilgore, also a Democrat from Texas; Benjamin Butterworth, a Republican from Ohio; Thomas M. Bayne, a Republican from Pennsylvania; Charles Boutelle, a Republican from Maine; and Dwight M. Sabin, Republican senator from Minnesota.[18]

Turner returned to St. Louis from the May meeting with Dawes's subcommittee and remained there until January 1886, when he again went to Washington. He stayed there for nearly eight months. He had, by that time, become impatient with the slowness of the legislative machinery. In an attempt to speed up the process, he addressed an eighteen-page petition to Pres. Grover Cleveland on February 8, 1886, hoping that the president might make it possible for him to bypass the Congress. The petition was a cogent rehearsal of the narrative of events from the signing of the 1866 Treaty to June 1886. The treaty provisions, the black "lawyer" argued, were clear. The freedmen were entitled to "all the rights of native Cherokees," including an equal share in all tribal wealth. And, he continued, the federal Constitution clearly recognized the preeminence of treaty provisions over statutory enactments. Turner concluded his petition by asking the president to issue an executive order forcing the Cherokee Nation to end its discrimination against blacks.[19]

Although the president rejected the idea of an executive order, he did submit a letter of recommendation to the commissioner of Indian affairs, endorsing Turner's position and employing much of Turner's language to encourage approval of the remedial legislation. A few days later, Turner went with Missouri Democratic Congressman

18. Henry E. Cuney to Secretary of the Interior John W. Noble, August 16, 1889, Special File 298, frames 145–52; Richard Harvey Cain to Henry E. Cuney, August 16, 1889, Special File 298, frame 170; Henry M. Cuney to Sen. Constantine B. Kilgore, August 18, 1889, Special File 298, frame 174; Sen. Dwight May Sabin to Henry E. Cuney, August 28, 1889, Special File 298, frame 181. Turner later denied having hired Cuney, although the evidence is heavily weighted against Turner's contention. There never was a formal contract drawn up between the two men.

19. Turner to Pres. Grover Cleveland, February 8, 1886, Letter No. 15802, Letters Received, L.D., BIA, R.G. 75, NA; *Indian Chieftain*, February 11, 1886.

John J. O'Neill to the office of the commissioner of Indian affairs, J. D. C. Atkins. Atkins pronounced the freedmen's claim to be "manifestly just" and forwarded the president's correspondence to the Senate, along with a draft of a bill, prepared by the commissioner, that would grant the freedmen a share in the three-hundred-thousand-dollar payment. Ultimately, it was this bill drafted by the commissioner that became law. Within scarcely more than a month, the bill was introduced into the Senate, and Turner had appeared before a special Senate committee on its behalf. The bill passed the Republican Senate by midsummer but ran into trouble in the Democratic House, where it failed to be considered before the expiration of the Forty-ninth Congress.[20]

That setback shattered Turner's hope of a speedy timetable for the passage of his bill. He had written in July that he expected the bill to be passed quickly by the House and signed by the president. The legislative wheels ground slowly, however, and by November 1886 Turner had given up hope of seeing the freedmen's bill passed that year. So frustrated was he, in fact, that he told a *St. Louis Post-Dispatch* reporter that he intended to abandon politics. "I am satisfied," he said, "that the colored man will never achieve his rightful place in society through the door of politics." Black political agitation, he explained, was offensive to whites. Black powerlessness dictated "that [blacks try] some other means of raising themselves than through politics." Alternatively, Turner returned to the familiar self-reliance theme. He argued that what a black person needed "to make him a valuable citizen" was "education and money." Moreover, in a statement that reveals a hardening of his position since the 1879 exodus, he stated that blacks could get neither money nor education as long as they remained in the South. The hatred of blacks and whites for each other ran too deep. Blacks had to be separated "from the old influences," in order to restore initiative and "get an impetus toward the improvement of themselves."

Just as important, Turner argued, blacks needed to become land-

20. "Messages from the President of the United States," Senate Executive Document No. 82, March 3, 1886, Special File 298, frames 604–14; *Indian Chieftain,* February 18, April 1, July 15, 22, 1886; Henry L. Dawes wrote on September 4, 1886, that though Senate Bill 1800 had passed the Senate, "the condition of business in the House made it impossible to get action upon it." H. L. Dawes to Joseph Bralay, Special File 298, frame 727.

owners, not just farm laborers. Land ownership entitled one to "a real interest in the government." Indeed, he went so far as to ask rhetorically whether "a colored man" who possessed no property had any business "imposing taxes by legislation upon property." He went on to say, "When the negro owns land and helps to make the wealth and worth of the country, he will have a right to say something besides casting his vote, in the government of the country." Turner proposed to test this premise by establishing a colony in Butler County, Missouri, about one hundred eighty miles south of St. Louis in the Missouri Bootheel. In terms reminiscent of the aims of his Freedmen's Oklahoma Association, he noted that southern blacks who moved there would "have an opportunity of getting both land and education under the most favorable circumstances." He made a vague claim to having access to twenty-five thousand acres of "very fertile" soil in the area. His plan was to give black emigrants jobs harvesting timber, presumably paying them with the profits, and providing them with an opportunity to accumulate a down payment on a homestead. He acknowledged that the colony had not really gotten started yet but noted, "I will send some carpenters down in a day or two to build houses." He wanted it understood that "there is nothing communistic or socialistic in the plan." Quite the opposite—it was a means by which he believed blacks could become capitalists. "All we want is to give our people a chance to buy homes."[21]

Although Turner claimed that "there are now some actual settlers on the lands," there is no evidence that this colony was ever established. Indeed, there is no evidence that any serious effort to establish it occurred. The only mention of it is in the November 19, 1886, *Post-Dispatch* interview. Turner's formulation of a colonization scheme is perhaps best understood as a short-lived, impulsive reaction born out of his frustration over a lack of lobbying success rather than as an operational plan for another exodus of southern blacks. Turner was desperate for the freedmen's bill to pass. He had suffered serious financial problems throughout the time the legislation was pending and could count on little or no income until the bill was passed—a reality that must have made the postponement of its passage in 1886 a harsh blow.

The colonization scheme was not the only manifestation of frus-

21. Turner to Editor of *Indian Chieftain,* July 15, 1886, *Indian Chieftain,* July 22, 1886; *St. Louis Post-Dispatch,* November 19, 1886.

tration over the failure of the Congress to enact a freedmen's bill. By spring 1887 Turner had devised another plan by which he hoped to gain the seventy-five-thousand-dollar settlement for the freedmen, along with his own fee. The freedmen's case had become one of the issues dividing the two major political parties in the Cherokee Nation. The National party included in its platform a provision to grant the freedmen their claim to seventy-five thousand dollars and full tribal rights. By contrast, the Union party opposed both of those proposals. Turner campaigned actively for the National party.[22]

The 1887 Cherokee election, according to historian Morris Wardell, was "one of the bitterest in the history of the Nation." Turner did nothing to assuage the bitterness. He traveled throughout the Indian Territory making strong speeches in favor of the National party and virulently attacking the opposition. His political speech-making created a furor that culminated in a petition by fifty-four members of the Union party (eight of whom were black) to the United States Indian agent at Muskogee, Robert L. Owen, asking to have Turner physically removed from the territory. Their major point of contention centered on Turner's allegedly being paid to deliver votes to the National party. In support of their argument, they submitted to Owen sworn testimony from two persons. Ilo Martin testified, "On or about the twentieth day of May, 1887, J. Milton Turner told me that he was to get two hundred dollars a district" for making political speeches throughout the nation. Columbus McNair also testified that Turner told him "he was employed to make a political canvas [sic] of this nation in the interests of the National Party for which he expected to be paid." Turner readily admitted his involvement in Cherokee Nation politics but adamantly denied having received any money for the venture. In fact, he argued that the trip to Oklahoma cost him one hundred and twenty dollars instead of profiting him. Whatever the truth of the charges, Turner stood to gain if the National party won, both for himself and for the cause he represented. In spite of criticism, Turner continued his active involvement in Cherokee politics.[23]

22. Turner to the commissioner of Indian affairs, June 8, 1887, Letter No. 14942, Letters Received, L.D., BIA, R.G. 75, NA.

23. Wardell, *Political History,* 343; Petition to the commissioner of Indian affairs, n.d., received June 7, 1887, Letter No. 14871, Letters Received, L.D., BIA, R.G. 75, NA; Aleck Hawk, Affidavit, September 19, 1889, Special File 298, frames 277, 278; see also, *Indian Chieftain,* June 2, 1887. The *Chieftain* advised

The National party lost the 1887 election. This defeat, combined with Turner's growing disbelief in the ability of the Fiftieth Congress to pass the freedmen's bill, led to a slightly different gesture of frustration: Turner decided to try to regain the Liberian ministership. When one recalls the antipathy he had developed for that position only a decade before, his effort to return is all the more shocking. Charles H. J. Taylor of Kansas, who had been appointed minister to Liberia on March 11, 1887, resigned on November 11, 1887. By December, Turner had a number of his friends and political acquaintances submit letters of support on his behalf. The first of those, written on December 3 by C. F. Schultz of St. Louis, noted simply that he had known Turner for a number of years and that he was pleased to recommend him for the position.[24]

On December 6, 1887, James H. Wear, a St. Louis dry-goods wholesaler, wrote to Missouri Democratic Sen. Francis M. Cockrell and asked him to use his "influence in having the President consider [Turner's] application favorably." Sometime in early December "a large and enthusiastic meeting of negro citizens of St. Louis" was held during which "it was resolved that J. Milton Turner is the choice of Missourians for Minister to Liberia." Out of that meeting came a six-person committee charged with the responsibility of requesting "Missouri senators and members of congress to urge the appointment of Turner upon [the] president."[25]

On December 10, 1887, Cockrell received another pro-Turner letter, this time from his friend, St. Louis attorney William B. Thompson. Thompson remarked, "Several of your warm friends and friends

---

Turner "not to monkey with the politics of the country," and exclaimed that his actions had "the appearance of being that of one who is paid for what rumor says he is doing." See also, Turner to the Reverend Lawrence Ross, May 26, 1887, and *Indian Chieftain,* June 16, 1887; Petition to Commission on Indian Affairs, Letter No. 14871, Letters Received, L.D., BIA, R.G. 75, NA; Turner to the commissioner of Indian affairs, June 8, 1887, Letter No. 14942, Letters Received, L.D., BIA, R.G. 75, NA.

24. Padgett, "Ministers to Liberia," 74–75; C. F. Schultz to Pres. Grover Cleveland, December 3, 1887, Applications and Recommendations for the Cleveland Administration, R.G. 59, NA.

25. J. H. Wear to Hon. F. M. Cockrell, December 6, 1887; M. J. Britton, P. H. Murray, George J. Wood, Charles H. Tyler, J. L. Turpin, George Long, and S. Y. Jordan to F. M. Cockrell, December 7, 1887. This was a telegram which also carried with it the note, "Please show (senator) Vest & the president." Applications and Recommendations for the Cleveland Administration, R.G. 59, NA.

of mine have urged me to join in a letter to the President, as well as to yourself, in favor of the appointment of J. Milton Turner as Minister to Liberia." He indicated that he had known Turner only by reputation, noting that the latter was "a shrewd politician." Thompson revealed that it was his understanding that Turner had "openly and publicly announced his adhesion to our [Democratic] principles," adding, "I think him the most intelligent man among the colored people of the country, and I believe that his appointment would attract universal attention and would give universal satisfaction." Thompson concluded by asserting that he thought "there would be no difficulty in securing a petition signed by almost all of the prominent men here in St. Louis or in the State in favor of his appointment." In addition to these letters, Cockrell received correspondence endorsing Turner from St. Louis Comptroller Robert A. Campbell and Oscar W. Collet of the Missouri Historical Society, the latter of whom commented, "As a life long democrat, [I] consider Mr. Turner's appointment would be appropriate."[26]

Turner did not receive the appointment. Instead, Ezekiel Ezra Smith, a black North Carolina newspaper publisher, was appointed on April 24, 1888. It is possible that Turner did not receive the position because "by some oversight [his endorsements] were not sent to [the State] department," but it is impossible to say for certain why he did not receive the post. Perhaps his prior appointment by a Republican president made the Democrat Grover Cleveland wary of him. Perhaps, too, Ezekiel Smith was simply a stronger candidate. Whatever the case, one of the most interesting things about Turner's attempt to return to Liberia was that he sought Democratic patronage and led at least some Democrats, notably William B. Thompson, to believe that he had switched party alliances. And, indeed, he had invoked the assistance of Cockrell, a member of the "Confederate faction" of the Democratic party that he had so vigorously opposed a decade before. Turner's courting of prominent Democrats foreshadowed the intensity of his political machinations during the following year's national election.[27]

26. William B. Thompson to Hon. Francis M. Cockrell, December 10, 1887, ibid., R.G. 59, NA; R. A. Campbell to Hon. F. M. Cockrell, December 16, 1877; Oscar W. Collet to Hon. F. M. Cockrell, no date, ibid., R.G. 59, NA.
27. Padgett, "Ministers to Liberia," 75; F. M. Cockrell to Assistant Secretary of State G. L. Rives, July 3, 1888; Turner to the State Department, April 28, 1888, ibid., R.G. 59, NA.

Turner still proved unsuccessful in his attempts to get the freed-men's bill passed as the 1888 political season rolled around but developed a new tactic as late spring turned to summer. In July of 1888 he called for a convention of black Independent and Democratic voters to be held in Indianapolis. The purpose of the convention, as he expressed it, was to register a protest against the Republican party and acknowledge the Democrats as the better friends of blacks. Even though both the Democratic president and the Democratic commissioner of Indian affairs had supported his proposed legislation, it still needed to pass through a Democratically controlled House; so Turner praised the Democrats, asserting that the election of Cleveland to the presidency had brought political emancipation to blacks. In return, he argued, blacks ought to support Cleveland's bid for reelection.[28]

Such a political reversal of his intense pro-Republican stand of the previous decade did not, of course, occur overnight. Its inevitability was inherent in the position Turner took in his speech before the Independent Republicans when he aspired to the Republican congressional nomination in 1878. He had become increasingly aware of the Republicans' resistance to rewarding him as they had done in the early seventies. Besides, they were no longer in power, and there were concrete benefits to be gained by catering to the Democrats. Turner's longtime friend George B. Vashon, himself a black Democrat, wrote in 1901 that Turner became a Democrat in 1885 as part of a strategy for getting the Cherokee bill passed into law. He indicated that in that year Turner made a "radical Democratic speech" at Union City, Tennessee—an event that marked his desertion of the Republican party. Henry Cuney wrote in 1890 that Turner had only turned Democratic "in order to pass his Bill." According to Cuney, Turner "decided to get up a convention of colored Democrats," thereby ingratiating himself with the party hierarchy and ensuring the passage of his bill. The evidence surrounding Turner's apostasy overwhelmingly supports the statements of Vashon and Cuney.[29]

Early in June 1888 Turner began distributing a letter to potential participants in the July convention. The gathering was to be held in

28. "A Wrangling Convention," *New York Times,* July 26, 1888; Lawrence Grossman, *The Democratic Party and the Negro: Northern and National Politics, 1868-1892.*

29. George B. Vashon, "Progress of Negroes in Their Efforts to Free Themselves from Republicanism," *Republic* [St. Louis], August 4, 1901; H. E. Cuney to Col. Robert Christy, January 20, 1890, Special File 298, frames 0178-87.

Indianapolis. Turner affixed the names of eighteen nationally known black leaders to this letter. Enclosed along with this piece of correspondence was another circular, calling blacks to the convention and headed with the caption "Attention Colored Voters!" This call proclaimed the 1888 election to be "unequaled by any political contest that has . . . transpired since the formation of our Government." The Republican party, Turner wrote, needed to use "Herculean efforts to regain what it lost in 1884. . . . Defeat to the Republicans this year will no doubt lead to a disintegration of their party and its relegation to join other like organizations that have lived, flourished for a time, and, having outlived their usefulness, are now 'numbered among the things that were.'"[30]

The pertinent question insofar as black people were concerned, Turner challenged, was "what part are *we* going to act in the great political drama of 1888?" He continued: "Are we to stand 'up and be counted by this party or that,' like so many dumb driven cattle, or . . . are we going to act as men, each in accordance with his own uncoerced conviction and vote with that party which he may deem most likely to promote the interests of himself and [his] race?" Turner called for "more individuality and less clannishness on the part of the colored people in politics," arguing that such a position would "place them on a higher plane in the estimation of the dominant race of this country" than they had enjoyed since the passage of the Fifteenth Amendment. Turner closed his "call" by asking blacks to assemble in Indianapolis on July 25, 1888, "for the purpose of consulting and considering upon what recommendations may be decided upon as best to promulgate to the colored electors of the country." Perhaps in an effort to anticipate criticism that he was calling the convention to gain personal advantage, he assured his readers, "The proposed conference is not called in the interest of any particular party or individual but purely of the negro."[31]

Even though Turner claimed that the convention was not being called "in the interest of any particular party," the gathering was subsidized by the Democrats, whose platform claimed that under Cleve-

30. Printed letter from Turner, June 12, 1888, Enclosure 1; William Calvin Chase to Benjamin Harrison, July 9, 1888, Benjamin Harrison Papers, Reel 9, Series 1, Library of Congress; J. Milton Turner, "Attention Colored Voters!" Enclosure 3, ibid.
31. *Washington Bee,* August 18, 1888.

land "the rights and welfare of all the people have been guarded and defended, every public interest has been protected, and the equality of all our citizens before the law, without regard to race or section, has been steadfastly maintained." Eager to sway the majority of black voters to the Democratic camp, party officials courted prominent black leaders such as Peter Clark, T. Thomas Fortune, George T. Downing, James M. Trotter, James C. Matthews, T. McCants Stewart, and J. Milton Turner.[32]

Before the convention even met, however, a wave of criticism arose against Turner and James Monroe Trotter in particular. The old charge of opportunism resurfaced. Turner was accused of conspiring to sell black votes to the Democratic party. The *Washington Bee* claimed that the idea of the convention had originated with James Monroe Trotter, a black man who held the coveted position of Recorder of Deeds for the District of Columbia. Trotter, the *Bee* reported, had been asked by the president to devise a scheme to take black votes away from the Republicans in the 1888 election. Trotter, eager to please his patron, seized upon the idea of an Independent or Democratic conference and employed Turner to assist him. Turner, unable to get the Cherokee bill passed, and generally disillusioned with Republicanism, welcomed the convention as a grand opportunity to win the favor of key Democratic leaders and get his bill through both houses, while also, in a sense, punishing the Republicans for their betrayal of both him and black people.

Unfortunately for Turner and Trotter, word circulated among members of the black community that they were attempting to betray black interests for their own selfish gains. Emotions were further raised when it was discovered that Turner had signed the names of prominent black political leaders as endorsers of the convention without their permission or knowledge. The call issued by Turner bore the names of eighteen prominent black men from Missouri, Massachu-

---

32. Grossman, *The Democratic Party and the Negro*, 144–45. Significantly, as Grossman points out, Turner's calling card turned up in a letter from Missouri Democratic Sen. F. M. Cockrell to Democrat Daniel S. Lamont. Cockrell's letter introduced "Capt. W. D. Mathews," one of the signatories to the June 12 letter, and about "whom I spoke to the President Saturday." Cockrell was arranging a meeting for Mathews with the president already in late May. F. M. Cockrell to Daniel S. Lamont May 28, 1888; F. M. Cockrell to Pres. Grover Cleveland, May 28, 1888, Grover Cleveland Papers, Series 3, May 18 to June 9, 1888, Reel 12, Library of Congress; see also, *Cleveland Gazette*, July 28, 1888.

setts, Illinois, Tennessee, Kansas, North Carolina, Virginia, Michigan, Ohio, and Indiana. Only three of them had been contacted prior to the distribution of the call, and several expressed great indignation over being "made responsible for a political scheme that Turner is endeavoring to operate solely in his own interest."[33]

After several days of charges and countercharges, Charles H. J. Taylor of Kansas City, a nationally recognized leader of black Democrats, decided to go to the Indianapolis convention and thwart the efforts of Turner and Trotter. Taylor, himself a former minister to Liberia and the editor of the Democratic journal *Public Educator,* asserted that he did not propose "as a representative of the pioneer negro Democrats, whose democracy commenced before the elevation of Cleveland to the Presidency, to allow gentlemen who have just entered our ranks to take charge and lead." The confusion, unavoidable in a leadership fight, was compounded by a Republican attempt to sabotage the July meeting. William Calvin Chase, black Republican editor of the *Washington Bee,* wrote to Benjamin Harrison on July 9, 1888, urging that the Indianapolis convention be stopped. He asked for the candidate's "aid in this matter, *immediately,* as we have no time to loose [*sic*]." He offered Harrison a "plan of operations" to throw the Democratic convention into an uproar and asked that it be kept confidential. Chase maintained, "The real object of the proposed meeting is to sow the seeds of dissatisfaction in the minds of the colored voters of the country and to so act upon them as to cause a diversion . . . in the interest of the Democratic Party." Chase explained that one of the persons planning the convention was a friend of his who had joined the movement only to keep tabs on its operations. That friend told Chase that "arrangements [had been] made to pay the fare of those invited to attend both to and from the conference, as well as their care whilst there, all at the expense of the Democratic Party." Chase was adamant in his conviction that "*we must capture this* conference . . . [and we] can do it by and with the assistance of the [Republican] National Committee." Chase's inside friend was chairman of the Credentials Committee and had the power "to send out invitations to whomsoever he may chose [*sic*]." While Turner and Trotter were "inviting those who are of their way of thinking . . . my friend will invite only those he knows as true and tried Republicans and with them we will capture the meeting . . . [and]

33. *Washington Bee,* August 18, 1888.

adopt resolutions endorsing the nominees of the Republican party, County, State and National."[34]

The desire of Turner and Trotter to make the convention a success, combined with Taylor's resolve to wrestle control away from them and Chase's efforts to disrupt the whole proceedings, made conflict inevitable. When Turner arrived in Indianapolis he faced a number of openly hostile delegates rather than the uniformly warm, receptive group he had anticipated. Clearly, a number of the delegates had been persuaded by Taylor's labeling of Turner as a usurper, and when Turner was asked his opinion of the Kansas Citian's influence among black Democrats, he replied bitterly: "Taylor is a national buffoon and a national ass. He is an empty barrell rolling down a rocky hill. I have no words to waste upon him."[35]

The conference opened at 10:00 A.M., Wednesday, July 25, at the Hendricks Club rooms in Indianapolis. Turner served as the convener with approximately sixty of the seventy delegates present. He prefaced the proceedings by reiterating his reasons for issuing the call. It was time, he said that "the negroes were asserting themselves, or at least time they had begun to think independently." Having completed his introductory remarks, Turner tried to move the convention into executive session, thereby excluding "all persons not holding credentials as delegates." That caused a stir, as the *Indianapolis Freeman* said, over "whether the convention should go into temporary organization during its temporary organization." After considerable discussion, Turner's suggestion was rejected in favor of the view "that all the proceedings should be known to the outside world."[36]

During the afternoon session, the Committee on Permanent Organization offered its majority report to the gathering. It recommended that Peter Clark, a veteran black Democrat and a nominee

---

34. "A Wrangling Convention," *New York Times,* July 26, 1888; William Calvin Chase to Benjamin Harrison, July 9, 1888, Benjamin Harrison Papers, Reel 9, Series 1, Library of Congress. Whether the Republican National Committee provided any money or not, a number of Republicans did attend the convention, though they were not able to obtain endorsements for Republican officeseekers. *New York Age,* July 28, 1888.

35. "A Wrangling Convention," *New York Times,* July 26, 1888; *Cleveland Gazette,* July 28, 1888, reported that upon his arrival in Indianapolis, Turner discovered that "his position among the sixty-two Negroes who constituted the representation of delegates was that of a distinguished high private."

36. *Freeman,* July 28, 1888.

acceptable to the Taylor faction, serve as permanent chairman. A minority report, offered by Joseph Hauser of Illinois, recommended that Turner hold that position. A heated debate followed, with partisan speakers making pleas for one or the other of the candidates. When the roll call was finally taken, the wrangling and confusion proved so great that balloting took more than an hour. The tellers came up with two different tallies: one showing Clark the victor, the other showing the two candidates tied. When the secretary reported only the tie, pandemonium broke loose. Charges of cheating and subterfuge filled the room, leading to a melee of flying fists and drawn revolvers and ending in the arrest of several delegates.

Ultimately, Clark was declared the winner. The next day, amid what *The Freeman* called an "auspiciously peaceful" session, T. Thomas Fortune asked Turner to explain "the position of himself and [his] friends . . . in the interests of peace and harmony." The black orator rose to speak amid shouts of "Turner, Turner." Under normal circumstances, he declared, he would give no expression of his feelings "after suffering such an overwhelming defeat as I did yesterday"; however, his loyalty to his supporters forced him to speak. His followers, he proclaimed, "are Western men, and as Western men saved, in a great measure, this country, there is a determination on their part now to save the Negro." Because that could only be accomplished without strife, he said, "We bow to the will of the majority." He spoke flatteringly of his opponent, Clark, before warning the Republicans that black Democracy would defeat them at the polls in November. "I will say to our Republican friends," he continued, "who are so solicitous about us, that we are not being enticed away from the Republican fold. We are simply coolly and deliberately walking away."

Having explained his motives to his own satisfaction, Turner concluded by saying, "Ask me for no further speech-making but show me how I can aid in the election of Cleveland and Thurman and no effort of mine will be spared to accomplish that end." During the closing session that afternoon, however, chaos threatened to return. While the question of whether to establish a national executive committee was considered, F. V. Anderson of Pennsylvania introduced a resolution to make J. Milton Turner its chairman. Turner, however, seemed eager to avoid another conflict. He argued for the appointment of the committee by the convention, but suggested that the committee be allowed to select its own chairman. He was apparently confident that he could gain the chairmanship by committee vote, without risking a floor fight that involved the entire convention. His confidence was borne out when the executive committee selected him as its chairman an hour later. That ended the business of the convention, which adjourned so that its participants could take part in a mass meeting at which Clark, Turner, and others spoke. Turner was the last speaker and, in what *The Freeman* called a "brief but forcible plea," he called "for a division of the Negro vote." Later, on board a train en route to Washington, Turner expressed regret over the turmoil at Indianapolis. He was committed to doing what was necessary to get the freedmen's bill passed and spent much of the following fall making political speeches on behalf of the Democratic candidates.[37]

While Turner was overtly maneuvering in Democratic circles, he had a colleague working more quietly but with equal, if not greater, success among Republicans on behalf of the Cherokee bill. By January of 1888, the bill had been floundering for nearly two years in the House, held up largely by the lobbying of Cherokee Elias C. Boudinot, who sought to have the whole case referred to the courts as an alternative to trying to resolve the problem through the legislative process.[38]

Turner became increasingly desperate and in January asked Washington attorney and businessman Garrett H. Ten Broeck for help. He told Ten Broeck that up to that time he had been able to find work in Washington to cover his expenses, that he "was entirely out of funds, [with] no prospect of employment in Washington and that unless he could secure some outside assistance he would lose all that he had put into the case." Ten Broeck quietly lobbied for the bill among congressional leaders known to him through his business contacts and after a ten-month effort, primarily with the help of Republican Congressman David B. Henderson of Iowa, was able to have the bill voted upon favorably on October 19, 1888.[39]

The new law provided for the distribution of seventy-five thou-

37. Ibid.; "A Wrangling Convention," *New York Times,* July 26, 1888; "Attention Colored Voters!" *Washington Bee,* August 18, 1888; *Indian Chieftain,* August 23 and September 27, 1888.

38. Henry E. Cuney to Secretary of the Interior John W. Noble, August 16, 1889, Special File 298, frame 147; Richard Harvey Cain to Henry E. Cuney, August 16, 1889, Special File 298, frame 170; Elias C. Boudinot to secretary of the interior, July 6, 1889, Special File 298, frames 0495–0502; *Indian Chieftain,* September 12, 1889.

39. Garrett H. Ten Broeck to Secretary of the Interior John W. Noble, January 11, 1890, File 298, frames 0802–5.

sand dollars among the Cherokee freedmen and other "adopted citizens," specifically the Shawnee and Delaware Indians who lived in the Cherokee Nation, under Cherokee rule. The significance of that step was best summed up by Turner in December when he wrote, "The passage of this act settled [the freedmen's] condition, relieves their apprehension that they will be forced to leave, defines their status, confirms their title to an interest in the 11,035,000 acres of land held by the Cherokees, and in fine to all the rights of the native Cherokees as provided for under the Treaty of 1866."[40]

It had been a long, hard-fought battle getting the bill passed, but at last the goal had been accomplished. All that remained was for Turner to collect his fee for the legal services he performed. That would be the least difficult part of all. Or so he thought.

40. *Cherokee Freedmen Act. Statutes at Large* 25 (1888): 608. According to Turner's attorney, Congress learned from Turner's efforts that certain adopted Delaware and Shawnee were entitled to the same considerations as the former black slaves. Hence, they lumped them all together for the sake of uniform legislation. J. H. McGowan to Secretary of the Interior John W. Noble, April 5, 1889, Special File 298, frames 0474–76; Turner, Affidavit filed with commissioner of Indian affairs, incomplete date, 1888, Special File 298, frame 41.

CHAPTER VIII
A Pyrrhic Victory

There is already a conspiracy on foot to beat [Turner] out of his attorneyship and give it to other parties. This looks like very bad policy indeed for there is not a man in the country who has given the cause of the freedmen the attention which Turner has and there is hardly a possibility of their getting a lawyer to take this case who possesses the ability which Turner does.

—*Indian Chieftain*
January 1, 1891

The Cherokee Freedmen's Act, which James Milton Turner lobbied for, became law on October 19, 1888, and created as many problems as it solved. Despite Turner's confidence that the act had settled the condition of the freedmen, the "settling" had only begun. Indeed, Turner's own status as the attorney for the freedmen was an open question. He had spent nearly five years of his time, along with thousands of his own dollars, furthering the freedmen's claims. Once the act was passed and it became apparent that the attorney for the freedmen was entitled to a large payment for services rendered, challenges to Turner's claim surfaced. These challenges led to an investigation that revealed that Turner, as the attorney of record for the freedmen, had engaged in questionable maneuvers to get the statute enacted. These ploys included promising financial rewards to many who helped him—a commitment that he failed to keep. The investigation confirmed what many had long charged: Turner was an opportunist.[1]

Other problems arose as well. The 1888 freedmen's act provided for the distribution of seventy-five thousand dollars among the Cher-

1. *Cherokee Freedman Act. Statutes at Large* 25 (1888): 608.

okee freedmen, but who were they? How would they be identified? How would they be paid? What did the future hold for the freedmen in Cherokee Territory? What would happen if the Cherokee Nation continued to deny the freedmen full tribal rights? Would legislative remedies be needed each time a new land cession was made?

The Fiftieth Congress sought to answer those questions in 1889 by means of two additional legislative enactments. The secretary of the interior was granted five thousand dollars to cover the expense of compiling a list of persons who were entitled to participate in the per-capita distribution. The secretary of the interior, in turn, appointed Special Agent John W. Wallace to conduct this census-taking operation. Wallace traveled to the Indian Territory, compiled a list of names, and turned them over to the Indian agent of the Union Agency at Muskogee, Oklahoma, to carry out the provisions of the 1888 legislation. Congress referred the question of the freedmen's future status to the United States Court of Claims. It would decide "what are the just rights in law or in equity of the . . . Cherokee freedmen, who are settled and located in the Cherokee Nation under the provisions and stipulations of article nine of the aforesaid treaty of eighteen hundred and sixty-six."[2]

Turner's involvement with the 1888 act obliged him to deal with the problems of claimants against the Cherokees and other Indian nations for the rest of his life. Confident after his victory on behalf of the Cherokee freedmen, and hopeful of continued success with the court case, he tried to extend the logic of the 1888 act to black-Indian relations in nations other than the Cherokee. Whatever combination of altruism, opportunism, and righteous indignation over justice denied had gotten him involved with the freedmen in the first place, he now made a career out of challenging the attempts by the Five Civilized Tribes to confine citizenship rights to full-blooded Indians. As the government continued to pay the Indians for land cessions, the potential profits to be made by the freedmen's attorney increased. Turner's subsequent efforts, however, were less successful than his initial appeals on behalf of the Cherokee freedmen. Even his attempts

2. *Act for Fulfilling Treaty Stipulations with Various Indian Tribes. Statutes at Large* 25 (1889): 994. Turner to the commissioner of Indian affairs, January 13, 1892, Letter No. 1920, Letters Received, L.D., BIA, R.G. 75, NA; *Act to Refer Cherokee Freedmen's Claims to the Court of Claims. Statutes at Large* 26 (1890): 635.

to admit more Cherokee freedmen to per-capita payments proved largely unsuccessful. Ultimately, his career as an attorney for the freedmen ended in frustration when he not only lost the last case he worked on but also was unable to collect any fees from his clients and ended up suing the very people whom he had been trying to help.

Nine days after the passage of the 1888 Cherokee Freedmen's Act, Turner's lawyer, J. H. McGowan, wrote to Secretary of the Interior William F. Vilas asking that no "final settlement of this matter" be made until his client had an opportunity to file his account and be heard. Turner submitted his claim in early December 1888. It was a detailed, itemized account of his expenditures, extending back to January 1884 and amounting to $12,210.61, plus the 25 percent commission he had been promised, for a total of $30,960.51.[3]

Turner's claim was referred to the office of the commissioner of Indian affairs on December 12, 1888. While the claim was pending, Commissioner John H. Oberly drafted a resolution that was presented to Congress and ratified on March 2, 1889. Among other things, this new law provided for a fifteen-thousand-dollar payment to be made to "any duly authorized agent or agents acting for said freedmen and rendering them aid in obtaining the allowance of said seventy-five thousand dollars." An assistant attorney general assigned to the Department of the Interior offered the opinion in June 1889 that "no formal authority of the appointment of said committee of Cherokee freedmen is filed with the papers, nor is there sufficient evidence before me that the parties who signed the contract were authorized to do so or to bind the Cherokee freedmen for the payment of the sum stipulated to be paid to said Turner." He did, however, indicate his belief that Turner was entitled to the fifteen-thousand-dollar fee.[4]

Others, however, were less convinced. In July 1889 the secretary of the interior, John W. Noble, received the first of several challenges to Turner's claim. On July 23, 1889, Noble ruled that seventy-five hundred dollars should be paid to Turner immediately, with the bal-

3. J. H. McGowan to Vilas, October 27, 1888, Special File 298, frame 0004; see also, F. M. Cockrell to Vilas, October 18, 1888, Special File 298, frame 006. Why Turner hired an attorney when he claimed to be a lawyer himself remains a mystery. Account of Turner, Fees and Expenses, Special File 298, frames 0027–33.

4. George Shield to secretary of the interior, June 7, 1889, Special File 298, frames 0445–57.

ance to be paid only after those contesting Turner's claim had an opportunity to do so. For the remainder of the year, as a result, the Interior Department accepted counterclaims from people who argued that they were entitled to a share of the fifteen thousand dollars. Some alleged that Turner had promised to pay for services they had rendered him, but that he later reneged on the promise. Others stated flatly that they had done things on behalf of the act for which Turner claimed credit.[5]

The principal challenger to Turner's claim was Elias C. Boudinot, a Cherokee Indian. Boudinot claimed to have become involved in the attempt to gain tribal rights for the Cherokee freedmen immediately after the May 1883 decision confirmed the distribution of three hundred thousand dollars to full-blooded Cherokees. He argued that it was upon his advice at meetings at Lightning Creek and Fort Gibson that Turner was selected to serve as the freedmen's attorney. Boudinot explained, "I put J. Milton Turner forward in this matter because I knew him to be a colored man of reputation and ability. . . . It was expressly understood that I would continue my services in this behalf at my own expense, and that if successful in whatever fee might be paid by the freedmen or allowed by the United States we should share equally."

Boudinot clearly did work on behalf of the freedmen. There is even considerable evidence that Boudinot introduced Turner to the freedmen's case and was instrumental in getting him appointed as attorney. Boudinot was also the principal figure behind the presentation of a memorial on the freedmen's behalf to the House of Representatives during the Forty-eighth Congress. That document contributed to the establishment of a subcommittee of the House Committee on Indian Affairs to investigate the treatment of the freedmen. The secretary concluded, however, that Turner was "the authorized agent" and that if Boudinot had any relationship to the case it was, at most, as Turner's assistant. Consequently, Boudinot's claim was against Turner and not under the jurisdiction of the secretary of the interior.[6]

5. Affidavit of Secretary of the Interior John W. Noble, July 23, 1889, Special File 298, frames 0459–63. Special File 298 was compiled as a result of claims made by persons who argued that they had a right to share any fees Turner received. It contains more than one thousand frames of letters and other affidavits pertaining to the case.
6. For affidavits filed for and against Boudinot's claim, see the following frames of Special File 298: 0082–89, 0095–0102, 0122–32, 0142–44, 0187–91,

In addition to Boudinot's claim, Charles Journeycake submitted a petition to the department on July 26, 1889, arguing that as attorney for the Delawares, he and his three partners should receive money that was to be paid to Turner on behalf of those Indians. In the case of Journeycake et al., the secretary ruled that their claim had arisen only after Boudinot had written to Journeycake's partner on July 12, 1889, complaining that "Turner, 'the black-son-of-a-gun,'" was claiming to have rendered services for the Delawares, even though he "was a mere figure-head and deserves nothing." Boudinot followed with a second letter on July 24, 1889, stating clearly that his purpose was "to defeat the nigger Turner from getting what belongs to you and Journeycake." The secretary concluded that the claim of Journeycake and his partners was not legitimate.

In August 1889, Henry E. Cuney filed a claim for thirteen hundred dollars in compensation for his assistance in securing the passage of the Cherokee Freedmen's Act. Cuney said he had a verbal contract with Turner. By his own admission, Cuney was not a "duly authorized agent" of any of the beneficiaries of the 1888 act and therefore only had a personal contract with Turner, "to whom he must look for his compensation." Cuney's argument that he was hired by Turner is persuasive and offers the clearest example of how Turner refused to acknowledge help he had received. Cuney filed a sworn statement from A. W. Kellogg, an assistant postmaster of the Senate, who not only testified to Cuney's interest in the matter but acknowledged that at Cuney's request he had lobbied on behalf of the freedmen's act with Illinois Republican Congressman Lewis E. Payson. Mr. N. W. Cuney filed an affidavit in which he swore that Turner admitted to him the employment of Henry E. Cuney and promised to pay the latter. Fred G. Norris, private secretary to former Republican Sen. Dwight Sabin, stated that Henry Cuney introduced Turner to the senator, "with a view of obtaining his support of the Indian bill." W. H. Smith, assistant librarian of the House, said that he frequently saw Turner and Cuney "in consultation during the pending legislation relative to the Cherokee claims" and added that he thought Cuney

---

0196–0204, 0205–11, 0212–26, 0227–35, 0236–59, 0260–63, 0264–0321, 0325–38, 0339–42, 0344–52, 0358–65, 0390–0425, 0428–35, 0435–41, 0486–88, 0495–0507, 0508–22, 0523–24, 0527–75, 0659–63, 0758–67, 0810–11. Final Decision of Secretary Noble in the Claim of J. Milton Turner, March 26, 1890, Special File 298, frames 0895–0944.

had rendered valuable services. Ezra N. Hill stated that Turner had told him he had employed Cuney to assist him and that Cuney was to be well paid. George B. Giddings, one of the few people whom Turner did acknowledge hiring, swore that Cuney greatly helped Turner, that Turner had been quite pleased with his services, and that Turner had promised to pay Cuney the same one-thousand-dollar fee that Giddings had been promised. Democrat Congressman William Crain testified that Cuney introduced Turner to him and asked him to call up the Indian bill, which he had declined to do. Democrat Congressman Constantine B. Kilgore was also introduced to Turner by Cuney and admitted to being persuaded to withdraw his opposition to the bill because of Cuney's lobbying.[7]

All of these testimonials notwithstanding, Turner steadfastly refused to acknowledge having received any help from Cuney or having promised to pay him anything. In fact, he mounted a counteroffensive against Cuney's eminently persuasive argument. Turner instructed his lawyers to discredit Cuney by informing the secretary of the interior of Cuney's indictment on a criminal charge in the District of Columbia. Such a maneuver made Cuney furious, and he replied in kind: "Turner and his counsel must be desperate when they descend to such baseness as cooking up evidence against my character." Such behavior did not surprise him, for he professed to believe that Turner "is capable of anything." Although Cuney claimed to be averse to mudslinging, he made it clear that he could engage in it as well. "I know," he wrote, "of several whorehouse bills outstanding against Turner as well as money that he borrowed and refused to pay. There are some liquor bills too."[8]

One of the few people who did have a written contract with Turner was George B. Giddings. Giddings, however, claimed that Turner owed him one thousand dollars, whereas Turner was only willing to pay five hundred. Giddings's claim met the same response as the others: "He must," the secretary of the interior wrote, "look to Turner, and not to this Department." Garrett H. Ten Broeck had a claim of a

7. For affidavits filed for and against Journeycake's claim, see the following frames of Special File 298: 0102–5, 0366–75, 0716–17, 0771–95. For affidavits filed for and against Cuney's claim, see the following frames of Special File 298: 0145–86, 0262, 0654–58, 0703–12, 0752–57. Final Decision of Secretary Noble in the Claim of J. Milton Turner, March 26, 1890, Special File 298, frames 0895–0949.

8. Cuney to Christy, January 20, 1890, Special File 298, frames 0178–87.

slightly different nature: he advanced Turner large sums of money "to pay his personal expenses whilst advocating the passage of the appropriation of $75,000." Additionally, he also claimed to have "used his personal influence with members of Congress to secure the said appropriation and the further one of $15,000." As in the case of Giddings, Turner acknowledged his liability, stating that he owed Ten Broeck $5,212.01. Despite the fact that Turner acknowledged the legitimacy of the debt, he paid Ten Broeck only two thousand dollars, leaving his benefactor to plead with the secretary of the interior to take the balance of $3,212.01 out of the amount still due Turner. The secretary rejected Ten Broeck's claim for the same reason that he rejected all of the others: Ten Broeck's complaint against Turner was the result of a private contract and was not subject to the provisions of the 1888 legislation.[9]

William Brown, one of the original members of the committee that hired Turner, also claimed he was entitled to two thousand dollars "for expenses and services as committee-man in securing the appropriation for the freedmen." Brown claimed to have been responsible for securing the job for Turner, for which the black lawyer promised him four thousand dollars, although Brown was willing to settle for only half that amount. Brown filed affidavits from Roswell Machey, George W. Elliott, and Joe Douglas all corroborating his story. Again, the secretary of the interior concluded, "Apart from any question about the morality of the transaction, the case is one of an entirely private and personal contract between the parties . . . and in no way comes within the purview of the act authorizing the payment of compensation." Having rejected all attempts to garnish the remaining seventy-five hundred dollars previously assigned to Turner, but held in escrow until his challengers could be heard, the secretary finally ordered "that the remainder of the fund of $7,500 be paid to J. Milton Turner, as follows: $3,750 at this time, and $3,750 on July 10, 1890."[10]

9. For affidavits filed for and against Giddings's claim, see the following frames of Special File 298: 0106–21, 0353–57, 0525–26, 0713–15, 0718–21. Final Decision of Secretary Noble in the Claim of J. Milton Turner, March 26, 1890, Special File 298, frames 0895–0944. For affidavits filed for and against Ten Broeck's claim, see the following frames of Special File 298: 0482–87, 0768–70, 0796–0809. Final Decision of Secretary Noble in the Claim of J. Milton Turner, March 26, 1890, Special File 298, frames 0895–0944.

10. For affidavits filed for and against Brown's claim, see the following

It was something of a hollow victory for Turner. Even though he emerged from the affair with the full payment of fifteen thousand dollars, it was less than half the amount he had hoped to collect. Moreover, Turner's machinations had finally caught up with him. He had obviously broken commitments with a number of persons who had helped him to get the bill passed, and his already dubious reputation had suffered further defamation as a result. There were even indications in the latter stages of the push for the bill that his increasingly intense lobbying efforts were jeopardizing his goal. In September of 1888, for example, one observer, J. E. Bruce, offered the following assessment of Turner's activities on behalf of the Cherokee bill. "Mr. Turner," he wrote, "is a brilliant and scholarly man, a very poor lobbyist and an excellent judge of fire-water, which he samples too often and as a result it loosens his tongue too much." Bruce claimed that Turner had "succeeded admirably in talking his bill to death by boasting of his sharp practices to secure its passage." Indeed, Bruce maintained that the bill would not pass the House "so long as Turner has anything to do with it." Henry Cuney quoted Republican Congressman Robert La Follette as saying that Turner's activities during the late summer and early fall of 1888 actually postponed the passage of the bill. Garrett Ten Broeck also wrote that Turner "complicated himself politically and secured the opposition of the Republicans and found he could make no progress whatever."[11]

Even when successful, Turner was criticized both by his colleagues and by those he purported to serve. Looking back in 1889 on the previous six years, he must have wondered why he had undertaken to process the Cherokee freedmen's claims. What had seemed to him in 1883 to be a simple, straightforward case of asserting the freedmen's claims and collecting his fee had become immensely drawn out and complicated. His efforts to speed up the process, particularly his involvement in Cherokee politics and his work on behalf of the Indianapolis convention, brought him extensive criticism. Even after the bill was passed, he had to settle for an amount less than half of

frames of Special File 298: 0090–94, 0131–41, 0322–24, 0376–89, 0438–41. Final Decision of Secretary Noble in the Claim of J. Milton Turner, March 26, 1890, Special File 298, frames 0895–0944.

11. J. E. Bruce to the Editor of the *Cherokee Advocate,* September 9, 1888, quoted in the *Indian Chieftain,* September 27, 1888. H. E. Cuney to Robert Christy, January 20, 1890, Special File 298, frames 0178–87. Garrett Ten Broeck to secretary of the interior, January 11, 1890, Special File 298, frames 0802–5.

what he thought he was entitled to and was paid only after a delay of more than one year, during which time he had to suffer the challenges of people who contested his claim. The disappointment of the 1889 fee settlement, combined with the harsh criticism of Turner's detractors, must have been a stark contrast to the black lawyer's expectations.

Whatever his disappointment might have been, Turner continued to work on behalf of the freedmen. Another cession of land in 1890 brought an additional payment of three hundred thousand dollars to the Cherokee Nation, with the prospect of more to come. The potential personal profit for an attorney was enormous. The 1890 law that referred the question of the freedmen's future status to the courts also authorized them to hire attorneys, "the amount of compensation of such attorneys and counsel fees, not to exceed ten percent of the amount recovered." Almost immediately, rumors circulated about who the attorney for the freedmen would be. The *Indian Chieftain* reported on November 6, 1890, that "J. Milton Turner has secured a contract from the colored citizens for the prosecution of all their claims against the Cherokee Nation." The announcement was premature, however, and there was a good deal of anti-Turner sentiment still present among the freedmen. On November 13, Luster Foreman, who described himself as the "president of the Freedmen brotherhood of the Cherokee nation," declared that "no such contract exists." Moreover, he exclaimed, "The Cherokee Freedmen don't need any attorney and if Mr. Turner has any such contract it is a spurious and bogus one." A week later the *Chieftain* noted that "the colored people are becoming involved in an acrimonious controversy as to who shall represent them in the court of claims." Interestingly the *Chieftain,* which had spoken so critically of Turner's political maneuvering in the 1887 tribal elections, now wrote glowingly of the black lawyer. It suggested to the freedmen "that Turner probably accomplished in their behalf what no other man in the country could and there is no telling what his resources are."[12]

Late in November, a call was issued for a convention to be held in the Cherokee Nation to discuss pursuing claims in the courts. The

12. *Act to Refer Cherokee Freedmen's Claims to the Court of Claims. Statutes at Large* 26 (1890): 635; U.S. Court of Claims, *Whitmire, Trustee, v. Cherokee Nation and the United States, Cases Decided in the Court of Claims of the United States at the Term of 1894–1895,* 30:138–59; *Indian Chieftain,* November 6, 13, 20, 1890.

convention recommended Moses Whitmire, a member of the original committee of blacks that had hired Turner, to the secretary of the interior as the official representative of the freedmen. He was to act as their trustee. Whitmire's role as representative of the freedmen had been vigorously challenged by William and Joseph Brown, who felt that Turner controlled Whitmire. William Brown claimed Turner still owed him money for his assistance in the passage of the 1888 Freedmen's Act. Nevertheless, Whitmire was accepted officially by the secretary in mid-December and authorized to employ counsel to pursue the case before the court of claims. Turner's questionable tactics of the previous seven years made him an extremely controversial prospect. Again on January 1, 1891, the *Indian Chieftain* encouraged the freedmen to "secure the most able attorneys if they expect to participate in the proceeds from the sale of the strip lands," asserting "J. Milton Turner has already won half the fight for the freedmen." Despite Turner's victory, the *Chieftain* noted, "There is already a conspiracy on foot to beat him out of his attorneyship and give it to other parties. This looks like very bad policy indeed for there is not a man in the country who has given the cause of the freedmen the attention which Turner has and there is hardly a possibility of their getting a lawyer to take this case who possesses the ability which Turner does." The *Chieftain* concluded its editorial support of Turner by noting, "The very fact of his being a colored man gives him an especial advantage when appearing in behalf of his own race which his white competitor could not hope for."[13]

On January 22, 1891, the *Chieftain* announced that Turner had prevailed in his attempt to be named as the attorney for the freedmen and would "at once take steps to secure for the colored people a share in the next Cherokee payment." Simultaneously, on January 21, 1891, the Missouri Pacific Railway Company issued a circular to Cherokee freedmen announcing reduced rates for round-trip tickets from twelve points in Indian Territory to the town of Braggs, where they could presumably attempt to include themselves among the freedmen who were entitled to the per-capita distribution. Turner arranged the rail-

13. *Indian Chieftain*, November 20, 1890; January 1, 8, 1891. Presumably the white competitor referred to by the newspaper was John W. Wallace, who sought, according to Daniel Littlefield, "to take J. Milton Turner's place as attorney for the freedmen in future suits." Littlefield, *The Cherokee Freedmen*, 155. For the Browns' opposition to Whitmire and Turner, see 165–68.

road "scheme," as it was called by his critics. Most of the people who traveled to Braggs were blacks who had been left off the so-called Wallace Roll, compiled by Special Agent John W. Wallace in 1889, and were attempting to have their names added. In March 1891 a citizen of Indian Territory, Fred M. Strout, complained to the acting commissioner that "J. Milton Turner collected hundreds of dollars . . . from 'to-late' [sic] niggers who he has managed to get on the roll."[14]

Strout was not the only person who complained of Turner's appointment as attorney. Joseph and William Brown wrote to the acting commissioner on March 17, 1891, making, as the commissioner wrote, "sundry charges of extortionate practices said to have been indulged in by Mr. Turner upon the colored people of the Cherokee Nation." The commissioner replied to the Browns' complaint by indicating "that all the charges against Mr. Turner referred to by you in your letter were canvassed by the Secretary of the Interior at the time when he had the selection of Moses Whitmire under consideration." He told the Browns that "the matter will not now be re-opened" but added that they were free to submit facts pertaining to Turner's alleged "unprofessional conduct" to the court of claims.[15]

Despite the fact that he was surrounded by an atmosphere of distrust, and even hatred, Turner spent a good deal of time in Indian Territory during 1891. In January 1892 he offered his assessment of the inadequacy of the job done by Special Agent Wallace to Commissioner Thomas J. Morgan. He complained, "Many persons entitled to a per-capita share of [the original $75,000 and subsequent payments] had been, for lack of complete evidence and various other reasons . . . unjustly dropped from the rolls made by Commissioner Wallace." To illustrate his point, Turner proclaimed that on the Wallace Roll "a son was frequently paid and a father denied recognition; the same was true of a daughter while the mother was denied." According to Turner, he had complained to the secretary of the interior of this "incongruous and confusing spectacle." The secretary had promised "to make another supplemental roll . . . to the one already

14. *Indian Chieftain*, January 22, 1891. H. C. Townsend to Turner, January 21, 1891, Enclosure 1, Fred M. Strout to the acting commissioner of Indian affairs, March 18, 1891, Letter No. 10705, Letters Received, L.D., BIA, R.G 75, NA.

15. Acting commissioner of Indian affairs to Joseph and William Brown, March 25, 1891, Letter No. 10925, Letters Sent, L.D., BIA, R.G. 75, NA.

made by United States Commissioner Wallace." The compilation of a new list was delayed, however, because Wallace had exhausted the five-thousand-dollar appropriation provided for that purpose. Hence, the secretary had committed himself to making the supplemental roll "whenever the Department was in possession of the funds necessary to defray the expenses."

The time period for the new roll to be taken was fixed for January 1892, and the Indian agent at Muskogee published notices that he would receive applications from black freedmen omitted from the Wallace Roll until January 28. Turner complained that the "inexperience of the parties interested" made the time too short. He was "of the opinion that easily from 6 to 1200 persons are laboring under this particular hardship and unless granted ample opportunity to maintain their rights they will be ultimately debarred by undue . . . process." In view of that fact, he requested an extension of the January 28 deadline. He also asked the secretary of the interior to "recommend to the proper Committee of Congress that the necessary appropriation be made to perfect and complete the so-called Wallace roll." Turner concluded with a frank explanation of his concern about the number of freedmen to be added to the role. He noted that an extension "seems to the attorneys of the Cherokee freedmen necessary . . . in view of the fact that in much of their cause already brought before the Court of Claims . . . [the attorneys'] interest will turn largely and indeed with great significance . . . upon the numerical aggregate of human souls whom they shall be able to prove are included within the solemn treaty stipulations of the 9th Article of the Treaty of 1866."[16]

Commissioner Morgan replied to Turner's letter on January 21, 1892, saying that "Special Agent Wallace gave ample time, nearly nine months, to every freedman in the Cherokee Nation, to present their claim to enrollment with the evidence on which it was based." Morgan acknowledged that certain claimants "failed to complete or perfect their evidence" because of their "gross ignorance and lack of knowledge of business methods," but he argued that such claims could be adjusted through the Indian agent. He noted that much correspondence had already gone on with freedmen who felt that they had been unjustly excluded, "and wherever the proof has been [sufficient] . . . parties have been instructed how to complete their

16. Turner to commissioner of Indian affairs, January 13, 1892, Letter No. 1920, Letters Received, L.D., BIA, R.G. 75, NA.

chain of evidence, by furnishing them a series of questions to be answered under oath, in accordance with fact."

The commissioner declared that, while Wallace's work was not perfect, the job he had done was commendable. The apparent incongruities to which Turner referred, he said, could be explained in most, if not all, cases and cited the case of Martha Sales to illustrate his point. Mrs. Sales was fifty-three years old when she appeared before Special Agent Wallace on October 23, 1889. She had been born in the Cherokee Nation, the slave of Joe Riley. During the Civil War she fled to Kansas and did not return until 1881. Clearly, the commissioner argued, that was more than the six months stipulated by the 1866 treaty. Mrs. Sale's daughter, Anna Harris, on the other hand, was in the Cherokee Nation at the time of the treaty and remained there. Her claim was admitted.[17]

Not all freedmen in Indian Territory were eager to have the Wallace Roll tampered with. Many blacks who were on the original roll feared that any reopening might result in their subsequent exclusion. Isaac Rogers and George W. Vann, both Cherokee freedmen, wrote to Secretary Hoke Smith in December 1893, indicating "there are numerous complaints against [Moses Whitmire] and great dissatisfaction among the freedmen." First of all, they wrote, Whitmire was appointed the freedmen's trustee "without their consent and we believe in col[l]usion with J. Milton Turner to compromise the suit against our will and to our disadvantage." Rogers and Vann were fearful that the activity of Turner and Whitmire would jeopardize the gains already made by the freedmen. They complained that the trustee and his attorney were trying "to disturb the 'Wallace Roll' and throw out a great many freedmen who are recognized and legally placed thereon; and if [they persist and succeed] in [their] efforts it will cause many poor freedmen to be made homeless and endure many hardships." There is no evidence to support the contentions of Rogers and Vann. But by this time, Turner had been charged with so much wrongdoing that many freedmen assumed the worst of any venture in which he was involved.[18]

Despite opposition, Turner and Whitmire continued to challenge

17. Commissioner to Turner, January 21, 1892, Letter No. 1920, Letters Sent, L.D., BIA, R.G. 75, NA.
18. Dew M. Wisdom to secretary of the interior, December 26, 1893, Letter No. 47939, Letters Received, L.D., BIA, R.G. 75, NA. G. W. Vann and Isaac Rogers to secretary of the interior, incomplete date, December, 1893, Enclosure, Wisdom to secretary of the interior, December 26, 1893, Letter No. 47939.

the Wallace Roll. The fact that in 1894 another land cession was made for the staggering sum of $6,640,000 encouraged their persistence. The Cherokee freedmen's case was finally heard by the court of claims in March 1895. After becoming involved in the case in 1891, Turner had recruited four prominent white St. Louis attorneys, Robert H. Kern, Frederick W. Lehmann, Wells H. Blodgett, and Henry D. Laughlin, to assist in preparing the case for the court of claims. Kern, an active Democrat, was Turner's chief partner in the case, and he and Lehmann argued the case before the court of claims.[19]

The two attorneys focused their arguments on the constitution of the Cherokee Nation and the Treaty of 1866 and pleaded that those documents entitled the freedmen to "all the rights of native Cherokees." The attorney for the Cherokee Nation responded that the intention of the Cherokees was "to confer upon the colored people in the Cherokee Nation, and all who might become residents thereof, such rights, and such rights only, as were conferred upon the colored people in other parts of the United States." Hence, the Cherokee Nation "was certainly under no obligation to provide for this class of persons." Any other interpretation, the Indians argued, "would place a penalty upon the Cherokee Nation not imposed upon any other people within the broad domain of the United States and one with no parallel in its history." In addition, the Cherokees argued that the entire affair was an internal matter and "that the Cherokees possess the sole and exclusive right to manage their own internal affairs, and of control of the persons and property of their citizens, there has been no question for more than half a century."

The court of claims rejected the Cherokees' plea but postponed a final decree in the case until it could be informed of "the number of persons who were entitled to participate, or of the number of persons who constitute the body of the present claimants." Two weeks later the court met again, with Kern and Wells H. Blodgett arguing the case for the freedmen. By that time there had been three monetary distributions totaling $7,240,000. The court ruled that the Wallace Roll should be used for deciding who among the freedmen should receive per-capita payments. However, the court declared that the original

19. Lawrence O. Christensen, "J. Milton Turner: An Appraisal," 17; U.S. Court of Claims, *Whitmire, Trustee,* v. *Cherokee Nation and the United States, Cases Decided in the Court of Claims of the United States, at the Term of 1894–1895,* 30:138–59.

Wallace Roll compiled in 1889 should not be used. Rather, the so-called corrected Wallace Roll, compiled subsequent to the sending of two agents into Cherokee Territory in 1890, would be used.[20]

Counsel for the Cherokees challenged the accuracy of the Wallace Roll and its revisions. They argued that the number of freedmen in the nation should be drawn from a census "made by the nation at some time between 1880 and 1882." That number was 2,052, whereas the revised Wallace Roll insisted that the true number of freedmen living in 1883 was 3,524. The court of claims found in favor of Kern and Blodgett's argument that the revised Wallace Roll should be used. In addition, it provided for additional amendment to the roll by instructing the secretary of the interior to "cause the Wallace roll to be further corrected by adding thereto descendants born since March 3, 1883, and prior to May 3, 1894, and striking therefrom the names of those who have died or have ceased to be citizens of the Cherokee Nation." To carry out that task, the court authorized the secretary of the interior to appoint a commissioner to go to Cherokee country and determine the facts necessary for the correction of the roll. The newly revised roll became known as the Kern-Clifton Roll. Using the number of 3,524 freedmen out of a total Cherokee population of 28,243 and taking the total sum to be $7,240,000, the court ruled that $903,365 was to be distributed among the freedmen. The total represented, as the court pointed out, "more than $250 for each person—more than $1000 for every family of the freedmen." Moreover, the court directed the Cherokee Nation to pay the "attorney of the complainants" $18,067.30 in expenses. In addition, the attorneys were to be paid a fee of 4 percent of the settlement, or $36,134. Moses Whitmire, the trustee for the freedmen was to be paid $5,000.

Not only was the present status of the Cherokee freedmen clearly defined, but their future was as well. The court ruled that "the freedmen and free colored persons aforesaid and their descendants, are entitled to participate hereafter in the common property of the Cherokee Nation in the same manner and to the same extent as Cherokee citizens of Cherokee blood or parentage may be entitled." The Cherokee Nation appealed the verdict. Whitmire, Turner, and the other four attorneys responded by declaring that if the Cherokees refused

20. U.S. Court of Claims, *Whitmire, Trustee, v. Cherokee Nation and the United States, Cases Decided in the Court of Claims of the United States at the Term of 1894–1895*, 30:138–59.

to accept the validity of a revised Wallace Roll, they would themselves appeal the case and attempt to add more persons to the list than even the revised Wallace Roll allowed. The six men published an open "Address to the Freedmen" in the *Indian Chieftain* on September 19, 1895. They warned the freedmen that the Cherokee nation "has kept the Freedman out of his money for years in court, and now that it is well-whipped, is trying its further knavery." Indeed, the freedmen's representatives expressed confidence that they could win a $150,000 distribution increase in a Supreme Court fight. They were particularly incensed over the actions of Ike Rogers and Chief Harris, who, they complained, had called a convention for September 15, 1895, for the purpose of "prolong[ing] the payment of the Freedmen their just rights under the decree of the court of Claims." The address closed with a warning to the freedmen "to have nothing to do with Mr. Ike Rogers, nor the Cherokee nation in this matter, but leave it to the court where they are sure to win."[21]

Even after the new roll was completed there was controversy. Payment was finally made in February 1897, but only after mutual recriminations of "alleged crookedness" and "alleged misconduct." The department of interior charged William J. McConnell with the responsibility of investigating the manner in which the rolls had been compiled. The special agent concluded that "the entire transaction of the enrollment of the Cherokee freedmen and free colored persons, together with the appropriation of the money by the Cherokee council for the purpose of equalizing payments, was a disgraceful affair." McConnell noted that "men high in the councils of the Cherokee nation, as well as others trusted by the Cherokee freedmen and free colored persons, have grossly and outrageously betrayed the confidence of a too-confiding people." Congress responded to McConnell's report by deciding that yet another roll should be taken, this one by a senate committee headed by Henry Dawes. Hence, the whole question of who was and who was not entitled to per-capita payments was again reopened. Although the Dawes commission's new roll was not accepted formally by the secretary of the interior until March 4, 1907, Turner and others became aware much earlier that the new list excluded a number of freedmen whose names were on the Kern-Clifton Roll.[22]

21. Ibid., 189–96; *Indian Chieftain*, September 19, 1895.
22. *Indian Chieftain*, February 16, 1899; *Curtis Act. Statutes at Large* 30

As early as 1903, Turner tried to ascertain the status of those people whose names had either been added to or deleted from the Kern-Clifton Roll by the Dawes commission. More than one year later, he wrote again to the office of Indian affairs, indicating, "I am still in a way interested as an attorney in fact for the interests of the Cherokee Freedmen." He noted that the Cherokee chief had said recently, in reference to the roll of freedmen retaken by the Dawes Commission, "that 2,008 of said Freedmen had been placed upon a so-called doubtful list." Turner indicated that he had been intimately concerned with the fate of those 2,008 blacks and asked what their present status was in the Indian office. The acting commissioner of Indian affairs responded that his office did not know of the exact number of rejected applicants, but that the accepted enrollment of Cherokee Freedmen had risen to 3,881.[23]

Turner continued for the next five years to seek clarification on the disparity between the Kern-Clifton Roll and the Dawes roll. In addition, he made repeated, although unsuccessful, efforts to further the claims of blacks who had been excluded unjustifiably from the 1897 payment. Eventually he submitted the names of thirty-one persons who, he claimed, belonged in this latter category. In every case, the commissioner of Indian affairs ruled that the persons in question were either not entitled to payment or had already received payment. Meanwhile, Turner and his legal colleagues translated their concern about the incongruity of the Kern-Clifton and Dawes rolls into a formal petition to the court of claims in May 1909 on behalf of those persons whose names appeared on the former list "and prayed that the action of the Dawes commissioner and of the secretary of the interior to be declared unlawful." The court of claims ruled in their favor. That victory was reversed in 1912, however, when the United States Supreme Court overturned the court decision to reject the Dawes roll, thereby ending further attempts to add persons to the list of freedmen receiving payments. The Court noted that the Kern-

---

(1898): 495; U.S. Court of Claims, *Whitmire, Trustee, v. Cherokee Nation and the United States, Cases Decided in the Court of Claims of the United States at the Term of 1894–1895,* 30:115.

23. Turner to secretary of the interior, July 7, 1903, Letter No. 43298, Letters Received, L.D., BIA, R.G. 75, NA. Turner to Willis Smith, February 7, 1905, Enclosure, Letter No. 12075, Letters Received, L.D., BIA, R.G. 75, NA. Acting Commissioner to Turner, February 25, 1905, Letter No. 12075, Letters Sent, L.D., BIA, R.G. 75, NA.

Clifton Roll "had been made up with haste and under circumstances which caused question of its correctness." Consequently, it affirmed the roll compiled by the Dawes commission to be the most accurate and the one from which future distributions were to be made.[24]

At the same time, Turner tried to apply the maxims established with regard to the Cherokee Nation elsewhere in the Indian Territory. Having long since become convinced that the prosecution of claims such as those of the Cherokee freedmen could be financially rewarding, Turner tried to help Indians who were making claims against the United States: the Wea, Peoria, Kaskaskia, and Piankeshaw Indians who resided on the Quapaw reservation. When one recalls his earlier condemnatory statements about Indians, Turner's purely financial motive becomes clearly transparent. In an age when "Robber Barons" ruled the economic world, Turner sought fortune however he could find it. He also tried to help Choctaw and Chickasaw freedmen to gain more land from their respective tribes. But that effort, like those on behalf of the disgruntled Indians, failed. In spite of that failure, Turner and a new partner, S. T. Wiggins, tried to collect a twelve-thousand-dollar legal fee from the Choctaw and Chickasaw freedmen. The freedmen balked at paying, and Turner and Wiggins sued in an Oklahoma district court. The court awarded the two lawyers six thousand dollars, a decision that was appealed to the Oklahoma Supreme Court, where it was upheld. Turner was still trying to collect his share of the six thousand dollars up until he died.[25]

Turner's nearly thirty years of legal maneuvering for the Indian

24. File 57818, L.D., BIA, R.G. 75, NA, contains a dozen pieces of correspondence between Turner and the commissioner of Indian affairs extending from 1907–1909; U.S. Supreme Court, *Cherokee Nation and United States* v. *Whitmire et al.,* 116–117. U.S. Court of Claims, *Whitmire, Trustee,* v. *Cherokee Nation and the United States, Cases Decided in the Court of Claims of the United States at the Term of 1908–1909,* 44:453–68.

25. Turner to Champ Clark, April 5, 1900, Letter No. 17428, Letters Received, L.D., BIA, R.G. 75, NA. Acting commissioner of Indian affairs to Turner, April 16, 1900, Letter No. 17428, Letters Sent, L.D., BIA, R.G. 75, NA. Turner to commissioner of Indian affairs, April 20, 1900, Letter No. 19823; Turner to commissioner of Indian affairs, April 20, 1900, Letter No. 19805, Affidavit of J. Milton Turner, April 20, 1900, enclosed with Letter No. 19805; Letters Received, L.D., BIA, R.G. 75, NA. Report of commissioner of Indian affairs to the president, April 17, 1906, Letter No. 31811, Letters Sent, L.D., BIA, R.G. 75, NA. Secretary of the interior to the president, March 10, 1910, File No. 10406, L.D., BIA, R.G. 75, NA. *Daily Ardmorite,* November 2, 1915.

freedmen effectually came to an end with the closing of the rolls. He could count as his major accomplishments the passage of the 1888 Cherokee Act, the expansion of the Wallace Roll, and the clarification of the future status of the Cherokee freedmen. It had been an expensive odyssey. His scheming had seriously damaged his reputation, and he was singularly unsuccessful in his attempts to advance freedmen's claims after the court victory. Undoubtedly, he collected considerable sums of money in attorney's fees despite his lack of success in his later years. That money, however, was never able to restore him to the position of power and status that he had enjoyed in Reconstruction Missouri.[26]

26. *Washington Bee,* November 15, 1915. The *Bee* declared that Turner had made more money in attorney's fees than any other black man in the history of the country.

CHAPTER IX
A Final Effort Fails

I am wearied with you negro voters. . . . For years you have given 9,000 votes for 60 janitorships, and if you continue to do as you have done in the past you will never gain for yourselves and for your sons the political liberty which is more valuable to you than the name of citizen which is empty if you don't make your rights at the polls effective.

—James Milton Turner
October 29, 1898

Although his efforts on behalf of Indian freedmen occupied much of James Milton Turner's time after 1883, he maintained other interests. He continued to try to exercise the political power that he had wielded in the early 1870s, and which he had tried to regain at the Indianapolis convention in 1888. He adhered to his decision to leave the Republican party as a gesture of defiance against the organization, which did not take blacks seriously as a political force. When Theodore Roosevelt appeared on the political scene, he switched his allegiance again hoping that Roosevelt would revive the old Radical party of the Grant days.

Increasingly, however, both blacks and whites paid less attention to Turner. Party leaders seemed not to care whether he was a Republican or a Democrat, and he alienated many would-be followers by his sharp dealing, opportunism, and criticism of the black folk culture. The racism of white society precluded his movement into the white mainstream as well. One of the results of this rejection by both blacks and whites was that Turner became involved in a black fraternal organization that had institutionalized the very self-reliance philosophy that his early life experiences had instilled in him: Prince Hall Freemasonry. In the last third of his life, masonry provided a disappointed

Turner with an oasis of familiarity and friendliness in a desert of hostility and hate. Even though the status-conscious Turner did achieve some recognition within the limited community of black Missouri masonry, it never mollified the disappointment over not achieving his political and social aspirations. He withdrew from most masonic activities and spent his last days in near isolation, feeble and sickly much of the time, living out of a boardinghouse in St. Louis in a very strained relationship with a common-law wife.

Politics still remained one of the focal points of Turner's attention. He followed his 1888 effort to organize and unite the Independent and Democratic black vote in the country with an appearance at the National Negro Convention held in Washington, D.C., in February 1890. Turner was one of the delegates to this convention, which was made up primarily of persons wavering between continued support of the Republicans or a new alliance with the Democrats. His influence, however, was minimal. In fact, his only effort to speak to the largely Republican group was under the guise of seconding a nomination. As Turner was speaking, the audience, aware of his recent efforts on behalf of the Democratic party, reacted with hostility to the black orator's comments and interrupted him with cries of "Order! . . . What way do you vote? . . . Didn't you vote for Cleveland?" Ultimately, according to the *St. Louis Globe-Democrat,* a motion to limit all seconding speeches to five minutes prevailed, and Turner sat down.[1]

Whether in direct response to that humiliating experience or not, some months later Turner announced another colonization plan. This one echoed his 1886 proposal to establish a black settlement in Butler County, Missouri. There is no evidence that the 1890 scheme was anything more than an imaginary hope, for the only references to it seem to be confined to two back-to-back issues of the *New York Times.* Still, it is worth considering because it reveals something of a change in Turner's vision of a black utopia.

Up to this time Turner had maintained that the future of black people in the United States was tied to their ability to adjust to life in some part of their native land, either in the South or in the West. This current colonization scheme's location was outside the United States

---

1. *St. Louis Globe-Democrat,* January 25, February 1890; see also, Beatty, "Political Response," 210, and Larry H. Grothaus, "The Negro in Missouri Politics, 1890–1941," 11–12.

in Mexico because, Turner explained to a reporter, "the plan is being promoted by a firm of coffee dealers in New York, who have a capital of about $5,000,000." The purpose of the firm would be "to put the negroes to raising coffee and sugar." According to Turner, the white benefactors of the plan owned about two million acres of land, "which will be divided up among the colonists." He emphasized that no rent would be charged for the land and that "the firm will furnish a means of support for the negroes until they can get their grounds under cultivation and become self-sustaining." Turner revealed that the benevolent capitalists were "willing to spend $2,000,000 or $3,000,000 in that way."

Turner further emphasized that he was only the attorney for the firm in the matter. The directors of the firm had asked for plans to carry out their program, and "the one presented by me pleased them the most." He asserted that blacks were very optimistic that "the movement can be made very beneficial" for them and claimed that he had already received a large number of applications from blacks who were eager to go. He closed by stating significantly, "All these applications are from negroes in the North, where the negro is supposed not to be suppressed." The New York Times of the next day reported that Turner had acknowledged that both the scheme and the firm involved were fictitious. But his utopia reveals his frustration over the barriers against blacks in the United States—even in the North—and his continued belief that white Americans owed blacks assistance in their struggle for civil and political rights.[2]

Later in the year, Turner spoke at a black political rally in St. Louis and urged blacks to be politically realistic and to support the Democrats, whatever their ideological preferences. Turner especially encouraged young blacks to revolt against the Republican party, arguing that it allowed blacks neither a voice in the selection of candidates nor a meaningful share of party honors and patronage. His encouragement toward apostasy went largely unheeded because of the general awareness of the Democratic party's lack of concern about blacks. As Prof. Larry Grothaus has stated, "A possible alliance between Negroes and Democrats failed in the early 1890's [in Missouri] because the chief concern of the party was its rural constituency and not the urban Negro."[3]

2. New York Times, August 6, 7, 1890.
3. Grothaus, "Negro in Missouri Politics," 11–13; Republic [St. Louis] October 23, 1890.

With the Missouri Democrats unwilling to do anything to attract black voters, and with the black voters unmoved by Turner's appeals, there was really very little political activity that he could engage in. In 1892 he joined a nonpartisan movement by "the leading colored men of St. Louis" to call national attention "to wrongs that were being heaped upon them and to the frequency with which negroes [were] being lynched or burned alive on the mere accusation of crime, without the process of law." Turner and a committee of seventeen other black St. Louis leaders called for "a day [of] humiliation, fasting and prayer." They asked blacks all over the country "to meet on this day [May 31] at their places of worship . . . and to unite in prayer for the removal of the cause of these wrongs."[4]

That nonpartisan activity aside, Turner played no part in politics again until 1898. In that year black discontent with the Republican party erupted into what Professor Grothaus has called "an important political revolt." When Chauncey Filley, St. Louis Republican leader, fell from power in 1896, patronage positions and even menial political jobs for blacks were almost totally wiped out. Blacks expected eight hundred of the eight thousand jobs available in St. Louis but only held seventy-six in 1898. Another event that fueled the revolt was the question of David Murphy's renomination as judge of the Court of Criminal Corrections. Blacks saw Murphy as a sympathetic advocate to their plight and wanted to renominate him. Murphy's renomination, however, was rejected by the Republicans. This blatant disregard of blacks as a constituency prompted them to form an independent political organization and also to move toward the Democratic party. A slate of black candidates that did not include Turner was offered for several elective positions. The Democrats, led by Gov. Lon V. Stephens, began making overtures to the black rebels. Governor Stephens wrote to several black leaders, Turner among them, hoping to sway them toward the Democratic party. He assured Turner and others that he would talk to the St. Louis Police Board about the appointment of a black policeman, and he made similar commitments to other leaders.[5]

Turner appears to have played a relatively minor part in the 1898 revolt. He, of course, needed no convincing. He had made the switch from Republicanism to Democracy a full decade before and could

4. *St. Louis Globe-Democrat,* April 23 and May 11, 1892.
5. Grothaus, "Negro in Missouri Politics," 7, 17–18.

not pass up the opportunity to chide those who were so slow in seeing the light. In October 1898 he delivered a speech at an "Independent negro rally," described by the *Republic* as "the most remarkable demonstration of political enthusiasm in St. Louis for many years." The newspaper reported that "the hall was jammed to the entrance and the enthusiasm was unbounded." Reiterating an argument first advanced by the Equal Rights League more than thirty years before, Turner charged that the only claim to black loyalty that the Republicans could make was that "they freed the American negro from slavery." Even that claim, he said, was untrue. "Democrats as well as Republicans," he noted, had fought against the slavocracy during the Civil War. Then, in an obvious slur on the German-Americans who represented a large segment of the Missouri Republican party, he exclaimed, "And I tell you . . . that when Julius Overreacher and Henrich Allgrabber come to you and say that he and only he is entitled to the negro vote, you can tell him in all truth and sincerity that he lies." Turner insisted that blacks had "no equal representation" and that the Republicans had made every effort to keep it that way. Bitter from his own unsuccessful attempts to gain political office, he continued:

> You never had one man in the legislature; you never have had a negro in a constabulary position. You have never known your power. But I have hoped, and not in vain, that when our young men began to come out of the public schools of Missouri and to know the rights which are theirs by the law of God and man, they would rise up in the power of the American ballot and see to it that they are recognized, if not by the party with which they have been allied, then by the Democratic party, or better still, by their own party.

He continued to tell them that their failure to stand up to the Republicans had made them the "political laughing stock of the world." The independent movement was needed to restore black dignity, and each black person who joined it would thereby "announce his political freedom, and in elevating himself . . . elevate his race." Despite Turner's exhortations, the 1898 political revolt had little immediate impact. Dr. David W. Scott, the independent black candidate for Congress from the Twelfth District, who had appeared as a speaker on the program in October with Turner, polled only six hundred votes.[6]

6. *Republic,* October 29, 1898; Grothaus, "Negro in Missouri Politics," 22.

The rebellion did not die, however, and as the 1900 election approached, the Democratic machine in St. Louis renewed its efforts to attract black voters. Notorious ward boss Ed Butler and his son Jim, who was running for Congress, organized black support. They were aided by a new political organization in the city run by Harry B. Hawes, the St. Louis police board commissioner, and known as the Jefferson Club. Through Hawes's efforts, an auxiliary Negro Jefferson Club was formed with Christopher C. Rankin, Crittenden Clark, William H. Fields, and J. Milton Turner as leaders. The Negro Jefferson Club rallied behind Democrat Rolla Wells in the mayoral contest of 1901. Wells was the man who claimed to have helped Turner get the Liberian ministership in 1871. The club had units in twenty-six of the twenty-eight city wards and held a public black Democratic convention for the first time.[7]

Not all Democrats were in favor of soliciting the black vote. Indeed, the urban machines of Kansas City and St. Louis were attacked by a loosely configurated but powerful "Confederate faction" made up largely of rural Democrats who countered the machine overtures by trying to legalize racism. In 1903, as segregation was becoming the law of the land throughout the South, a vigorous effort was launched to establish Jim Crowism in Missouri. Turner was one of a number of blacks who traveled to the state capital to testify against the legal sanction of segregation. The Jim Crow bill was defeated, but only after black urban voters pressured Kansas City and St. Louis machine leaders to oppose the measure.[8]

Turner's role was minor in the 1903 fight against the Jim Crow bill. Perhaps that fact, combined with the vicious manifestations of racism still present in the Democratic party, were the major factors that led him again to switch political allegiances as the 1904 election approached. He must have been disappointed at not being allowed to play a more important role in Democratic party affairs. Perhaps that is why he lied to a *Globe-Democrat* reporter when it was announced that he would deliver a series of speeches on behalf of the Republicans in September 1904. Turner told the reporter that as a Democrat he had traveled all over the United States "as one of the national speakers for that party." He told how "in 1896 and 1900 he accompanied Mr.

7. Grothaus, "Negro in Missouri Politics," 23–25, 27; *Republic*, March 25, 1901; Wells, *Episodes of My Life*, 20–23.
8. Grothaus, "Negro in Missouri Politics," 34.

Bryan on some of his tours, speaking to the negro voters from Bryan's car, and was the only colored man with the party." The next evening Turner addressed a group of Republicans and explained why he had switched his allegiance from the Democratic party. "Efforts to divide the negro vote have taught at least one useful lesson." They have, he continued, shown "how deep rooted and brutal in its quality is the prejudice that actuates and controls the party represented by such human monstrosities as Vardaman, Tillman, Davis and John Sharp Williams." By contrast, he advocated the election of Theodore Roosevelt "because this broad-minded, intellectual giant of true Americanism has inspired and reawakened in the grand old Republican party the memory of its traditions of the past." In spite of Turner's optimism about Roosevelt restoring the grand old party, there is strong evidence to suggest that he had essentially despaired of advantages, either personal or collective, to be gained from black political involvement. Although he lived for eleven years after the 1904 election, there is no indication that he was again involved in any political contest.

The most persuasive argument that Turner had lost much of his faith in the traditional political structure is his turn to black masonry in the 1890s. Even his attachment to the Democratic party had not brought him the power and status that he had known half a lifetime earlier under Radical rule in Missouri. In his impressionable years as an Oberlin student, whites had befriended and encouraged him. White politicians had once courted and then rewarded him with the Liberian appointment, and blacks had cheered his rousing orations. All that was gone now. Alienated from whites and blacks, Turner shifted to an in-between world, made up of people who shared his values and vision: the world of masonry. Turner did not turn to masonry until he had virtually given up on retrieving his lost status in the white community. He left behind no explanations about why he waited until 1890, fifty-one years after his birth, to become a mason. It is clear that, although he did not become a mason until 1890, he had repeated and prolonged contact with masons for thirty years or more. Many of the leaders of the Missouri Equal Rights League with whom he worked during the immediate postwar years were masons. Black masonry was extremely important in Monrovia, Liberia, where Turner lived from 1871 to 1878, but there is no evidence that he became a member. Indeed, in 1879 a committee of St. Louis masons was assigned the task of assessing the status of masonry in Liberia.

Turner had just returned to St. Louis the year before and would certainly have been expected to provide information if he had been a mason or even a friend of masonry. However, his name is not mentioned in the committee's report.[9]

Turner's failure to associate with the masons during the years of the sixties through the eighties corresponds with his optimism during much of that period that he would be accepted into the mainstream of white society. Black masonry was considered inferior by white society, and Turner was very reluctant to be associated with an inferior class. Not, at least, until the frustrations of the late eighties had sufficiently dulled his expectations and caused him to seek status and solace elsewhere.

Prince Hall Freemasonry was the logical place for him to turn. Here was a forum for political activity where he could act out all the roles he had once played in mainstream society. Institutionally, freemasonry accepted and endorsed the same standards of self-reliance that Turner had made part of his value system in antebellum Missouri. He entered the mysterious world of masonry slowly, simply being listed as one of eighty-two members in Widow's Son Lodge of St. Louis in 1890. He did not attend the Annual Communication that year. By 1893, however, he had risen to the level of second-ranking officer in Widow's Son Lodge. In 1894 Turner rose to the leadership of Widow's Son. As its Worshipful Master, he represented his lodge at the Twenty-eighth Annual Communication, held at Moberly, Missouri. He actively participated in the election of officers for the communication, no doubt relishing the opportunity once again to influence votes and persuade people. He also took particular interest in two measures designed to preserve the history of black masonry in Missouri.[10]

According to historian William Muraskin, the masonic sense of history is crucial to an understanding of the organization. By tracing its foundation to Prince Hall, a free black of the eighteenth century, the fraternity "erased from the mind of the black Mason his actual descent from slaves." In the process, it also gave him a new heritage,

9. *St. Louis Globe-Democrat,* September 15, 17, 1904. Among the Equal Rights members who had been active masons since the mid–1860s were Moses Dickson, Henry McGee, Francis Robinson, Charleton Tandy, William R. Lawton, John Wheeler, and Rev. John Turner. *Official Proceedings of the Fourteenth Annual Communication of the Most Worshipful Grand Lodge, A.F. & A.M., 1880,* 15, 27–28, 62, 87. Hereafter referred to as *Official Proceedings.*

10. *Official Proceedings, 1890,* 87; *1893,* 107; *1894,* 10, 37–40, 73, 111.

or, as Muraskin has written, it allowed the black man, as the inheritor of the masonic past, to cease "to be a poor, insignificant member of an oppressed group and . . . become a member of the most important and idealistic institution the world has ever seen!"[11]

On the first day of the 1894 convention an address was delivered by "Bro. W. P. Brooks, one of the oldest Masons in Missouri." Brooks, whom Turner had worked with in the Missouri Equal Rights League during 1865–1866, was the only living member of the original committee appointed for the purpose of founding the Grand Lodge of Missouri. His "impressive and interesting" recounting of the early days of the organization was followed by a resolution offered by Rev. George W. Guy and Turner. The resolution was subsequently adopted by the convention and called for Brooks to furnish a synopsis of the early history of the Grand Lodge of Missouri for publication in the *Official Proceedings*. The resolution also included the unusual honor of Brooks's photo being included in the same edition of the *Proceedings*.

That resolution was followed by another, offered by Joe E. Herriford, G. W. Guy, and J. Milton Turner. It recalled "with pride" the record of Missouri's Most Worshipful Grand Lodge and pointed out the necessity of maintaining a historical record of that proud past. It asked that a committee be formed to collect the proceedings of each of the previous twenty-eight annual communications of the Grand Lodge, bind them, and place them under the care of the Grand Secretary. Turner offered an amendment to the resolution calling for a copy of each of the *Proceedings* to be sent to the Missouri Historical Society in St. Louis and for W. P. Brooks to be a member of the committee formed to carry out that task.[12]

Turner was reelected Worshipful Master of Widow's Son Lodge in 1895 and again represented that lodge at the Annual Communication in Lexington, Missouri. He actively participated in the routine business of the convention and again joined with others to offer a special resolution for consideration by the entire body. This time they proposed "to establish a Masonic Home for indigent Master Masons, their widows and orphans." Although Turner was only one member

11. William Muraskin, *Middle-Class Blacks in a White Society: Prince Hall Freemasonry in America,* 132. My interpretation of Turner's masonic career draws heavily on Muraskin's conceptual framework.

12. *Official Proceedings, 1894,* 33–35; Mrs. E. A. Stadler, Missouri Historical Society archivist, told me in an interview on July 5, 1977, that those records were never made a part of the society's holdings.

of the committee that offered the resolution, he was clearly the force behind the effort to get it approved by the entire communication. Ultimately, the committee's proposal was amended by a six-person committee appointed by the Grand Master. Assigning the task to a committee temporarily stymied it, for the Masonic Home did not come to fruition for another decade.[13]

Turner's advocacy of the Masonic Home was significant. It came at a time when he was disenchanted and disillusioned with white America. If the poor and helpless were going to be cared for, blacks would have to do the caring. This realization influenced him to support the resolutions offered by the Committee on Masonic Relief, of which he was also a member. The committee had the responsibility of approving payments to indigent masons. In short, the Masonic Home and Masonic Relief committees provided masons with the opportunity to be frugal, save their money, and invest in projects that would contribute to the advancement of the race. It was something that they had complete control over, and for which they did not need to be dependent upon whites.[14]

The Thirtieth Annual Communication was held in Jefferson City, Missouri, in 1896, the scene of many of Turner's political triumphs more than a quarter of a century before. He again attended the communication, although he was no longer the Worshipful Master of Widow's Son. The communication was welcomed by Pres. Inman E. Page of Lincoln Institute. On the second day of meetings, Turner, whose status had been enhanced by an appointment to the rank of "Grand Orator," offered another resolution on behalf of a proposed Masonic Home. His resolution suggested that the Grand Lodge secure land "for the purpose of establishng a Masonic Orphan's Home." The resolution was referred to the committee on Masonic Relief. The committee endorsed his proposal, resolving to add a "department . . . to the Masonic Relief work known as the Masonic Home of the Grand Lodge of Missouri." A three-member committee was appointed "to devise ways and means of founding and maintaining said home." As a matter of procedure, however, the proposal had to be submitted for approval to each of the local lodges throughout the state.[15]

13. *Official Proceedings, 1895,* 14–15, 46, 60–61, 117.
14. Ibid., 52–54.
15. *Official Proceedings, 1896,* 7, 25, 42, 45, 66, 99. Although Turner's motion referred to an "Orphan's Home," subsequent discussion revealed his intention was for the home to be for indigent masons and their widows as well.

On the third day of the communication, meetings were temporarily suspended so that the masons could "take a drive to the principal points of interest in the city." Led by Special Grand Marshall
James Milton Turner, the lodge left the hall of the House of Representatives where it was meeting and moved onto the driveway encircling
the capitol where carriages sufficient in number to accommodate the
two hundred and fifty men waited. The caravan proceeded first to
cross "the great new steel bridge [spanning the Missouri River] connecting North Missouri with South Missouri." It continued on to the
state prison, then to Lincoln Institute, then to "other points of interest." The institute was the major attraction. The cortege gathered to
hear speeches in the institute's newly erected forty-thousand-dollar
Memorial Hall, at which point Grand Master Pelham urged "the
Brethen" to send their children "to this great institution of learning."
The tour over and the Grand Lodge back in session, Turner praised
"Lincoln Institute and its management." He called attention to the
institute as "the magnificent gift of the old soldiers and the generous
State of Missouri to the cause of education." Ever constant in his
belief that education was the key to black upward mobility, Turner
included in his resolution the assertion that the institute held "great
promise for the Negroes of the State of Missouri," adding, "We com-
mend it to the hearty support of the Negro Masons of the State."[16]

Turner again represented Widow's Son Lodge at the 1897 Annual Communication. He was on three regular committees that year:
Rules and Order of Business, Jurisprudence, and Grand Master and
Grand Lecturer's Address. One of the first orders of business was the
Grand Master's address, a good portion of which was devoted to an
endorsement of the proposed Masonic Home. The Grand Master
commended his listeners on masonic progress over the past decade,
reporting that their efforts had made it possible for sixty thousand
dollars to be paid to widows and orphans during that period. Such
efforts, however, were insufficient. "If it shall transpire," he said "after all our grand pretensions and phenomenal success, we permit a
Negro Mason to die in destitution or in the alms house of the State we
shall be disgraced." He urged his fellow masons to "take immediate
steps, as far as possible, to provide for the wants of our poor and
destitute Masons." That, he argued, was the real purpose of masonry.

16. Ibid., 41–42.

"As I comprehend its symbols," he said, "*this* is its teaching, and as I believe in its principles *this* is its design."[17]

A motion to refer the Grand Master's address to the Committee on the Grand Master's Address followed with an amendment offered by James Milton Turner. He was so moved by the speech that he called for its submission to the *St. Louis Globe-Democrat* for publication. Later, the committee on the address "heartily" endorsed the Grand Master's suggestion "with reference to the subject of Masonic Relief" and resolved "to entirely adopt the language of his address, and to request the M. W. Grand Lodge to set apart a day for a sermon, to be universally preached throughout this Jurisdiction upon the subject of Masonic Relief and Charity." It went on to recommend that the committee on the Masonic Home be "empowered during the ensuing Masonic year . . . to secure premises for such few indigent Masons, their widows and orphans as may be within the financial power of this M. W. Grand Lodge to care for."[18]

Turner was listed as a member of Widow's Son Lodge again in 1898, although he did not attend the communication that year. He was still a member of the same lodge in 1899, although he again did not attend the annual meeting. In addition, there is no further mention of the proposed Masonic Home in either the 1898 or the 1899 annual communications. Perhaps his work among the Cherokee freedmen and a short-lived farm implement business, begun in St. Louis in 1898, kept him too busy during that time.[19]

Turner's business venture in 1898 was eminently consistent with one of black masonry's major precepts that businesses run by blacks could raise the entire black population's standard of living, thereby helping to solve the race problem. In 1898 Turner listed his occupation as "Manager, Milton Turner Manufacturing Establishment and Attorney for the Cherokee Freedmen." Although the Milton Turner Manufacturing Establishment did not last long, it was an extremely ambitious enterprise. The business was located on Broadway Street in St. Louis. Turner apparently provided the money and the organizational skills necessary to turn an idea by George W. Murray, a black

17. *Official Proceedings, 1897*, 9, 21–23.
18. Ibid., 23, 28–29.
19. *Official Proceedings, 1898*, 11; *1899*, 91; *St. Louis Post-Dispatch*, March 6, 1898.

former member of Congress from Charleston, South Carolina, into a reality.

Murray's idea was to build a "multiplex machine" for farm work, a machine that would do a variety of tasks. It was an implement equipped with an assortment of attachments that purported to allow it to be a rye, oats, barley, or wheat planter, an ordinary drill, a corn planter, a grass mower, a cultivator, a cotton chopper, and, lastly, a potato digger. Interestingly enough, Turner emphasized that he employed only white laborers in his shop and had "half a dozen first-class white mechanics" who worked for him. The business folded the following year, a victim, no doubt, of a vision that promised more than it could deliver.[20]

Masonic records are unavailable for the years 1900 and 1901, so it is impossible to say how quickly Turner returned to active involvement in masonic affairs after his business failure. He did attend the Annual Communication held in 1902, at Cape Girardeau, Missouri. Still a member of Widow's Son in that year, Turner was nominated by J. A. Jordan for the post of Junior Grand Warden, although he curiously and inexplicably asked that he not be considered for the post. Again, there is no mention of the Masonic Home. One of the major topics of interest at this communication was the proposed 1904 World's Fair to be held in St. Louis. Turner was appointed to a special committee, along with six other masons, that was assigned the task of preparing for that event. The committee resolved to send an invitation "to all Ancient Free and Accepted Masons of the World to attend and participate" in a World Congress of masons. The committee acknowledged that the exposition to be held in St. Louis would bring "all the nations of the earth [to] contribute the best products of their minds and hearts—their arts, letters and sciences, as well as their most cogent evidences of progress in political, economic, social and spiritual elements." The committee saw the fair as an opportunity, like none available to blacks before, "in which the Negro may give to all the world the practical proof of his capabilities and possibilities in every relation that may effect his career as a citizen as well as the happiness of those with whom he is to associate as a citizen."[21]

20. *Gould's St. Louis Directory,* 1898, 1682; *St. Louis Post-Dispatch,* March 6, 1898.

21. *Official Proceedings, 1902,* 8, 36–40, 93. Turner's involvement with the effort to establish a convention to demonstrate black abilities presumably was at

The 1902 gathering also witnessed a pathetic display of a search for recognition by Turner that moved the entire convention. Turner, apparently feeling slighted and unappreciated, arose ostentatiously during the middle of the convention and asked permission to bid the members of the Grand Lodge good-bye, "because imperative duties called him away." In taking his leave, he asked that a special record be made of his desire "that Bros. Chinn, Pelham, Ricketts and Kenner [all high-ranking Masons] be selected to pronounce the Masonic Eulogy over his lifeless remains [should] death call him hence before the next session." According to the *Official Proceedings,* Turner then said good-bye, "with an impressiveness that lent solemnity to the scene . . . amid the tearful silence of numbers deeply affected."[22]

Whatever the explanation for his strange farewell, death did not call Turner before the next meeting, and he returned for the Thirty-seventh Annual Communication held in Richmond, Missouri. Whether as a result of his impromptu speech of the year before or not, the 1903 gathering conferred upon him an honor that was reserved for only a select few. For the first time, Turner's photograph appeared in the *Official Proceedings,* the same uncommon honor that he had recommended for William P. Brooks nine years earlier. In addition, Turner resurfaced as an active participant in the routine business of the lodge and also served on several committees.[23]

One of the committees Turner served on was charged with the responsibility of assessing the condition of black people in the country at the time. Its report offers further insight into Turner's view of the status of black people as of 1903. It began by asserting that the conditions confronting black people were "ominous and threatening." It emphasized that the United States was the home of American blacks, recalling Frederick Douglass's statement: "Now that he [the black man] is a free man [he] demands that he be allowed to rest beneath the protecting folds of the stars and stripes." Douglass's statement echoes Turner's adamant opposition nearly thirty years before to Liberian emigration schemes. The committee also emphasized that American blacks had been loyal to their government, recall-

---

the bottom of his letter to Booker T. Washington, whose aid he solicited in preparing for the World's Fair. Turner to Booker T. Washington, incomplete date, 1900, Booker T. Washington Papers, Library of Congress, Washington, D.C.

22. *Official Proceedings, 1902,* 47.

23. *Official Proceedings, 1903,* 8–9, 18, 20–22, 42.

ing how "the pages of history record no more brilliant achievements than Negro men exhibited at Valley Forge; at New Orleans under Gen. Jackson; at Chapultepee under Winfield Scott; at Petersburg and Ft. Wagner; with Dewey in Manila Bay, and with Roosevelt . . . at El Caney, Santiago and San Juan." It noted that black literacy rates had risen considerably between 1880 and 1890 and again by 1900. In keeping with its self-reliance philosophy, the masonic committee singled out Booker T. Washington as an exemplar of industry and virtue, labeled him "great," and identified Tuskegee as "a magnificent testimonial to the capability and genius of the greatest Negro educator of the age." It also paid tribute to the white businessman Andrew Carnegie and identified him as a "grand old philanthropist."[24]

The committee acknowledged that the country had been "wonderfully prosperous" during the previous six years and noted that blacks had clearly contributed to and benefited from that prosperity. Despite the efforts and successes of black people, however, the committee lamented the fact that "the humiliating conditions attempted to be forced upon the Negro have been more accentuated than at any time since the negro was clothed with the panoply of American citizenship." The most appalling example of those "humiliating conditions" cited by the committee was the spread of lynching in the South. The committee called upon high governmental officials to speak out against this "atrocious and indefensible crime" and noted with obvious satisfaction that Pres. Theodore Roosevelt had already done so. That action, it wrote, "once again stamps him as being one of the bravest and most courageous men that ever sat in the Presidential chair."

The committee acknowledged also that not all of the problems afflicting blacks were caused by white racism. In words reminiscent of Turner's comments during the 1879 exodus, the committee noted that the "moral condition" of blacks needed to be "decidedly improved," adding that "it behooves every Negro [who] desires the prevalence of a better condition of affairs, to bend their whole energies to instill in the masses higher ideals and more wholesome surrounds." It registered specific opposition to "destroyers of pure womanhood," white or black, insisting that speedy and certain punishment be meted out to rapists, no matter what their race. The committee's report on

24. "State of the Country," *Official Proceedings*, 1903, 59–61.

the "State of the Country" concluded with an appeal to all American citizens "to rally to the standard of fair play and equal opportunity."[25]

The topic of a Masonic Home was finally revived again at the 1905 Annual Communication, after being ignored for nearly ten years. Turner led discussion on the topic, serving as chairman of the Special Committee on the Masonic Home. His report to the communication argued that masonic charity was one of the fundamental principles upon which the masonic order rested. He believed one of the best ways to demonstrate a firm belief in the importance of "this great human principle" would be to create a fund "for the purchase of a Masonic Home for poor and indigent Master Masons, their widows and orphans." This could be done, he explained, by assessing each mason five cents per month. Turner's proposal was accepted by those present, and the Grand Master and Grand Secretary were given the responsibility of selecting a site for that purpose. A Masonic Home was in operation near Hannibal, Missouri, by the next annual meeting.

Turner's name appeared again on the Widow's Son Lodge roster in 1905. His role at the communication that year, in addition to his chairmanship of the Special Committee, was an active one. The gathering was held in Boonville, the site of one of Turner's early teaching positions nearly forty years before. The meeting opened with a welcoming speech by the Boonville mayor, and Turner was asked to respond. He stated that his long acquaintance with the town's residents made it possible for him to acknowledge "gladly" their "genuine character." He hinted that he would like to become the Most Worshipful Grand Master of the organization when he called attention to the fact that the previous three Grand Masters had been persons who were identified with the educational interests of Boonville. He went on to assure his listeners that "Boonville was the Masonic Mecca, dear to the hearts of all those who aspired to that position," an obvious statement about his own aspirations.[26]

Brother Turner also served as a cochairman of the Committee on Complaints and Grievances in 1905. This committee was an appeals court for masons dissatisfied with the justice handed out to them by local lodges. It also served to help the masons police themselves and enforce the higher moral standards called for by Turner's committee in its "State of the Country" message in 1903. Since image and out-

25. Ibid.
26. *Official Proceedings, 1905,* 10, 48.

ward behavior were important to the masons in their attempt to enforce morality among their members, brushes with the civil authorities were treated harshly. In 1905, for example, Turner's committee sustained a judgment by the William Henry Lodge No. 45 of Platte City, Missouri, expelling William Pearson for criminal conviction by the courts of the state of Missouri. It sustained a similar ruling by True Blue Lodge of St. Louis against Thomas Sanders. It also recommended the indefinite suspension of Dr. William S. Carrion, who was found guilty by Wilkerson Lodge "of shooting with intent to kill . . . J. R. A. Crossland."[27]

Official Proceedings for the years 1906 and 1907 are missing, but the *Proceedings* for 1908 reveal that Turner was again an active participant in masonic affairs when the lodges were called together at Hannibal, Missouri, for the Forty-third Annual Communication. His photograph appeared in the publication of that year along with the following notation: "Bro. Turner is a national character. He has held many responsible positions as representative of his people. He is deservingly popular with the craft for his suave manner and unselfish devotion to the elevation of his fellow man." Appropriately enough, there also appeared in the 1908 *Proceedings* a photograph of the new Masonic Home that Turner had been instrumental in establishing. The home was a going concern by that time. The Grand Master, in his annual address, said, "The purchase of property and the establishment of a home for the old and decrepit members of this Jurisdiction [was] the most creditable thing [we] have ever done." He congratulated those present and offered them an invitation to visit the home, a short distance from where their convention was being held.[28]

Turner participated in other ways as well in 1908. Early in the convention he addressed the entire body, recalling again the importance of masonic history, speaking "eloquently of the sacrifices of the Masonic pioneers with whom he was acquainted." He emphasized to the craft, "We owe to those heroes a debt of gratitude which we should be ever ready to pay." Again, he participated in the election process, seconding Brother Ricketts's nomination to the office of Grand Master. Brother Ricketts, in turn, appointed Turner to serve again as Grand

27. Ibid., 7, 31–32. Turner served on similar committees in 1897 and 1903. See *Official Proceedings, 1897,* 37; *1903,* 18.
28. *Official Proceedings, 1908,* 18–19, 24–25, 124–25.

Marshall in the Public Parade. In addition to those activities, Turner also served again on the Committee on Complaints and Grievances.[29]

Turner appears to have become quite inactive after that 1908 meeting, although the evidence is inconclusive. *Official Proceedings* for the period 1909 through 1915 are not available, except for 1910. The record of the annual gathering in that year includes Turner's name as a member of Phoenix Lodge No. 78 in St. Louis. He did not, however, attend the annual meeting. Turner's will, written only a few weeks before his death on November 1, 1915, suggests that he had ceased masonic activities several years prior to 1915.[30]

One can only speculate about why Turner's masonic career ended so abruptly. Perhaps he had been hopeful of rising to the leadership of the Missouri masons, as his speech of 1905 suggests, and simply gave up on that hope by 1910. If that was the case, even the position of Grand Marshall, the honor of having his photograph published in the *Official Proceedings,* and whatever plaudits that could have been offered him, would have been disappointing. Perhaps status in a segregated organization was no longer desirable to him. His repeated failure during this period to win the battles he waged against the commissioner of Indian affairs might have soured him on a number of things, including masonry. Certainly his health was poor during the last five years of his life.

Whatever the reason for his withdrawal, Turner obviously became less involved in masonic activities. After his death from an accident in Oklahoma in 1915 the *Official Proceedings* included a brief obituary of Turner, noting that he was a member of Phoenix Lodge. Significantly, it spoke of Turner as a hero out of the somewhat distant past, identifying him as "for many years Grand Marshal of the Grand Lodge." His name had been a household word among blacks in the early eighties, it said, implying that he had been much less known, if not forgotten, after that. The obituary concluded by noting that he was "as an orator . . . gifted as a few men this race and country have ever known."[31]

Turner's name appeared in the *Official Proceedings* for the last

29. Ibid., 10, 23, 38, 40, 55–56, 59–60.
30. *Official Proceedings, 1910,* 177; Will of J. Milton Turner, Will No. 45591, St. Louis Probate Court, Civil Court Building, St. Louis, Missouri.
31. *Official Proceedings, 1916,* 18; *St. Louis Argus,* November 5, 12, 16, 19, 1915; December 5, 10, 1915.

time in 1917. George L. Vaughn, Grand Attorney for the Most Worshipful Grand Lodge of Missouri, reported that the lodge had become a litigant in the disposition of Turner's estate. His will had been contested by "persons alleging themselves to be his heirs." Turner had willed one thousand dollars to the Masonic Home at Hannibal, contingent upon his estate being worth twenty-five thousand dollars or more.[32]

A controversy over the division of Turner's estate offers insight into the turbulence of the once powerful black leader's personal life in his late years and suggests that the frustration he felt politically and socially affected his relationship with his family. The fight began in February 1916 when his will was filed in St. Louis Probate Court. Turner had left most of his material wealth to the daughter and grandchildren of his first wife. Ella Brooks Turner, who was not listed as one of Turner's beneficiaries, contested the will, claiming to be his wife. Her challenge to the will sent the case into circuit court.[33]

Pretrial depositions and trial testimony revealed that Turner lived with Ella Brooks after the death of his first wife in 1907, and that the two of them lived as husband and wife from late 1909 until just before Turner's last trip to Oklahoma. According to Estelle Montgomery, Turner's secretary, and William H. Hollam, Turner tried to get his "wife" to sign a document that would have allowed him to borrow money "from some man in Texas." Mrs. Brooks refused, greatly angering Turner. He left for Oklahoma soon after, trying to collect money from his Choctaw freedmen clients. Turner's annoyance with Mrs. Brooks's refusal to sign the deed seems to have been the major reason he failed to include her in his will. Even prior to that disagreement, however, theirs had not been the happiest of relationships. Despite the fact that Turner occasionally referred to Mrs. Brooks as Mrs. Turner, the elderly woman told the secretary to refer to her as Mrs. Brooks, "to keep the peace." John J. Jones, who testified that he knew J. Milton Turner for twenty-eight years, said that Turner "treated Mrs. Brooks just as though he owned her." Jacob Fishman, a peddlar from whom Turner often bought clothes, indicated that Turner and Brooks fought a lot.[34]

In addition to the friction between Turner and Mrs. Brooks, there

32. *Official Proceedings, 1917*, 60–61.
33. Will of J. Milton Turner, Will No. 45591, St. Louis Probate Court, Civil Court Building, St. Louis, Missouri, Case No. 2884B; see also, Appeals Court Case No. 15958, Missouri State Archives, Jefferson City, Missouri.
34. Testimony of Estelle Montgomery, John J. Jones, Jacob Fishman, and William H. Hollam, Case No. 2884B.

is also at least a hint of similar disquietude in Turner's relationship with his first wife and her daughter and grandchildren. Once, in 1896, Turner's stepdaughter and he came to blows in a dispute that lends itself to symbolic, albeit speculative, interpretation. One night in April of that year Turner came home not only quite late but evidently quite intoxicated. His wife, who asserted it her "custom for years to spread his meals in his room, no matter what time he came home at 1, 2, or even 3 o'clock in the morning," proceeded to prepare his dinner. Turner, meanwhile, went up to his room, making a good deal of noise in the process. At that point, his stepdaughter, whose four children were asleep in the house, asked Turner to be quiet. He swore at her, told her to mind her own business, and finally demanded that she leave his house with her children. She refused, saying that it was much too late at night. A physical confrontation ensued, resulting in Turner's being struck with a pitcher and rendered unconscious. Later, while recovering from a fractured skull in a hospital, he "loudly bewailed the girl's ingratitude," saying "her husband will not work . . . and I support the whole family, including four little girls."[35]

In many ways, in fact, that incident, apocryphal though it might be, sums up much of Turner's later life. He felt unappreciated and ignored, convinced that he could have accomplished much more save for the barriers of white racism and the provincialism of the black masses. Late in life he retreated to the more comfortable world of black masonry, which, in a sense, institutionalized the alienation that he felt. Although the masons hoped that their brotherhood would eventually uplift the race, moving blacks into the mainstream American culture, the masons' very existence confirmed blacks' marginal status. Even though Turner left little direct evidence about his thoughts during the last years of his life, the indirect data suggest he had come to understand this no-win situation, and the frustration of that realization adversely affected his personal life.

35. Ibid.; *New York Times*, April 15, 1896.

EPILOGUE
Legacy and Tragedy

He was a man of great ability and rendered fine service to his country and race.

—Congressman Leonidas L. Dyer
Eulogy of James Milton Turner
November 15, 1915

James Milton Turner was in Ardmore, Oklahoma, in the fall of 1915, still trying to collect fees due him from his Choctaw and Chickasaw freedmen clients. His trips to Oklahoma had been more infrequent during the last five years of his life. The closing of the freedmen rolls gave him less cause to return than before, and his declining health made travel exceedingly difficult.[1]

On September 27, 1915, Turner was standing in the vicinity of a railroad tank car in Ardmore when it exploded. Debris from the explosion struck his right hand. The wound bled profusely, but it appeared not to be serious. That wound never healed, and Turner became progressively sicker and weaker as he developed blood poisoning. He died on November 1, 1915. Although he had been out of the public eye for some years, throngs of blacks turned out to mourn him as a memory and a symbol.[2]

His funeral proved to be one of the largest ever held for a black person in St. Louis. The masons came out in force, causing many to comment "upon the magnificent and beautiful manner in which the order conducted his services." Several weeks later, a "Citizens' Me-

1. Testimony of J. W. McClelland, Turner's personal physician the last five years of his life, Case No. 2884B.
2. *New York Times* and *Daily Ardmorite*, November 2, 1915; *Washington Bee*, November 15, 1915.

morial" was held to honor the dead hero. Turner would have relished the occasion. At long last, those who had ignored him had come to pay their respects. There were two hundred honorary vice-presidents of the memorial, a list that read like the "who's who" of prominent Missouri blacks. One of the people present was Leonidas C. Dyer, a white United States congressman from St. Louis. Congressman Dyer eulogized Turner as "a man of great ability [who] rendered fine service to his country and race." The dead orator would, no doubt, have agreed. He would have also concurred with the assessment of his life offered by an anonymous editor who proclaimed that "J. Milton Turner was a leader who moved among the masses—none being too lowly; who marched with intellectuals—none being his superior." Several years later, prominent black leader Charleton H. Tandy, who had known Turner since the two of them were teenagers together in St. Louis in the 1850s, and who had often been his foe, told a judge trying to decide the disposition of Turner's estate that the latter had been "one of the foremost leading negroes in the State of Missouri." Those postmortem accolades notwithstanding, James Milton Turner died a tired, lonely, dejected, disappointed man. And yet, in the seventy-five years of his life, he accomplished many things that fundamentally changed the lives of subsequent generations of Missourians, and of Americans generally.[3]

He established schools for blacks all over the state of Missouri and was responsible for gaining state support for Lincoln Institute. That school became a college in 1887 and a university in 1921. For two generations after Turner's death, Lincoln University was the only public institution of higher education in Missouri that blacks could attend.

Turner wielded political power in the border state of Missouri that has been, arguably, unrivaled by a black person since. Certainly no other black leader of the nineteenth century was courted by politicians as he was. And no twentieth-century black political leader in Missouri has been able to coalesce the black vote in the state better than he did more than a century ago.

Turner became America's first black minister to Liberia, and the second black person in the history of the country to become a foreign

3. *Kansas City Sun*, November 15, 1915; Moore, "James Milton Turner, Diplomat, Educator, and Defender of Rights, 1840–1915," 201; Testimony of Charleton H. Tandy, Case No. 2884B.

diplomat. As such, he was and is a role model for African-Americans who desire a professional career. He is a role model, too, as an orator of great power and renown. From the time he emerged on the political scene in the mid–1860s until his death, he was recognized by both blacks and whites as an uncommonly gifted speaker. In September 1890, the *Indianapolis Freeman* polled its seven thousand readers in an effort to identify "the Ten Greatest Negroes" in American history. When the poll was completed, there, beside Frederick Douglass, T. Thomas Fortune, Toussaint L'Overture, and Peter Clark, was James Milton Turner, "Orator." The *Freeman* editor summarized Turner's abilities:

> Every settlement has its "best talker" and "brilliant speakers" nowadays as thick as leaves in Valombrosia, but this man with a halt in his gait and a most un-reassuring countenance, plays havoc with your tenderer feelings at will, by the witchery of his tongue and the lulling mellifluousness of his diction. . . . As an orator . . . his equal belongs not in the Negro race to-day.[4]

During the 1879 exodus, long before there were discussions about "welfare" or "workfare" or "learnfare," Turner talked about the need not only to help the victims of racism to satisfy their basic human needs but also to provide them with the opportunity and skills necessary to help themselves. Turner's efforts on behalf of the Cherokee freedmen secured monetary settlements for thousands of blacks who would otherwise have been ignored by the Cherokee Nation. When one considers that he accomplished this as a self-taught lawyer, the feat seems all the more extraordinary. Indeed, although Turner's educational training was good for a mid-nineteenth-century African-American, it is clear, in retrospect, that his formal education was minimal and that much of what he learned, he taught himself. In that regard, he truly was a self-made man.

Turner's racial pride is also a positive legacy. At a time when little was known about the historical contributions of blacks, and even less was being done in a systematic way to publicize those contributions, he tried to ensure that future generations would be proud of their black forebears. His support of black masonic relief efforts, and par-

4. Ebenezer Basset was the first black diplomat. Benjamin Quarles, *Frederick Douglass,* 321. *Freeman,* September 20, 1890.

ticularly the Masonic Home, resulted in countless black Missourians being cared for at a time when there was nowhere else for them to turn.

Turner also left us a sobering legacy. His life reminds us that believing in the promise of America, and preparing oneself to be a beneficiary of that promise, is not enough. He taught us that hope encouraged, then deferred, eventually becomes hope betrayed. He taught us how wasteful it is when a country, by word, encourages all people to move into the mainstream of its society and then, by deed, places obstacles into the path of that movement. He taught us that one can pay a high personal price for possessing a finely tuned sense of social responsibility.

The wonder is not that he eventually succumbed to frustration and despair—that he became manipulative and opportunistic. The wonder is that he, born a slave in a racist society, believed so deeply for so long. James Milton Turner seemed to believe that America was more than the sum of its parts, that Americans as a people were better than Americans as individuals. He believed that the role of government was to inspire and even force people to adhere to and abide by a higher law—the law that was implicit in a literal interpretation of the Declaration of Independence. Turner was, oddly enough, more American in his hopes—in his outlook and vision—than the white racists who opposed him. He constantly appealed to the American government, even as his white opponents sought to subvert it.

Turner's perception of what freedom for African-Americans meant was a far cry from that of whites. He believed that intelligence and accomplishment on the part of blacks would soften, even eliminate, white hostility. The advancement of African-Americans as a group would follow apace the progress of the elites of the race, such as himself. The flaw in Turner's reasoning, of course, was that he misunderstood the intransigence of white American racism. There was no place of equality in late nineteenth-century American society for a black man, no matter how intelligent or accomplished.

But if Turner misunderstood white America, just as assuredly he failed to understand the folk culture of the black masses. He was at his best in the early postwar days when, as a spokesman for former slaves, he could articulate in general terms their hopes for civil and political rights. Arrayed against the white power structure in the early days of Reconstruction, he was both eloquent and formidable in his advocacy of black causes. His power diminished, however, the more specific the discussions became. Just what should black people learn and who should teach them? Who should vote and who should hold office? Who should decide who held what job? How exactly should black people live? Turner's answers to those questions differed markedly from the answers of the black masses. He ceased to be a leader, except in the minds of a few whites and elite blacks, as lower class blacks began to understand what he stood for. Clearly, he had no constituency after the 1870s, and he had no organic relationship with the black masses through which to reestablish one.

Turner's class biases separated him from most African-Americans just as the whites' racism separated them from him. One suspects, for example, that he never fully understood the former slaves' passion to own land or their perception that freedom would make them landowners. As historian Leon Litwack has written, "To apportion the large landed estates among those who worked them and who had already expended years of uncompensated toil made such eminent sense to the ex-slave that he could not easily dismiss this aspiration as but another 'exaggerated' or 'absurd' view of freedom. . . . The expectation of 'forty acres and a mule' may have been sheer delusion, but the freedmen had sufficient reason to think otherwise."[5]

Although he seems never to have addressed the issue publicly, and here is where the absence of private papers is especially frustrating, one assumes that Turner would have been intensely opposed to the confiscation of slaveowners' land and the distribution of it to freedmen. He was too much of a capitalist to endorse such an idea. When he addressed the land issue at all, it was to encourage blacks to be farm laborers and, through thrift and industry, save their money to buy land. When blacks were unable to do so, he tended to blame their thriftlessness and improvidence as much as he blamed the discriminatory practices of the white landowners. His constant exhortations to hard work and frugality fell on the unreceptive ears of African-Americans who had heard white folks preach the same message all of their lives. James Milton Turner, they must have thought, was just another person who wanted to change them.

Some historians have criticized Turner and others like him for allowing themselves to be co-opted as leaders by white society. This school of thought criticizes the elite African-American leaders of the postwar period as "assimilated blacks," who are to be condemned for

5. Litwack, *Been in the Storm So Long,* 401.

their own assimilation and for their propensity to ask "unschooled Blacks to change their way of life." This position fails, however, to appreciate the fact that it was the very different socialization process experienced by middle-class black leaders that caused them to seek assimilation, to fight white racism in the particular way that they fought it, and, quite often, to find that their education alienated them from the masses and neutralized them as effective leaders. They were as much victims as they were oppressors.[6]

Rather than summarily condemning Turner and others like him, an effort should be made to understand them. An understanding of their plight will provide greater appreciation for the complexity of immediate post–Civil War black life. Turner saw white racism as clearly as anyone else alive during his lifetime. He believed implicitly, however, in the nineteenth century's "idea of progress" that education moved human beings steadily and inevitably toward greater achievement and understanding, even hostile, white, racist human beings. In 1870, writing to F. A. Seely of the Freedmen's Bureau of his efforts to establish schools for blacks in the face of white opposition, Turner could suggest as a solution only "the daily spread of more enlightened ideas as a permeating ingredient of an advanced civilization." Nowhere, of course, was the promise of that happening greater than in republican America. Ultimately, that promise failed Turner and African-Americans. He was neutralized as a spokesman for freedmen at precisely the time that they needed him most. Therein lies the great tragedy of James Milton Turner and a host of other black leaders of the post–Civil War generation.[7]

6. One of the harshest critics of Turner and other "assimilationists" is Painter, *Exodusters,* 14–16, 226–27.

7. Turner to Seely, February 28, 1870, "Freedmen's Bureau Records." Howard Rabinowitz, in a biographical essay on Holland Thompson of Alabama, writes, "A surprising number of black Reconstruction leaders throughout the South, whether because of death, disillusionment, poor health, emigration, or other interests, ended their political careers prematurely, depriving other blacks of much needed leadership" (Rabinowitz, ed., *Southern Black Leaders of the Reconstruction Era,* 269).

APPENDIX A
St. Louis Post-Dispatch *Interview (1911)*

This account of James Milton Turner's life, written in 1911 and carried as a Sunday feature in the *St. Louis Post-Dispatch,* is the only detailed autobiographical statement extant. It is, however, problematic. First of all, interviews such as this one were often embellished by journalists of the era who wanted to increase Sunday paper circulation. Secondly, this interview was done late in Turner's life, at a time when he felt insufficiently rewarded for his public service and, therefore, sought to compensate by exaggerating. It is for that reason as much a statement of what he *wished* his life had been as it is a statement of what his life was really like. There is a touch of truth in much of what Turner told a reporter in this interview, although he expanded the narrative in such a way as to enhance his own reputation. Some of what he said is patently false; probably the truth of the bulk of what he said cannot be corroborated.

SAINT LOUIS EX-SLAVE, ONCE SOLD
FOR $50, EARNS $1,000,000 FEE

Wrapped in meditation, a patriarchal black man may often be seen sitting on the south steps of the St. Louis Courthouse. When asked the reason of his preoccupation, he will reply: "On these steps I was sold as a slave for fifty dollars, 67 years ago." By one of the fairy tales of emancipation, this $50 helot arose to be a Minister of the United States, with the rank of Brigadier-General in the army and of Commodore in the navy. He became the friend of King Edward VII, of Bismarck and of Emperor William of Germany and one of the imperial carriages was placed at his disposal in Berlin. Through his remarkable ability he and his legal partners today stand to win a million dollar fee in Indian land cases. His rise, as his beginnings were lowly, may be compared with that of Benjamin Franklin, as related in his autobiography. It is a romance of "Up From Slavery."[1]

1. Turner's position as minister to Liberia carried no military rank, and

James Milton Turner was born 71 years ago on a plantation near the St. Charles road, in St. Louis County, 12 miles west of St. Louis. His father claimed descent from a Moorish prince and his mother was derived from the Vey tribe in Africa, which is said to have invented a system of writing and elaborated a grammar. His father was a nephew of Nat Turner, leader of the slave insurrection in Virginia in 1831, and, although he had no part in the conspiracy, would have lost his life but for the devotion of his young master, Benjamin Tillman. For the sake of his slave, Tillman obtained his share of the family estate, hastily converted it into movables and emigrated to St. Louis. In defiance of the law, Tillman had taught his servant to be a veterinary surgeon. They set up a partnership in Carondelet.[2]

Reverses coming, Turner was sold to Frederick Colburn, and continued in the business for himself. For 25 years he paid $9 a month to Mrs. Colburn for control of his own time—a system of semi-freedom which was then practiced. As "Black John, the horse doctor," he was familiarly known by Ulysses S. Grant, then an obscure peddler of cordwood; Frank P. Blair, Dr. Joseph Nash McDowell, the late William J. Lemp, the elder Wainwright and the elder Anheuser.

His wife had been a wedding present to the bride of the Rev. Aaron Young of Kentucky, and later of St. Louis County. Having purchased his own freedom, Turner was anxious to liberate his wife, but the price set upon her, $3,000, was beyond his means. It happened that she broke a bone in one of her wrists. Dr. Tiffen, a free soiler, said to Turner: "I will report to your wife's owners that her hand must be amputated. This will depreciate her value, and you can buy her." The plot was successfully carried out, and the negro bought his wife for $400, on the Courthouse steps. James Milton, being then 4 years old, was thrown in for an extra $50. He declares that his mother was willing to suffer the loss of her hand had it become necessary to free herself and her child.

The fear of being sold South then possessed all slaves in the border states, and as the commercial value of negroes in St. Louis was much less than their value on the cotton plantations, their owners

---

there is no evidence that he even met the dignitaries mentioned here, much less became friends with them.

2. In 1932, Turner's stepdaughter, Lillie B. Mason of Fulton, Missouri, categorically denied that her stepfather was related to Nat Turner. Irving Dilliard, "James Milton Turner: A Little Known Benefactor of His People," 373.

were often tempted to sell them, although the sale meant a breaking up of families. Turner relates that his father always attended the big slave auctions in St. Louis on the first of January, and sometimes prevented a wife's being torn from her husband and children by purchasing her with his own money.

The boy's education was the anxiety of his parents. A tallow candle school, instituted secretly for negroes, was broken up by the police. At the Old Cathedral on Walnut street, a band of nuns, in open opposition to the law, conducted a school for the children of slaves. Here the boy attended three years.

While working as an office boy at $6 a month for Dr. McDowell, Robert H. Whitelaw and others, young Turner satisfied his passion for learning by studying their books secretly, with a watchful ear cocked for the footsteps of those who might detect him and denounce him to the authorities. When he grew older his father sent him for three years to Oberlin College, in Ohio, where he became acquainted with John Brown. On his return he was that prodigy in a slave state, an educated negro.

On the outbreak of the Civil War, the youth attended Col. Madison Miller of St. Louis as his body servant, as he had formerly been his employee in a railroad office. He was at the battle of Wilson's Creek and saw the death of General Nathaniel Lyon.

After the battle of Shiloh, Turner found that he had had his fill of war and came to St. Louis, conveying $4,000 which belonged to Col. Miller, who, he thought, had been killed. The negro delivered the money to Mrs. Miller, sister of the late Gov. Thomas C. Fletcher of Missouri. Miller returned to St. Louis some weeks later, on parole from Libby Prison, believing that he did not possess a cent in the world. He was so overjoyed to find his money awaiting him that he gave Turner $500.

The latter devoted himself to "running off" slaves to the North. Often, at night, he tied a skiff containing a fugitive slave to the stern of a steamboat and was towed to the Illinois shore. There the slave would be entrusted to the Rev. John Anderson of Brooklyn, Ill.

In 1866 Turner went to Jefferson City and by his own efforts helped obtain the passage of a law establishing the present system of negro schools in Missouri. He himself opened the first colored school in the state, at Kansas City. Almost the only negro with education in the entire state, he was appointed Second Assistant Superintendent of State Schools, with the duty of establishing negro schools all over

Missouri. As an assistant in the work, he obtained a salary of $225 a month and traveling expenses from Gen. O. O. Howard, head of the Freedman's Bureau in Washington.

The great difficulty was the lack of instructors. White teachers, imported from the Northern states, found their condition intolerable because of the contempt in which they were held by their white neighbors. Turner saw that it was necessary to provide training for negro teachers.

How he helped raise the first money for this end is an engaging story. A negro regiment, composed mainly of Missourians, was stationed in Arkansas. On their pay day, Turner appeared before them and delivered a speech instead of the customary religious exercises, it being Sunday. At the close of his appeal, the soldiers within a few minutes contributed $5,000. The money was delivered to R. B. Foster, Captain of the regiment, and with it he purchased the present site, at Jefferson City, of the Lincoln Institute, the state normal school for negroes.[3]

Turner then went before the Legislature and asked that the proposed school be made a State Institution. A resolution was passed to the effect that as soon as the promoters of the college raised $15,000, the State would contribute $15,000 more for buildings and appropriate $15,000 annually for its maintenance.

With Capt. Foster, Turner went East to solicit the money. In Pittsburg, he was introduced to William Thaw, father of Harry Thaw. After listening to the negro's plea, Thaw gave him a check for $1,000, and his sister, who was present gave him $500 more. Capt. Foster obtained the rest of the required $15,000 in Massachusetts, and successive Missouri Legislatures, Democratic as well as Republican, have made generous annual appropriations for the support of Lincoln Institute.

Turner likes to recall that the very first sum, $20, towards the establishment of Lincoln Institute, was contributed by the Rev. Samuel A. Love, now advanced in age, but for many years prominent

3. There is no evidence that Turner was involved, as he claimed, in the *establishment* of Lincoln Institute. Likewise, Turner was the third, not the first, teacher in Kansas City's black school. His salary as a Freedmen's Bureau agent was one hundred dollars. There is no record of his being paid by the State Department of Education. All the existing evidence weighs against Turner having had any contact with the black soldiers of the Sixty-second and Sixty-fifth Colored Infantries. Kremer, "Biography of James Milton Turner," 57–59.

among negro Baptists in Missouri. Love was Major of the Eleventh Volunteer United States Infantry, composed of negro troops.

Turner's position as State Superintendent of negro schools was turned by him to political advantage in 1870, the first year in which negroes voted in Missouri. The State Republican convention, which met in Jefferson City, had 220 black delegates, who knew just enough to vote solidly as Turner in that the negro leader held the balance of power in the convention "The Republicans learned a lesson that week," says he. "They haven't allowed the negroes 220 delegates since."[4]

Carl Schurz, United State Senator from Missouri, endeavored to put through a plank for the re-enfranchisement of ex-Confederates. Although approving for the measure, Turner found minor phrases of the bill which alarmed him and he threw the solid phalanx of the negro delegation against Schurz, who was therefore defeated again and again. Such pressure was placed upon Turner that he telegraphed President Grant for instructions. The reply came: "You don't seem to know that I hear every speech in the convention by means of a wire on my desk. You are right. Who cares for Carl Schurz? Stand pat. U. S. Grant"

That dispatch, read by Turner on the floor of the convention, split the Republican party in Missouri wide open. B. Gratz Brown was elected Governor. Schurz failed of renomination for Senator and the honor went to Frank P. Blair, who was afterwards elected. Brown, who was editor of the *St. Louis Democrat,* was wounded at Selma in the last duel in Missouri in which blood was shed. His opponent was Thomas J. Reynolds, afterwards Acting Governor of Missouri.[5]

Turner's defeat of Schurz won him an appointment by President Grant as United States Minister to Liberia. After the appointment had been made, Grant discovered, to his astonishment, that Turner was "that black boy, Jim, who brought me the famous whisky at Shiloh."

In fact, when President Lincoln inquired what brand of whisky Grant drank, so that he might give some of it to the rest of the Union

4. There were 180 delegates, not 220.
5. It is doubtful that Turner ever received such a telegram, much less read it on the floor of the convention. However, Col. C. Q. Ford, United States Internal Revenue Collector of the St. Louis district, did present a message to the convention from President Grant that was similar in spirit to the one reported by Turner. Kremer, "Biography of James Milton Turner," 82.

generals, he could have learned the secret from Turner. While the negro was a boy, Grant, after selling a load of wood before the Planter's Hotel, often went to the home of "John Turner, the horse doctor."

Grant's brand was sold by a Frenchman, named Bertrand, who kept a shop at Second and Valentine streets. Thither the boy would be sent to buy a "Long Picayune's" worth of whisky. This coin was 6¼ cents, and it bought a quart of the beverage. Grant, according to Turner, abhorred the new-fangled method of coloring whisky brown, and always insisted upon having his white, like moonshine. Before he started on the errand, Turner relates, Grant would usually call to him: "Remember, now, and get it white."

While Minister at Monrovia, Turner frequently had to obtain the intervention of United States warships and marines to protect the black republic from the inroads of savage tribes. As a Commodore in the navy, a rank which his position carried with it, he was from time to time the superior officer of "Fighting Bob" Evans, Rear Admiral Sampson and Admiral Schley, who were then all young officers.

Turner relates a story of a picturesque African prince, named Seyton, whose father was chief of a large tribe, with 40,000 warriors, on the border of Liberia. Seyton was sent to Oxford and then studied military tactics with the German army. On his return he smuggled in many rifles and assiduously drilled his army after the German fashion. When the time was ripe, he seized Cape Palmas County, a Liberian territory.

The Liberian army of 4,000 men was dispatched to expel him. Forming an ambuscade with great skill after the best Prussian tactics, Seyton captured the whole Liberian army, bag and baggage.

"The President appealed to me," relates Turner, "to go get his army. I had to wire to Madeira, thence to Lisbon, thence to London and thence to Washington for permission to intervene. In 30 days Commander Schley, with several ships, came sailing into the harbor from Lisbon.

"I went out with some marines, under Midshipman Winslow, later distinguished in the Spanish American War, to see the chief of the tribe. He was every inch a king, in stature and bearing.

"You your King's little boy—humph?" He asked me. Yes, said I. "Then why no your king come to me hisself?" thundered the chief. "Why send little boy?" I explained that it wasn't convenient just then for the President of the United States to join him in a conference, and added that unless he turned the Liberian army loose I would hang him and Seyton too.

There could have been a terrific battle in a minute, but I instructed Schley to fire several broadsides from the fleet. At the same time I told Winslow to turn loose a Gatling gun upon the forest. The effect was tremendous. The land shook and the roar of the guns and 400 bullets a minute from the Gatling gun tore trees to shreds. The chief leaped straight in the air and shouted: "Your King big man—whoo-ee! Me fight such big man? No!"

Soon afterwards the Liberian army was once more free and marching back to the capital. When President Grant gave Turner his credentials, he said: "I shall hold you just as responsible as I do the Ambassador at the Court of St. James." The negro took the hint, and by assiduous reading made himself an authority on international law, so much so that he was once chairman of a committee of arbitration to settle a dispute between England and Spain as to the boundaries of Sierra Leone and Liberia.

He made several trips to Europe while Minister, and at Berlin was presented to Bismarck, Kaiser Wilhelm, then Crown Prince, and his father, the Emperor. Said the Emperor to the slave: "Welcome to Germany!" "I'm very glad to see you," roared Bismarck, the man of blood and iron, in his thunderous voice. The Crown Prince, now the Emperor, was more loquacious. He inquired particularly as to the condition of the negroes in the United States and paid Turner the compliment of expressing astonishment at his career.

In England Turner was presented to the late King Edward VII, who had not then succeeded to the throne, and was entertained at Windsor Castle.

In the first year of President Hayes' administration Turner was recalled at his own request as he could no longer withstand the deadly climate of Liberia. He had been the first negro to be appointed a Minister of the United States accredited to a foreign government.[6]

He was instrumental in obtaining for freedmen of the Cherokee na-

6. Turner's 1911 account of his Liberian career is greatly exaggerated. There is no evidence in the dispatches that Turner sent to the State Department or in the instructions that the department sent to him that a European trip was ever made. His 1911 version of the Grebo War totally contradicts his dispatches written in 1875 and 1876. Turner did not, for example, accompany Captain Semmes to Cape Palmas, and the peace agreement was reached with only a show of force that did not include any violence or even the firing of weapons. Kremer, "A Biography of James Milton Turner," 159–61. Turner was the second black man to hold such a ministerial position.

tion about 1,400,000 acres of land and approximately $1,400,000. He is now interested with Judge Laughlin and Robert H. Kern of St. Louis in a suit favorably decided Feb. 20, 1911, by the United States Court of Claims, establishing the title to oil lands in Oklahoma valued at between $10,000,000 and $12,000,000. He is also prosecuting claims for negroes formerly the slaves of the Choctaw and Chickasaw tribes, in which he has already won for them 100,000 acres of land. Associated with him in these last cases are ex-Probate Judge Thomas B. Crews and Harry J. Cantwell of St. Louis. Should they be successful, it is predicted that they will divide among them as fees a round million of dollars.[7]

Under the administration of President Cleveland, Turner won the last suit in these Indian cases, involving a property of $75,000. For this service Congress voted $15,000 to the negro. The sum was paid to him by Gen. John W. Noble of St. Louis, then Secretary of the Interior under President Harrison, and through Judge George H. Shields, also of St. Louis, who was at that time Judge Advocate of the Interior Department. For the last 30 years he has acted as the Washington representative of the Five Civilized Tribes of Indians in Oklahoma.

"The suits in which Turner is interested," says Attorney Cantwell, "all turn on the recognition of the Indian-negro descendants of the Five Civilized nations as legal members of the tribes, with full property rights."

In the Cherokee Nation, 2,600 names of persons of mixed negro and Indian blood, which were striken from the rolls by the Department of the Interior, have been ordered restored by the United States Court of Claims. The Government has appealed to the Supreme Court, which is certain to affirm the decision of the lower court.

"In this case property amounting to from $10,000,000 to $12,000,000 is involved. The legal fees in which Turner will share will be approximately $1,000,000.

"Another sum, possibly as large, may come to him through the Choctaw-Chickasaw cases. Bills are now pending in Congress for the reopening of the rolls, so as to admit the names of about 5,000 persons of Indian and negro descent who are now excluded from tribal rights. It is probable that the bills will be acted upon next autumn: and if the legislation is favorable, about 10,000 cases will be filed. In

---

7. Turner grossly exaggerated both what he had accomplished and the compensation he received for his efforts.

all, property worth approximately $10,000,000 is concerned in the Choctaw-Chickasaw case."

Despite his acquaintances with many of the illustrious men of the world and his own remarkable career, Turner has remained as modest and unassuming as when he ran chores for [General] Grant. In all the negotiations which he has conducted with the various departments of [our] Government, he has permitted his white colleagues to take the prominent roles, while he was content to suppress himself in the background until summoned to come forward.

J. MILTON TURNER'S STORY OF HOW HE CARRIED WHISKY TO GEN. GRANT AT SHILOH.

Here is the story of the whisky consumed at the battle of Shiloh by Gen. Grant as revealed by J. Milton Turner, the negro who served the historic beverage to the Federal chieftain. Newspaper reports concerning Grant's alleged intoxication upon the field of battle provoked him into a determination to resign from the army, and he would have done so, he admits in his memoirs, but for the entreaties of Gen. Sherman.

"I was body servant to the Colonel of a Missouri regiment," Turner related, "and on the morning of the battle of Shiloh fled across country eight miles to escape the confederates. Once I lay in the muddy water of a creek, submerged to my chin, and thanked Heaven I was black. Had I been white I should certainly have been seen.

"When I got near the river, the commander of a battery of artillery told me to go to the wharf and see whether Gen. Grant had arrived. He had just come, and I showed him the way to the battery. You should have been here two hours ago, the commander shouted to Gen Grant." He replied slowly: "I was fixing things for Sherman to turn the flank of the rebel charge. Have you got anything to drink?" "The artillery man told me to go to his tent and fill three quart bottles with white whisky from the barrel. When I returned Gen. Grant poured a pint of the liquid into a big cup and drank it at one draft."

"Several newspaper correspondents were with Gen. Grant, and I saw them busily taking notes. One was Joseph B. McCullough, afterwards editor of the *St. Louis Globe-Democrat.* I heard one of the correspondents say to him: "'Give Grant h__l in your paper, Joe.'"

"General Grant wanted me to carry whisky for him whenever he wanted it from the river to the front, but I was too frightened by the grape-shot. Finally, he had one of his orderlies do it for him. Although Gen. Grant drank quantities of whisky, it did not seem to affect him in the least. To my knowledge, he was perfectly sober at the battle of Shiloh."

HOW JESSE JAMES HELPED J. MILTON TURNER MAINTAIN HIS SCHOOL.

The first negro school in Missouri was founded in Kansas City by J. Milton Turner in 1868. The school commissioners, were ex-Confederates and refused to appropriate a salary for him.

Every Saturday night or so, he says, Jesse James, the celebrated bandit rode over from Liberty, Mo., shot up Kansas City and robbed its citizens. Then he would gallop to the negro school, discharge his pistols in the air and shout: "Where's that nigger school teacher?" "I would go out in fear and trembling," Turner relates, "and say: 'Here I am, boss.' 'Haven't those commissioners done anything for you yet?' James would yell. And I would answer: 'No, boss.' "Then I'll have to help you,' he would roar, and give me $10, $15 or $20. But for Jesse James I could not have kept up the school."

APPENDIX B
Dispatch on Immigration to Liberia (1877)

This dispatch was James Milton Turner's response to the increasing numbers of southern blacks immigrating to Liberia in response to white violence in 1877. Portions of this dispatch were reproduced in newspapers in the United States, causing consternation among pro-migration groups, especially the American Colonization Society.

Mr. Turner to Mr. Evarts
No. 273 Legation of the United States Monrovia, Liberia, September 3, 1877
    Sir: I have read in the New York Semi-weekly Evening Post of the 17th July this paragraph, viz:
    The promoters of a Liberian emigration scheme in Charleston assert that they have enrolled the names of two thousand five hundred colored persons in that city, and thirty thousand in the State, who consent to emigrate.
    And in the New York paper *Le Messager Franco-Américain,* of Tuesday, 17 July, 1877, viz:
    Il parait que les Sud-Caroliniens ne voient pas avec plaisir cette entreprise d'emigration nègre.
[Translation] It seems that the South Carolinians do not view with pleasure this enterprise of negro emigration.
    I found also in the Washington *National Republican,* July 20, the following, viz:
    . . . Nevertheless some families did go, but from the report which they sent back they found Liberia anything but an El Dorado. A few of them wrote urgent appeals to their friends at home to assist them to return and by means of subscriptions so obtained managed to make their way back.
    The reasons which have influenced me to omit in my correspondence to notice the scheme for the emigration to Liberia of negro citizens of the United States, as propagated by the organizations in the

United States known as the American Colonization Society, &c., are manifold; the principal one of which is, no doubt, obvious to the Department. But as the determined agitation of the agents of those associations appears of late to attract the attention of a class of Americans whose ignorance of all the real facts in the case leaves them exposed to *ex parte* statements, which, in many instances, may induce them to leave homes and situations in life where they enjoy, at least, comparative comfort, and are able at the same time to supply an important demand for labor, only to experience disappointment in a foreign land, without hope, in nine cases in ten, of even being able to acquire the means to return to their homes, it now suggests itself as my duty to give only a very few of the more cogent reasons why I cannot advise or encourage the emigration by subscription of negro citizens of the United States to Liberia.

American philanthropists, influenced by the belief that they are assisting the elevation and well-being of an unfortunate class, and at the same time aiding the evangelization and civilization of Africa, contribute of their means to support a scheme which is not alone impolitic, but, in a majority of instances, absolutely injurious in results. It is far from my purpose to condem or cause to be misunderstood the well-meaning intentions of persons who merely contribute their money to be used by others in this enterprise to colonize the American negro in Africa. This entire enterprise is kept alive in the United States by a few active agents of those societies who represent, usually, to the more inexperienced of the class they desire to operate upon as emigrants, only what is of a nature best adapted to deceive the unwary into the belief that the abundant wealth which nature has lavished upon Africa is not locked securely within the environs of these deadly climatic influences. These agents speak the truth when they represent that emigrants will find the soil fertile; that constant summer prevails; that there are mineral wealth, beautiful landscapes, luxurious vegetation, tropical fruits of every description, &c. Such a thing as a plow is not to be found in use in Liberia. It has been demonstrated that neither horses, mules, nor donkeys can withstand the climate on the sea coast. Horses are found in the interior, but, when brought to the coast, they sicken and die. Although constant summer prevails, as to temperature, the miasmatic influence, caused by the heavy rain alternating with hot sunshine, causes sickness during six months of the year, and, during the remaining six months of the year the power of the sun is such that it is almost impossible for any one except a native to work, as it produces inertia, lassitude, want of energy. Indeed, after a man has once had the fever, he never, in Africa, regains the energy he was possessed of before. Only a very few of the most robust constitutions ever regain, after leaving the climate, their former physical status. It is impossible to direct the sight anywhere without its resting upon the "beautiful landscapes," and upon hills and dales covered with virgin forests, the sea and rivers margined with that "luxuriant vegetation" always peculiar to the deadly mangrove swamps. It is true there is mineral wealth, but the procuring of this wealth is more than counterbalanced by the sacrifice and difficulty necessary for a people poor in the knowledge of the economy of government, and poor as well in individual competence. Rich as the country is naturally, Liberia has never been independent to loose herself from other countries enough to produce food sufficient for her daily home consumption. Although a rice growing land, rice is imported from England and other countries and sold at $4 per bushel when better rice can be grown and sold at half the price. Rice is the principal breadstuff. I have never seen flour of a less price than $14 per barrel; butter, at $1 per pound; hams, from $5 to $8 each; other provisions proportionably high. In the face of these facts the American emigrant has to compete with the native for labor. The native is strong and hardy, with a very few wants, and able, at fifty cents per day, to perform the labor usually assigned to horses in other countries.

When these agents, by reason of such *ex parte* representations, have succeeded, first, in producing discontent, thereby inducing these unsuspecting persons to quit homes and surroundings, already known and possessed, and to migrate across an ocean to a land unknown to themselves and the world, impossible hopes are afterward raised, superinduced by these distorted statements of empire and national greatness. They are left, at the expiration of six months of (so-called) support, without money or any means of livelihood, with little, if any, communication with their former friends and homes, without knowledge of the customs and nature of the country to which they have come, suffering from the despair and discouragement occasioned by the acclimation fever, and, alas! In too many cases, mourning the loss of perhaps their entire families, save the one thus left a mourner; such are only anxious to return from whence they came. I may here remark, I have never known of the departure of a vessel to America, without receiving, frequently, a dozen applications to be sent back. Under the law I am powerless to help them. If, perchance, the chil-

dren of a family survive, as is frequently the case, the guardians are
alarmed when they discover that they have left a country where a
public school system prevails for one where their children will be
deprived of this benefit. Thus, confronted on every hand by discouraging circumstances, the emigrant naturally turns to the agent in the
United States, whose representation led to this condition of things. I
have been sorry before now to believe that the agent loses much of his
zealous interest in the emigrant with the conclusion of the contract
for the provisions for the support of the emigrant for six months. The
agent generally replies, with the gratuitous advice to the emigrant to
push his way as far to the interior of Africa as possible and there
settle.

Travelers to the interior of Africa agree that some distance inte-
rior-ward from the sea coast we may reach healthier localities. But
when we reflect that there are no roads, only foot paths cut by the
natives, and the only means of transporting their goods is on the
heads or backs of native carriers, we are not surprised to find that
after so long a time as sixty years, the emigrant has not penetrated the
interior more than four or five hours' travel, especially considering
that the forests are almost impregnable, being matted together with a
thick undergrowth of vines. The facts show that these poor people
cannot go to the "high hills and undulating plains" said to be in the
interior of Africa, without means to provide themselves with roads,
and without treaties of commerce and friendship with the numerous
petty kings, who are, in many instances, either openly or covertly
hostile. It would frequently be necessary to enforce these treaties by
means of an armed force, as England and all European powers who
have colonies find from experience, as witness the recent difficult
march of the English upon Coomassie, and the capture and execu-
tion of four or five African kings by the colonial government of Sierra
Leone for obstructing the roads.

It is worthy of observation that even the majority of those powers
have not been able to conquer the dense obstruction, which lie on the
way to the interior of Africa, but comparatively short distances. And I
would also remark that the theory that the negro of America, after
three centuries of absence from Africa, the long weary years of which
were not altogether devoted to training him in the things which pertain to the higher walks of knowledge, is better prepared than other
foreigners, physically or otherwise, to carry civilization to this unfortunate people, is in my opinion and experience as fallacious as it is

unreasonable. In fine, my experience has been that when the American negro is brought face to face in contact with this work, he is, for all practical purposes, as much a foreigner as any other people and can only extend to the barbarous African the same philanthropic sympathy. It is not to be wondered at that when the emigrant is met by the unexpected obstructions referred to, his interest and ardor to realize the dream of evangelizing, civilizing, and colonizing Africa, himself being the immediate means, often changes into the desire to return to his home. After sixty years we find that those who have remained with praiseworthy determination, if possible, to conquer these obstructions, have not assimilated a single tribe of native Africans, but have caused the extinction as such of perhaps as many of the aborigines. Instead, the continual cry is for "more, more" from America to come, and, I suppose, do as they have done toward the grand consummation—nothing. Without a census in the country it is easy to observe that our mortality is greater than our increase from all sources; our children born in the country are weaker, therefore, more short-lived, than their parents, and our need today is more men. Would it not be reasonable to suppose that another sixty years, the number supplied being equal, the want of Liberia will then, as now, be "more men"? Now, seeing that the result of these trying experiences is not the furtherance of the object aimed at, does it not seem advisable that philanthropy should be discouraged rather than promoted in this mistaken direction? None would have American benevolence discontinue the effort to make "sunshine in the shady places" of this republic, nor cease seeking to mitigate the wants of the unfortunate children of Africa; on the contrary, would it not seem time for that benevolence to show increased effort in the development of Africa's vast resources, and that this effort should not only be increased, but take to itself an interest in Africa as broad as Charity, kind as sympathy, and as comprehensive as the work is extensive and just. Neither is it intended to disparage the Spartan like patriotism and stoic indifference to suffering, put forth so persistently by the first settlers of Liberia. They gained a foothold upon the shores of this country by persuasion when possible and by conquest when necessary. When taken comparatively, the policy employed by the English and other Europeans seems productive of as great, if not greater results than the plan adopted by Americans. They seem to realize the necessity of supplying light from without Africa; but at this point their policy appears to diverge from the plan of Americans, inasmuch as they intrust the continuation, indeed the completion, of the work to the indigenous inhabitant himself. At first it was their policy to take from the tribes the children of greatest intellectual promise and place them in the universities of Europe that they might become qualified to train their fellow countrymen. It was discovered that this method furnished the pupil with ideas of civilization ill adapted to the purpose for which he was destined. Then the English adopted the plan of the Fourah Bay College, of Sierra Leone, where the student may acquire that kind of education necessary without leaving Africa. The result of this and other efforts in like direction is the production of men suitable for the work. For example, from schools thus established hundreds of young Africans with common training are graduated every year. It is pleasant to notice that Bishop Browther, of the Church of England, takes to the new field of labor which he has opened on the Niger many young men and women from these schools, who in their turn become co-laborers for the elevation of their people. The students from these schools may be found in all the professions, in commerce, and in all the several vocations of life. Africa is their home, and for them the climate possesses beauties, where others find only terror and premature death.

It does seem that the mission of Liberia is to form the nucleus about which to culminate the very tractable tribes residing upon their territory. Since the want of Liberia at the present time is men, would it not be a better economy to expend the moneys now being used for the migration of the class of emigrants described, in the establishment of manual labor schools which would supply the class of men needed in the country, free from all the drawbacks consequent upon emigrating from America?

We have at our very doors, only forty miles from Monrovia, at Cape Mount, the Vei tribe,[1] with perfect physical organization, and with an inventive genius which has won for them the reputation of being the only tribe known on this coast to have invented an alphabet, by means of which they were found in communication with the interior. Their language has been reduced to grammar. This tribe desires to learn. Often when any of them were employed about this legation they would require in payment pens, ink, and paper; not, as the other nations, gin, rum, tobacco, cloth, &c.

After examining their traditions we find that this tribe has ab-

1. Turner's spelling of this tribe varies.

sorbed others, and that the Vei language is more extensive than that of any of the neighboring tribes. Vei is spoken by more of the surrounding aborigines than any other language. Therefore, I think this tribe the best vehicle for the propagation of civilization to the interior tribes of Africa.

One half of the cost of colonizing the 30,000 emigrants (if that were possible) would, within a very short space of time, prepare as many men from this people who are exactly suited to the kind of work required. And I may add that if Christian philanthropists loiter much longer in manipulating this chiliahedronic idea into shape, the Mandingoes, who, as Mohammedans, are indefatigable missionaries, will probably very soon disseminate the dogmas of the religion among this desirable people, and thus place their evangelization at least another half century farther in the future. This is evident when it is considered that the Mandingo teaches his religion at the same time he pushes forward his commerce; with him the two go hand in hand. The Mandingoes and Veis are in intimate communication, and this intimacy grows daily *pari passu* with their commerce.

Momorah, a Mandingo chief, from the interior, with a caravan of trade, usually to Sierra Leone, is often visiting this legation. He is a man noble in his deportment, six feet in height, as all his tribe are, athletic and well proportioned, with straight features, having none of the characteristics usually ascribed to the African; intellectual, speaking English, French, German, and Portuguese, from contact with the people of those colonies, where he has been accustomed to trade. He also reads Arabic from the religious training peculiar to his people, and Vei, acquired during his intimacy with that tribe. What I have ascribed to Prince Mamorah is true of many of his tribe. It is impossible to look upon this perfect type of manly physique and intellectual strength without being impressed by the superiority of the material of which his tribe is composed. They are the men of conquest in Africa, the commercial races dwelling far in the interior, making pilgrimages to Mecca across the continent, and whose treaty of friendship and whose passport over the domains of hostile tribes who dwell between their home and the sea-board are the Koran and the sword.

Speaking to this man of commerce, of the Koran, and of the sword, upon the subject upon which I am writing, his evident disposition to commiserate rather than admire the American negro as he sees him here, convinces me that it will be long before the abnormal can mold the normal man. His language forces upon me the recollection that human slavery is as old as human conquest; that it was the custom of the victor to enthrall the vanquished, and that many are slow to value the fact that human slavery was not the crucible to refine and enoble human nature and befit it for grand undertakings.

While my object is not to encourage the persuasion of citizens of the United States to exchange their homes and country for Liberia, neither is it desired to dissuade any from coming to Liberia who may wish to do so. It is merely desired to present the facts and difficulties attendant upon such a course, with a view that none, if possible, may emigrate without full knowledge of the probable result. And I may add, that a fact generally recognized by many thoughtful and prominent Liberians, and one in which I thoroughly acquiesce, is that men of any consequence to the wants of Liberia are able to pay their own expense of travel, and if desirous to come, would be willing and would prefer to do so.

Whether Liberia succeeds or fails, she cannot be accepted as a fair test of the negro's capacity or incapacity for self government.

This dispatch has exceeded the length intended. There are many things of interest which might be mentioned on a subject so important, but I must not occupy the time of the Department unnecessarily; hence, I have avoided any allusion to the condition of the government of Liberia—as to the security or insecurity of life and property; whether or not crime can be committed with impunity; whether the financial system employed is potent or impotent, &c.

Upon such topics the government is doubtless already informed through my previous correspondence.

I have, &c., J. Milton Turner.

BIBLIOGRAPHY

Books and Articles

Abbott, Martin. "Free Land, Free Labor, and the Freedmen's Bureau." *Agricultural History* 30 (October 1956): 150–56.

Abel, Annie H. *The American Indian under Reconstruction.* Cleveland: Arthur H. Clark Co., 1925.

Abingbade, Harrison Ola. "The Settler-African Conflicts: The Case of the Maryland Colonists and the Grebo 1840–1900." *Journal of Negro History* 66 (Summer 1981): 93–109.

African Repository. Vols. 47–54. Washington, D.C.: American Colonization Society, 1871–1878. Reprinted. New York: Kraus Reprint Corporation, 1967.

Anderson, Galusha. *The Story of a Border City during the Civil War.* Boston: Little, Brown & Co., 1908.

Andrews, Thomas F. "Freedmen in Indian Territory: A Post–Civil War Dilemma." *Journal of the West* 4 (July 1964): 363–77.

Armstrong, Warren B. "Union Chaplains and the Education of the Freedmen." *Journal of Negro History* 52 (April 1967): 105–15.

Athearn, Robert G. *In Search of Canaan: Black Migration to Kansas, 1879–1880.* New York: Oxford University Press, 1989.

Babchuk, Nicholas H., and Ralph V. Thompson. "The Voluntary Associations of Negroes." *American Sociological Review* 27 (October 1962): 647–55.

Barclay, Thomas S. "The Liberal Republican Movement in Missouri." *Missouri Historical Review* 21 (October 1926): 59–108.

Bardolph, Richard, ed. *The Civil Rights Record: Black Americans and the Laws, 1847–1970.* New York: Thomas Y. Crowell Co., 1970.

Beatty, Elizabeth Caldwell. "The Political Response of Black Americans, 1876–1896." Ph.D. diss., Florida State University, 1976.

Beisner, Robert L. *From the Old Diplomacy to the New, 1865–1900.* The Crowell American History Series. New York: Thomas Y. Crowell Co., 1975.

Bellamy, Donnie D. "The Education of Blacks in Missouri Prior to 1861." *Journal of Negro History* 59 (April 1974): 143–57.

Berry, Mary F. "Reparations for Freedmen, 1890–1916: Fraudulent Practices or Justice Deferred?" *Journal of Negro History* 57 (July 1972): 219–30.

Bigglestone, W. E. "Oberlin College and the Negro Student, 1865–1940." *Journal of Negro History* 56 (July 1970): 198–219.

Blackett, R. J. M., ed. *Beating against the Barriers: Biographical Essays in Nineteenth-Century Afro-American History.* Baton Rouge: Louisiana State University Press, 1986.

Blassingame, John. *Black New Orleans, 1860–1880.* Chicago: University of Chicago Press, 1973.

————. "Status and Social Structure in the Slave Community: Evidence from New Sources." In *Perspectives and Irony in American Slavery,* edited by Harry P. Owens, 137–52. Jackson: University Press of Mississippi, 1976.

Blight, David W. "Frederick Douglass and the American Apocalypse." *Civil War History* 31 (December 1985): 309–28.

Boles, John B. *Black Southerners, 1619–1869.* New Perspectives on the South. Lexington: University Press of Kentucky, 1983.

Brantley, Daniel. "Black Diplomacy and Frederick Douglass' Caribbean Experiences, 1871 and 1889–1891: The Untold Story." *Phylon* 45 (September 1984): 197–209.

Brawley, Benjamin. *A Social History of the American Negro.* New York: Macmillan Co., 1921.

Brier, Stephen. "The Career of Richard L. Davis Reconsidered: Unpublished Correspondence [February-August, 1891] from the National Labor Tribune." *Labor History* (Summer 1980): 420–29.

Brigham, Robert I. "The Education of the Negro in Missouri." Ph.D. diss., University of Missouri–Columbia, 1946.

Brock, Euline W. "Thomas W. Cardozo: Fallible Black Reconstruction Leader." *Journal of Southern History* 47 (May 1981): 183–206.

Brotz, Howard, ed. *Negro Social and Political Thought, 1850–1920.* New York: Basic Books, 1966.

Brownlee, Richard S. *Gray Ghosts of the Confederacy: Guerilla Warfare in the West, 1861–1865.* Baton Rouge: Louisiana State University Press, 1958.

Bullock, Henry Allen. *A History of Negro Education in the South: From 1619 to the Present.* Cambridge: Harvard University Press, 1967.

Bullock, Penelope L. *The Afro-American Periodical Press, 1838–1909.* Baton Rouge: Louisiana State University Press, 1981.

Burnham, John C. "The Social Evil Ordinance—A Social Experiment in Nineteenth Century St. Louis." *Bulletin of the Missouri Historical Society* 27 (April 1971): 203–17.

Caldwell, Dorothy J. "Vignettes of Famous Missourians, James

Milton Turner." *Missouri Historical Review* 54 (October 1959): 55–57.

Cassell, C. Abayomi. *Liberia: History of the First African Republic.* New York: Fountainhead Publishers, 1970.

Chapman, Berlin B. "Freedmen and the Oklahoma Lands." *Southwestern Social Science Quarterly* 29 (April 1949): 150–59.

————. "The Pottawatomie and Absentee Shawnee Reservation." *Chronicles of Oklahoma* 24 (August 1946): 293–305.

Cheek, William, and Aimee Lee Cheek. *John Mercer Langston and the Fight for Black Freedom, 1829–1865.* Blacks in the New World Series. Urbana: University of Illinois Press, 1989.

Christensen, Lawrence O. "Black St. Louis: A Study in Race Relations, 1865–1916." Ph.D. diss., University of Missouri–Columbia, 1972.

————. "J. Milton Turner: An Appraisal." *Missouri Historical Review* 70 (October 1975): 1–19.

————. "Race Relations in St. Louis, 1865–1916." *Missouri Historical Review* 78 (January 1984): 123–36.

————. "The Racial Views of John W. Wheeler." *Missouri Historical Review* 67 (July 1973): 535–47.

————. "Schools for Blacks: J. Milton Turner in Reconstruction Missouri." *Missouri Historical Review* 76 (January 1982): 121–35.

————, ed. "Cyprian Clamorgan: The Colored Aristocracy of St. Louis." *Bulletin of the Missouri Historical Society* 30 (October 1974): 3–31.

Christopher, Maurice. *America's Black Congressmen.* New York: Thomas Y. Crowell Co., 1971.

Cook, Samuel DuBois. "The Tragic Conception of Negro History." *Journal of Negro History* 41 (October 1960): 219–40.

Crockett, Norman L. *The Black Towns.* Lawrence: Regents Press of Kansas, 1979.

Cruden, Robert. *The Negro in Reconstruction.* Englewood Cliffs, N.J.: Prentice Hall, 1969.

Cummings, Melbourne S. "The Rhetoric of Bishop Henry McNeal Turner [Florida, 1857–1898]." *Journal of Black Studies* 12 (June 1982): 457–70.

Curry, Richard O. "The Civil War and Reconstruction, 1861–1877: A Critical Overview of Recent Trends and Interpretations." *Civil War History* 20 (September 1974): 215–38.

————, ed. *Radicalism, Racism, and Party Realignment: The Border States during Reconstruction.* Baltimore: Johns Hopkins University Press, 1969.

Davis, Allison. *Leadership, Love, and Aggression.* New York: Harcourt Brace Jovanovich, 1983.

Davis, Lenwood G. "Black American Images of Liberia, 1877–1914." *Liberian Studies Journal* 6:1 (1975): 53–72.

DeMarco, Joseph P. *The Social Thought of W. E. B. DuBois.* Lanham, Md., New York, and London: University Press of America, 1983.

Dilliard, Irving. "James Milton Turner: A Little Known Benefactor of His People." *Journal of Negro History* 19 (October 1934): 372–411.

―――. "They Came from Missouri and They Showed the World." *Missouri Historical Review* 36 (October 1941): 3–31.

―――, ed. "Dred Scott Eulogized by James Milton Turner." *Journal of Negro History* 26 (January 1941): 1–11.

Donald, Henderson H. *The Negro Freedman: Life Conditions of the American Negro in the Early Years after Emancipation.* New York: H. Schuman, 1952.

Drago, Edward L. *Black Politicians and Reconstruction in Georgia.* Baton Rouge: Louisiana State University Press, 1982.

Dreer, Herman. "Negro Leadership in St. Louis: A Study in Race Relations." Ph.D. diss., University of Chicago, 1955.

Dubois, W. E. B. *Dusk of Dawn: An Essay toward an Autobiography of a Race Concept.* New York: Harcourt Brace Jovanovich, 1940. Reprint. New York: Schocken Books, 1968.

Duncan, Russell. *Freedom's Shore: Tunis Campbell and the Georgia Freedmen.* Athens: University of Georgia Press, 1986.

Dwight, Margaret. "Black Suffrage in Missouri, 1865–1877." Ph.D. diss., University of Missouri–Columbia, 1978.

Edwards' St. Louis Directory for 1864. St. Louis: Richard Edwards, 1864.

Eisenberg, Bernard. "Only for the Bourgeois? James Weldon Johnson and the NAACP, 1916–1930." *Phylon* 43 (June 1982): 110–24.

Engs, Robert F. *Freedom's First Generation: Black Hampton, Virginia, 1862–1890.* Philadelphia: University of Pennsylvania Press, 1979.

Eriksen, Erik H. "The Concept of Identity in Race Relations: Notes and Queries." *Daedalus* 95 (Winter 1966): 145–71.

Evans, J. W. "A Brief Sketch of the Development of Negro Education in St. Louis, Missouri." *Journal of Negro Education* 7 (October 1938): 548–52.

Fellman, Michael. *Inside War: The Guerilla Conflict in Missouri during the American Civil War.* New York: Oxford University Press, 1989.

Fichter, Joseph H. "American Religion and the Negro." *Daedalus* 94 (Fall 1965): 1085–1106.

Filley, Chauncey I. *Some More Republican History of Missouri.* St. Louis: Christman Printing Co., 1902.

Finkenbin, Roy E. "'Our Little Circle': Benevolent Reformers, the Slater Fund, and the Argument for Black Industrial Education, 1882–1908." *Hayes Historical Journal* 6 (Fall 1986): 6–22.

Fischer, LeRoy H., ed. *The Civil War in Indian Territory.* Los Angeles: Lorrin L. Morrison, 1974.

Fleming, Walter L. "'Pap' Singleton, the Moses of the Colored Exodus." *American Journal of Sociology* 15 (July 1909; May 1910): 61–82.

Fletcher, Juanita D. "Against the Consensus: Oberlin College and the Education of American Negroes." Ph.D. diss., American University, 1974.

Fletcher, Ralph, and Mildred Fletcher. "Some Data on Occupations among Negroes in St. Louis from 1866 to 1897." *Journal of Negro History* 20 (July 1935): 338–41.

Flynn, John P. "Booker T. Washington: Uncle Tom or Wooden Horse." *Journal of Negro History* 54 (July 1969): 262–74.

Foner, Eric. *Reconstruction, 1863–1877.* New American Nation Series, edited by Henry Steele Commager and Richard B. Morriss. New York: Harper & Row, 1988.

Foner, Philip S., ed. *The Life and Writings of Frederick Douglass.* 4 vols. New York: International Publishers, 1950–1955.

Foner, Philip S., and Ronald L. Lewis, eds. *The Black Worker: A Documentary History from Colonial Times to the Present.* Vol. 2. Philadelphia: Temple University Press, 1978.

Foster, Richard B. *Historical Sketch of Lincoln Institute.* Jefferson City, Mo.: N.p., 1871.

Fox, Stephen R. *The Guardian of Boston: William Monroe Trotter.* Studies in American Negro Life. New York: Atheneum Press, 1970.

Franklin, John Hope. *George Washington Williams: A Biography.* Chicago: University of Chicago Press, 1985.

———. "Reconstruction and the Negro." In *New Frontiers of the American Reconstruction,* edited by Harold M. Hyman, 59–76. Urbana: University of Illinois Press, 1966.

Franklin, John Hope, and August Meier, eds. *Black Leaders of the Twentieth Century.* Urbana: University of Illinois Press, 1982.

Frederickson, George M. *The Arrogance of Race: Historical Perspectives on Slavery, Racism, and Social Inequality.* Middletown, Ky.: Wesleyan University Press, 1988.

Fullinwider, S. Pendleton. "The Emancipation of Negro Thought, 1890–1930." Ph.D. diss., University of Wisconsin–Madison, 1966.

Garvin, Roy. "Benjamin or 'Pap' Singleton and His Followers." *Journal of Negro History* 33 (January 1948): 7–23.

Gatewood, Willard B., Jr. "Alonza Clifton McClennan [1855–1912]: Black Midshipman from South Carolina, 1873–1874." *South Carolina History Magazine* 89 (January 1988): 24–39.

———. "Aristocrats of Color: South and North, the Black Elite, 1880–1920." *Journal of Southern History* 54 (February 1988): 3–20.

———. *Aristocrats of Color*. Bloomington: Indiana University Press, 1990.

———. *Free Man of Color: The Autobiography of Willis Augustus Hodges*. Knoxville: University of Tennessee Press, 1982.

———. *Slave and Freeman: The Autobiography of George L. Knox*. Lexington: University Press of Kentucky, 1979.

Gavins, Raymond. *The Perils and Prospects of Southern Black Leadership: Gordon Blaine Hancock, 1884–1970*. Durham: Duke University Press, 1977.

Gerlach, Russell. *Settlement Patterns in Missouri*. Columbia: University of Missouri Press, 1986.

Gillette, William. *The Right to Vote: Politics and the Passage of the Fifteenth Amendment*. Baltimore: Johns Hopkins University Press, 1965.

Gittinger, Roy. *The Formation of the State of Oklahoma, 1803–1906*. Publications in History, vol. 6. Berkeley and Los Angeles: University of California, 1917.

Goldstein, Michael L. "Preface to the Rise of Booker T. Washington: A View from New York City of the Demise of Independent Black Politics, 1889–1902." *Journal of Negro History* 72 (January 1977): 81–99.

Gould's St. Louis Directory. St. Louis: David Gould Publisher, 1870–1915.

Green, Dan S., and Earl Smith. "W. E. B. DuBois and the Concepts of Race and Class." *Phylon* 44 (December 1983): 262–72.

Greene, Lorenzo J., et al. *Missouri's Black Heritage*. St. Louis: Forum Press, 1980.

Grossman, Lawrence. *The Democratic Party and the Negro: Northern and National Politics, 1868–1892*. Blacks in the New World Series. Chicago: University of Illinois Press, 1976.

Grothaus, Larry I. "The Negro in Missouri Politics, 1890–1941." Ph.D. diss., University of Missouri–Columbia, 1970.

Gutman, Herbert. "Peter H. Clark: Pioneer Negro Socialist, 1877."
    Journal of Negro Education 34 (Fall 1965): 413-18.
Hare, Nathan. *Black Anglo-Saxon.* Introduction by Oliver C. Cox.
    New York: Collier Books, 1970.
Harlan, Louis R. *Booker T. Washington: The Making of a Black
    Leader, 1856-1901.* New York: Oxford University Press, 1972.
————. *Booker T. Washington: The Wizard of Tuskegee, 1901-
    1915.* New York: Oxford University Press, 1983.
Harlan, Louis R., and Raymond W. Smock. *The Booker T. Wash-
    ington Papers. Vol 12: 1912-1914.* Urbana: University of Illinois
    Press, 1982.
Hellwig, David J. "Building a Black Nation: The Role of Immigrants
    in the Thought and Rhetoric of Booker T. Washington." *Mis-
    sissippi Quarterly* 31 (Fall 1978): 529-60.
Higgins, Billy D. "Negro Thought and the Exodus of 1879." *Phylon*
    32 (Spring 1971): 39-52.
Hill, Mozell C. "The All-Negro Communities of Oklahoma: The
    Natural History of a Social Movement." *Journal of Negro History*
    31 (July 1946): 254-68.
Hill, Robert A. "The Foremost Radical among His Race: Marcus
    Garvey and the Black Scare, 1918-1921." *Prologue* 16 (Winter
    1984): 215-31.
————. *The Marcus Garvey and Universal Negro Improvement
    Association Papers.* 3 vols. Berkeley and Los Angeles: University
    of California Press, 1983-1984.
Hine, William C. "Black Politicians in Reconstruction Charleston,
    South Carolina: A Collective Study." *Journal of Southern History*
    49 (November 1983): 555-84.
Hogan, Daniel M. "The Catholic Church and the Negroes of St.
    Louis." Master's thesis, St. Louis University, 1955.
Holt, Thomas. *Black over White: Negro Political Leadership in South
    Carolina during Reconstruction.* Blacks in the New World Series.
    Urbana: University of Illinois Press, 1977.
Hosmer, John, and Joseph Fineman. "Black Congressmen in Recon-
    struction Historiography." *Phylon* 40 (June 1978): 97-107.
Howell, W. R. "The Colored Schools of Kansas City, Missouri." In
    Your Kansas City and Mine, edited by William H. Young and
    Nathan B. Young, 21-22. Kansas City: By the Editors, 1950.
Jones, Howard J. "Biographical Sketches of Members of the 1868
    Louisiana State Senate." *Louisiana History* 19 (Winter 1978):
    65-110.
————. "Images of State Legislative Reconstruction Participants in

Fiction [of Thomas Dixon, Margaret Mitchell, Joel Chandler Harris, Thomas Nelson Page, George Washington Cable, Albion Winegar Tourgee, Frank Yerby, and Howard Fast]." *Journal of Negro History* 67 (Winter 1982):318–27.

Joyce, Donald Franklin. *Gatekeepers of Black Culture: Black-Owned Book Publishing in the United States, 1817–1981*. Westport: Greenwood Press, 1983.

Kensell, Lewis Anthony. "Reconstruction in the Choctaw Nation, 1865–1870." *Chronicles of Oklahoma* 47 (Summer 1969): 138–53.

Klingman, Peter T. *Josiah Walls: Florida's Black Congressman of Reconstruction*. Gainesville: University Presses of Florida, 1976.

Kolchin, Peter. *First Freedom: The Response of Alabama's Blacks to Emancipation and Reconstruction*. Westport: Greenwood Press, 1972.

————. "Scalawags, Carpetbaggers, and Reconstruction: A Quantitative Look at Southern Congressional Politics, 1868–1872." *Journal of Southern History* 45 (February 1979): 63–76.

Kremer, Gary R. "Background to Apostasy: James Milton Turner and the Republican Party." *Missouri Historical Review* 70 (January 1976): 184–98.

————. "A Biography of James Milton Turner." Ph.D. diss., The American University, 1978.

————. "For Justice and a Fee: James Milton Turner and the Cherokee Freedmen." *Chronicles of Oklahoma* 58 (Winter 1981): 377–91.

————. "The World of Make-Believe: James Milton Turner and Black Masonry." *Missouri Historical Review* 74 (October 1979): 50–71.

Kremer, Gary R., and Antonio F. Holland, eds. "Some Aspects of Black Education in Reconstruction Missouri: An Address by Richard B. Foster." *Missouri Historical Review* 70 (January 1976): 184–98.

Lambert, Paul F. "The Cherokee Reconstruction Treaty of 1866." *Journal of the West* 12 (July 1973): 417–89.

Lamson, Peggy. *The Glorious Failure: Black Congressman Robert Brown Elliott and the Reconstruction in South Carolina*. New York: W. W. Norton Co., 1973.

Lange, Werner J. "W. E. B. DuBois and the First Scientific Study of Afro-America." *Phylon* 44 (June 1983): 135–46.

Leslie, James W. "Ferd Havis [1846–1918]: Jefferson County's Black Republican Leader." *Arkansas Historical Quarterly* (Autumn 1978): 240–51.

Lewis, Elsie M. "The Political Mind of the Negro, 1865–1900." *Journal of Southern History* 21 (May 1955): 189–202.

Littlefield, Daniel F. *The Cherokee Freedmen: From Emancipation to American Citizenship.* Contributions in Afro-American and African Studies, 40. Westport: Greenwood Press, 1978.

Litwack, Leon F. *Been in the Storm So Long: The Aftermath of Slavery.* New York: Alfred A. Knopf, 1979.

Litwack, Leon F., and August Meier, eds. *Black Leaders of the Nineteenth Century.* Urbana: University of Illinois Press, 1988.

Logan, Frenise A. "Black and Republican: Vicissitudes of a Minority Twice Over in the North Carolina House of Representatives, 1876–1877." *North Carolina Historical Review* 61 (July 1984): 311–46.

Logan, Rayford W. *The Betrayal of the Negro: From Rutherford B. Hayes to Woodrow Wilson.* 2d ed. New York: Macmillan Co., 1968. Originally *The Negro in American Life and Thought: The Nadir, 1877–1901.* New York: Macmillan and Co., 1954.

Low, W. A. "The Freedmen's Bureau in the Border States." In *Radicalism, Racism, and Party Realignment: The Border States during Reconstruction,* edited by Richard O. Curry, 245–64. Baltimore: Johns Hopkins University Press, 1969.

Lynch, Hollis. *Edward Wilmot Blyden: Pan-Negro Patriot, 1832–1912.* London: Oxford University Press, 1967.

McCandless, Perry. *A History of Missouri, 1820–1860.* Sesquicentennial History of Missouri Series, vol. 2. Columbia: University of Missouri Press, 1972.

McCullar, Marion Ray. "The Choctaw-Chickasaw Reconstruction Treaty of 1866." *Journal of the West* 12 (July 1973): 462–70.

McDaniel, Ruth Currie. "Black Power in Georgia: William A. Pledger and the Takeover [1880] of the Republican Party." *Georgia Historical Quarterly* 62 (Fall 1978): 225–39.

McMurry, Linda O. "A Black Intellectual in the New South: Monroe Nathan Work, 1866–1945." *Phylon* 41 (December 1980): 333–44.

McPherson, James M. "Coercion or Conciliation? Abolitionists Debate President Hayes's Southern Policy." *New England Quarterly* 39 (December 1966): 474–97.

————. "White Liberals and Black Power in Negro Education, 1865–1915." *American Historical Review* 75 (June 1970): 1357–86.

McReynolds, Edwin C. *Oklahoma: A History of the Sooner State.* Norman: University of Oklahoma Press, 1954.

Mann, George L. "The Development of Public Education for Negroes in St. Louis, Missouri." Ph.D. diss., Indiana University, 1949.

Manning, Kenneth R. *Black Apollo of Science: The Life of Ernest Everett Just.* New York and Oxford: Oxford University Press, 1983.

Martin, Waldo W., Jr. *The Mind of Frederick Douglass.* Chapel Hill: University of North Carolina Press, 1984.

Matthews, John M. "Jefferson Franklin Long [1836–1901]: The Public Career of Georgia's First Black Congressman [1867–1884]." *Phylon* 42 (June 1981): 145–56.

Meier, August. "The Beginning of Industrial Education in Negro Schools." *The Midwest Journal* 7 (Spring 1955): 21–44.

———. "Comment on John Hope Franklin's Paper." In *New Frontiers of the American Reconstruction,* edited by Harold M. Hyman, 77–86. Urbana: University of Illinois Press, 1966.

———. "The Negro and the Democratic Party." *Phylon* 17 (Second Quarter 1956): 173–91.

———. *Negro Thought in America, 1880–1915: Racial Ideologies in the Age of Booker T. Washington.* Ann Arbor: University of Michigan Press, 1963.

Mellinger, Philip. "Discrimination and Statehood in Oklahoma." *Chronicles of Oklahoma* 49 (Autumn 1971): 340–78.

Menake, John G. *Mulattoes and Race Mixture: American Attitudes and Images, 1865–1918.* Ann Arbor: UMI Research Press, 1979.

Mitchell, Theodore R. *Political Education in the Southern Farmers' Alliance, 1887–1900.* Madison: University of Wisconsin Press, 1987.

Moneyhon, Carl H. "Black Politics in Arkansas during the Gilded Age, 1876–1900." *Arkansas Historical Quarterly* 44 (Autumn 1985): 222–45.

Moore, Noah Webster. "James Milton Turner, Diplomat, Educator, and Defender of Rights, 1840–1915." *Bulletin of the Missouri Historical Society* 27 (April 1971): 194–201.

———. "John Berry Meachum: St. Louis Pioneer, Black Abolitionist, Educator and Preacher." *Bulletin of the Missouri Historical Society* 29 (January 1973): 96–103.

Moses, Wilson Jeremiah. *Alexander Crummell: A Study of Civilization and Discontent.* New York: Oxford University Press, 1989.

Moss, Alfred A., Jr. *The American Negro Academy: Voice of the Talented Tenth.* Baton Rouge: Louisiana State University Press, 1981.

Muraskin, William. *Middle-Class Blacks in a White Society: Prince Hall Freemasonry in America.* Berkeley and Los Angeles: University of California Press, 1975.

*Official Proceedings of the Annual Communications of the Most Wor-
shipful Grand Lodge, A.F. & A.M.* Hannibal, Mo.: Standard
Printing Co., 1880, 1887, 1890, 1892–1898, 1905, 1906, 1908,
1910, 1916, 1917.

*Official Proceedings of the Annual Communications of the Most Wor-
shipful Grand Lodge, A.F. & A. M.* Palmyra, Mo.: Sosey Bros.,
1902, 1904.

*Official Proceedings of the Thirty-third Annual Communication of
the Most Worshipful Grand Lodge, A.F. & A. M.* Fayette, Mo.:
Fayette Globe Printing Co., 1899.

Okonkwo, Rina L. "Orishatukeh Faduma [c. 1857–1946; leader in
Pana-Africanism]: A Man of Two Worlds." *Journal of Negro History* 68 (Winter 1983): 24–36.

Orofsky, Melvin. "Blanche K. Bruce: United States Senator 1875–
1881." *Journal of Mississippi History* 29 (May 1967): 118–41.

Padgett, James A. "Ministers to Liberia and Their Diplomacy." *Journal of Negro History* 22 (January 1937): 50–92.

Painter, Nell Irvin. *Exodusters: Black Migration to Kansas after Reconstruction.* New York: Alfred A. Knopf, 1977.

Parrish, William E. *A History of Missouri.* Sesquicentennial History
of Missouri Series, vol. 3. Columbia: University of Missouri
Press, 1971.

————. *Missouri Under Radical Rule, 1865–1870.* Columbia: University of Missouri Press, 1965.

————. "Reconstruction Politics in Missouri, 1865–1870." In *Radi-
calism, Racism, and Party Realignment: The Border States during
Reconstruction,* edited by Richard O. Curry, 1–36. Baltimore:
Johns Hopkins University Press, 1969.

————. *The Turbulent Partnership: Missouri and the Union, 1861–
1865.* Columbia: University of Missouri Press, 1963.

Patterson, H. Orland. "Slavery, Acculturation, and Social Change."
British Journal of Sociology 17 (June 1966): 151–64.

Perman, Michael. *The Road to Redemption: Southern Politics, 1869–
1879.* Chapel Hill: University of North Carolina Press, 1984.

Pitre, Merline. "Robert Lloyd Smith [b. 1861]: A Black [Texas] Law-
maker in the Shadow of Booker T. Washington." *Phylon* 46 (September 1985): 262–68.

————. *Through Many Dangers, Toils, and Snares: The Black Leadership of Texas, 1868–1900.* Austin: Eakin Press, 1985.

Pope, Christie Farnham. "Southern Homesteads for Negroes." *Agricultural History* 44 (April 1970): 201–12.

Primm, James Neal. *Lion of the Valley: St. Louis, Missouri.* The Western Urban History Series, vol. 3. Boulder: Pruett Publishing Co., 1981.

Quarles, Benjamin. *Frederick Douglass.* Washington D.C.: Associated Publishers, 1948. Reprint. New York: Atheneum Press, 1968.

Rabinowitz, Howard N., ed. *Southern Black Leaders of the Reconstruction Era.* Urbana: University of Illinois Press, 1982.

Rainwater, Lee. "The Crucible of Identity: The Negro Lower-Class Family." *Daedalus* 95 (Winter 1966): 172–216.

Rampersad, Arnold. *The Life of Langston Hughes.* Vol. 1, 1902–1941. *I, Too, Sing America.* New York: Oxford University Press, 1986.

Rampp, Larry C. "Negro Troop Activity in Indian Territory, 1863–1865." *Chronicles of Oklahoma* 83 (Spring 1965): 531–59.

Rankin, David C. "The Origins of Black Leadership in New Orleans during Reconstruction." *Journal of Southern History* 40 (August 1974): 417–40.

Reasons, George, and Sam Patrick. "James Milton Turner's Education Career Led to Politics." *Kansas City Star,* January 11, 1975.

Redkey, Edwin. "Bishop Turner's African Dream." *Journal of American History* 54 (September 1967): 271–90.

———. *Black Exodus: Black Nationalists and Back to Africa Movements, 1890–1910.* New Haven: Yale University Press, 1969.

Reid, George W. "Four in Black: North Carolina's Black Congressmen, 1874–1901." *Journal of Negro History* 64 (Summer 1979): 229–43.

Reimers, David M. *White Protestantism and the Negro.* New York: Oxford University Press, 1965.

Richardson, Joe M. "The American Missionary Association and Black Education in Civil War Missouri." *Missouri Historical Review* 69 (July 1975): 433–48.

———. *Christian Reconstruction: The American Missionary Association and Southern Blacks, 1861–1890.* Athens: University of Georgia Press, 1986.

———. *The Negro in the Reconstruction of Florida, 1865–1877.* Tallahassee: Florida State University, 1965.

Riddleberger, Patrick W. "The Break in the Radical Ranks: Liberals Versus Stalwarts in the Election of 1872." *Journal of Negro History* 44 (April 1959): 136–57.

———. "The Radicals' Abandonment of the Negro during Reconstruction." *Journal of Negro History* 45 (April 1960): 88–102.

Rigsby, Gregory. *Alexander Crummell: Pioneer in Nineteenth Century Pan-African Thought.* Westport: Greenwood Press, 1987.

Ripley, Peter, "The Autobiographical Writings of Frederick Doug-
lass." *Southern Study* 24 (Spring 1985): 5–29.
————. *Slaves and Freedmen in Civil War Louisiana.* Baton Rouge:
Louisiana State University Press, 1976.
Roberson, Jere W. "Edward P. McCabe and the Langston Experi-
ment." *Chronicles of Oklahoma* 51 (Fall 1973): 343–55.
Robinson, Walter G., Jr. "Blacks in Higher Education in the United
States before 1865." Ph.D. diss., Southern Illinois University–
Carbondale, 1976.
Rollin, Frank A. *Life and Public Services of Martin R. Delany.* Bos-
ton: Lee and Shepard, 1868.
Rose, Harold M. "The All-Negro Town: Its Evolution and Function."
Geographical Review 55 (July 1965): 362–81.
Savage, W. Sherman. *The History of Lincoln University.* Jefferson
City, Mo.: New Day Press, 1939.
————. "The Legal Provisions for Negro Schools in Missouri from
1865 to 1890." *Journal of Negro History* 26 (July 1931): 309–21.
————. "The Negro in the Westward Movement." *Journal of Negro
History* 25 (October 1940): 531–39.
Scarborough, W. S. "The Negro and the Louisiana Purchase Exposi-
tion." *Voice of the Negro* 1 (August 1904): 312–15.
Schwendemann, Glen. "The Exodusters on the Missouri." *Kansas
Historical Quarterly* 29 (Spring 1963): 25–40.
————. "Negro Exodus to Kansas: First Phase, March-July, 1879."
Master's thesis, University of Oklahoma, 1957.
————. "Nicodemus: Negro Haven on the Solomon." *Kansas His-
torical Quarterly* 34 (Spring 1968): 10–31.
————. "St. Louis and the 'Exodusters' of 1879." *Journal of Negro
History* 46 (January 1961): 32–46.
————. "Wyandotte and the First 'Exodusters' of 1879." *Kansas His-
torical Quarterly* 26 (Autumn 1960): 233–49.
Schweninger, Loren. *James T. Rapier and Reconstruction.* Chicago:
University of Chicago Press, 1978.
Seifman, Eli. "Education or Emigration: The Schism within the
African Colonization Movement, 1865–1875." *History of Educa-
tion Quarterly* 7 (Spring 1967): 36–57.
Seip, Terry L. *The South Returns to Congress: Men, Economic Mea-
sures, and Intersectional Relationships, 1868–1879.* Baton Rouge:
Louisiana State University Press, 1983.
Shapiro, Samuel. "A Black Senator from Mississippi: Blanche K.
Bruce (1841–1898)." *Review of Politics* 44 (January 1982): 83–
109.

Shick, Tom. *Behold the Promised Land: A History of Afro-American Settler Society in Nineteenth-Century Liberia.* Johns Hopkins Studies in Atlantic History and Culture. Baltimore: Johns Hopkins University Press, 1977.

———. "The Social and Economic History of Afro-American Settlers in Liberia, 1820–1900." Ph.D. diss., University of Wisconsin–Madison, 1976.

Shoemaker, Floyd C. "Some Colorful Lawyers in the History of Missouri." *Missouri Historical Review* 53 (January, April 1959): 125–31, 227–37.

Slavens, George Everett. "A History of the Missouri Negro Press." Ph.D. diss., University of Missouri–Columbia, 1969.

Spirey, Donald. *Schooling for the New Slavery: Black Industrial Education, 1868–1915.* Westport: Greenwood Press, 1978.

Starobin, Robert. "The Negro: A Central Theme in American History." *Journal of Contemporary History* 3 (April 1968): 37–53.

Stein, Judith. *The World of Marcus Garvey: Race and Class in Modern Society.* Baton Rouge: Louisiana State University Press, 1986.

Stevenson, Rosemary. "Black Politics in the U.S.: A Survey of Recent Literature." *Black Scholar* 19 (March/April 1988): 58–61.

Strickland, Arvarh E. "Toward the Promised Land: The Exodus to Kansas and Afterward." *Missouri Historical Review* 59 (July 1975): 376–412.

Sweet, Leonard I. *Black Images of America, 1784–1870.* New York: W. W. Norton & Co., 1976.

Thornbrough, Emma Lou. *T. Thomas Fortune: Militant Journalist.* Negro American Biographies and Autobiographies. Chicago: University of Chicago Press, 1972.

Thorpe, Earl E. *The Mind of the Negro: An Intellectual History of Afro-Americans.* Baton Rouge: Ortlieb Press, 1961.

Tindall, George B. "The Liberian Exodus of 1878." *South Carolina Historical Magazine* 53 (July 1952): 133–45.

Toll, William H. "The Crisis of Freedom: Toward an Interpretation of Negro Life." *Journal of American Studies* 3 (December 1969): 265–80.

———. *The Resurgence of Race: Black Social Theory from Reconstruction to the Pan-African Conferences.* Philadelphia: Temple University Press, 1979.

Tolson, Arthur L. "The Negro in Oklahoma Territory, 1889–1907: A Study in Racial Discrimination." Ph.D. diss., University of Oklahoma, 1966.

Tuchman, Barbara. *Practicing History*. New York: Alfred A. Knopf, 1981.

Tunnel, Ted. *Crucible of Reconstruction: War, Radicalism and Race in Louisiana, 1862–1877*. Baton Rouge: Louisiana State University Press, 1984.

Uya, Okon E. *From Slavery to Public Service, Robert Smalls, 1839–1915*. New York: Oxford University Press, 1971.

Vandersee, Charles. "Henry Adams and the Invisible Negro." *South Atlantic Quarterly* 66 (Winter 1967): 13–30.

Vincent, Charles. "Aspects of the Family and Public Life of Antoine Dubuclet: Louisiana's Black State Treasurer, 1868–1878." *Journal of Negro History* 66 (Spring 1981): 26–36.

———. *Black Legislators in Louisiana during Reconstruction*. Baton Rouge: Louisiana State University Press, 1976.

Voegeli, V. Jacques. *Free But Not Equal: The Midwest and the Negro during the Civil War*. Chicago: University of Chicago Press, 1967.

Wardell, Morris L. *A Political History of the Cherokee Nation, 1838–1907*. Norman: University of Oklahoma Press, 1938.

Warren, Hanna R. "Reconstruction in the Cherokee Nation." *Chronicles of Oklahoma* 45 (Spring 1967): 180–89.

Washington, Booker T. *Up from Slavery*. New York: Doubleday & Co., 1963.

Weaver, Valerie W. "The Failure of Civil Rights, 1875–1883, and Its Repercussions." *Journal of Negro History* 4 (October 1919): 368–82.

Wells, Rolla. *Episodes of My Life*. St. Louis: N.p., 1933.

West, Richard. *Back to Africa: A History of Sierra Leone and Liberia*. New York: Holt, Rinehart and Winston, 1970.

Wheeler, Edward L. *Uplifting the Race: The Black Minister in the New South, 1865–1902*. Lanham, Md., New York, and London: University Press of America, 1986.

White, Arthur O. "State Leadership and Black Education in Florida, 1876–1976." *Phylon* 42 (June 1981): 168–79.

Williams, George Washington. *History of the Negro Race in America*. New York: G. P. Putnam's Sons, 1883. Reprint. New York: Arno Press and the New York Times, 1968.

Williams, Henry S. "The Development of the Negro Public School System in Missouri." Master's thesis, University of Chicago, 1917.

Williams, Nudie. "Black Newspapers and the Exodusters of 1879." *Kansas Historical Review* 8 (Winter 1985–1986): 217–25.

Williams, Walter L. "Nineteenth Century Pan-Africanist: John Henry

Smyth, United States Minister to Liberia." *Journal of Negro History* 63 (January 1978): 18–25.

Williams, William Appleman. *History as a Way of Learning*. New York: New Viewpoints, 1973.

Williamson, Joel. *After Slavery: The Negro in South Carolina during Reconstruction*. Chapel Hill: University of North Carolina Press, 1965.

Willie, Charles V. "A Theory of Liberation Leadership [W. E. B. DuBois's Theory of Education]" *Journal of Negro History* 68 (Winter 1983): 1–7.

Wilson, Walt. "Freedmen in Indian Territory." *Chronicles of Oklahoma* 44 (Summer 1971): 230–44.

Woods, Randall B. "C. H. J. Taylor and the Movement for Black Political Independence, 1882–1896." *Journal of Negro History* 67 (Summer 1982): 122–35.

Woodward, C. Vann. *Reunion and Reaction: The Compromise of 1877 and the End of Reconstruction*. Boston: Little, Brown, 1951. Reprint [with a new introduction and concluding chapter]. Garden City, New York: Doubleday & Co., 1956.

Manuscript Collections

Columbia, Mo. State Historical Society of Missouri. Notes on James Milton Turner.

Jefferson City, Mo. Inman E. Page Library. Minutes of the Meetings of the Board of Curators of Lincoln University, 1866–.

Jefferson City, Mo. Missouri State Archives. Appellate Court Records. Case No. 15958. 1921.

Kansas City, Mo. Kansas City Public Library. Missouri Valley Room Collection. Cash Book for the School Board of Kansas City, 1868.

Little Rock, Ar. Arkansas Historical Commission. Enock K. Miller Papers.

St. Louis, Mo. Civil Courts Building. Probate Court, no. 45591, will of J. Milton Turner. Records of the Circuit Court, division 2, case no. 2884B. Records of the St. Louis Circuit Court, 1843–1844.

St. Louis, Mo. Missouri Historical Society. Dred Scott Papers. Ludlow Field-Maury Collection. P. Dexter Tiffany Papers, Bonds for Free Negroes. Walsh Collection.

Washington, D.C. Library of Congress. Benjamin Harrison Papers. Booker T. Washington Papers. Grover Cleveland Papers.

Washington, D.C. Moorland-Spingarn Research Center. Blanche K. Bruce Papers. Howard University, Washington, D.C.

Washington, D.C. National Archives. Bureau of Indian Affairs. Records Division. Record Group 69: Letters Received Relating to Choctaw and Other Freedmen. Record Group 75: Letters Received by the Office of Indian Affairs, 1880–1915. Land Division. Special Files of the Office of Indian Affairs, 1807–1904. M574, roll 81. "J. Milton Turner and others, claims for attorney fees for representing the Cherokee Freedmen, Shawnee, and Delaware in claim for share of proceeds of Cherokee lands, 1888–1890."

Washington, D.C. National Archives. Bureau of Refugees, Freedmen, and Abandoned Lands. Record Group 105. Missouri Chief Disbursing Officer. Letters Received. Vol. 2, 1867–1869, E–W.

Washington, D.C. National Archives. Interior Department. Appointment Division. File No. 784.

Washington, D.C. National Archives. M17, roll 63, vol. 139, State Department Registers of Miscellaneous Communications Received. M77, vol. 110, "Diplomatic Instructions of the Department of State, 1801–1906." M169, vol. 3, "Despatches from United States Consuls in Monrovia, Liberia, 1852–1906." M170, rolls T–2 through T–7, "Despatches from U. S. Ministers to Liberia, 1863–1906."

Washington, D.C. National Archives. Naval Records. M125, roll 392, "Letters Received by the Secretary of the Navy," Captains' Letters, 1805–1885. Record Group 45, Log of the U.S.S. *Alaska,* January–April 1876.

Washington, D.C. National Archives. Record Group 59. "Applications and Recommendations for the Cleveland Administration"; "Applications and Recommendations for the Grant Administration"; "Applications and Recommendations for the Hayes Administration."

Washington, D.C. National Archives. Records of the Education Division of the Bureau of Refugees, Freedmen, and Abandoned Lands. Letters Received A–P, June 1869–January 1870; M803, rolls 9 and 10, Records of the Education Division of the Bureau of Refugees, Freedmen, and Abandoned Lands. Letters Received A–F, January–December 1870; roll 25, Records of the Education Division of the Bureau of Refugees, Freedmen, and Abandoned Lands. Monthly and Other School Reports, Missouri, April 1867–July 1870.

Public Documents

Act for Fulfilling Treaty Stipulations with various Indian Tribes. Statutes at Large. Vol. 25 (1889).

Act to Refer Cherokee Freedmen's Claims to the Court of Claims. Statutes at Large. Vol. 26 (1890).

Cherokee Freedmen Act. Statutes at Large. Vol. 25 (1889).

Curtis Act. Statutes at Large. Vol. 30 (1898).

Missouri. Department of Education. Superintendent of Public Schools. *Fourth Report of the Superintendent of Public Schools of Missouri, 1869.* Jefferson City, Mo.: Horace Wilcox (1870).

Missouri. General Assembly. House of Representatives. *Journal of the House of Representatives of the Thirty-first General Assembly of the State of Missouri.* Jefferson City: State Journal Co. (1881). *Journal of the House of Representatives of the Thirty-second General Assembly of the State of Missouri.* Jefferson City: Tribune Printing Co. (1883)

U.S. Bureau of the Census. *Population Schedules of the 8th Census of the United States.* 1860. St. Louis, Missouri.

U.S. Congress. Senate. *Report and Testimony of the Select Committee of the United States Senate to Investigate the Causes of the Removal of the Negroes from the Southern States to the Northern States,* Report No. 693, part 2, 46th Cong., 2d sess., 1880.

U.S. Congress. Senate. Senate Executive Documents. S. Doc. 111, part 2, 47th Cong., 2d sess., 1881.

U.S. Court of Claims. *Whitmire, Trustee, v. Cherokee Nation et al. Cases Decided in the Court of Claims of the United States at the Term of 1894–1895.* Vol. 30 (1895).

U.S. Court of Claims. *Whitmire, Trustee, v. Cherokee Nation and the United States. Cases Decided in the Court of Claims of the United States at the Term of 1908–1909.* Vol. 44 (1909).

U.S. Department of State. *Papers Relating to the Foreign Relations of the United States.* 8 vols. Washington, D.C.: Government Printing Office, 1871–1879.

U.S. Department of War. *War of the Rebellion: A Compilation of the Official Records of the Union and Confederate Armies.* Series 1, vol. 52; Series 2, vol. 3. 128 vols. (1880–1901).

U.S. Supreme Court. *Cherokee Nation and United States v. Whitmire, Trustee for Freedmen of the Cherokee Nation. United States Reports: Cased Adjudged in the Supreme Court at October Term, 1911.* Vol. 301 (1912).

INDEX

(James Milton Turner is abbreviated here as JMT.)

Schmitt